MOLIÈRE

THE COMPLETE RICHARD WILBUR TRANSLATIONS

VOLUME 1

Molière

THE COMPLETE RICHARD WILBUR TRANSLATIONS

VOLUME I

The Bungler

Lovers' Quarrels

Sganarelle, or the Imaginary Cuckold

The School for Husbands

The School for Wives

Don Juan

A LIBRARY OF AMERICA *Special Publication*

MOLIÈRE: THE COMPLETE RICHARD WILBUR TRANSLATIONS
VOLUME I
Introduction and volume compilation copyright © 2021 by
Literary Classics of the United States, Inc., New York, N.Y.
All rights reserved.

Published in the United States by Library of America.
Visit our website at www.loa.org.

The Bungler, English translation copyright © 2010 by Richard Wilbur.
Lover's Quarrels, English translation copyright © 2009 by Richard Wilbur.
Reprinted by arrangement with Theatre Communications Group, Inc.

Sganarelle, or The Imaginary Cuckhold, English translation copyright
© 1993 by Richard Wilbur. *The School for Husbands*, English translation
copyright © 1992 by Richard Wilbur. *The School for Wives*, English
translation copyright © 1971, renewed 1999 by Richard Wilbur. *Don Juan*,
English translation copyright © 1998, 2001 by Richard Wilbur. Reprinted
by arrangement with Houghton Mifflin Harcourt Publishing Company.

An Interview with the Translator copyright © 2009 by Dana Gioia
and used by permission.

Distributed to the trade in the United States by Penguin Random
House Inc and in Canada by Penguin Random House Canada Ltd.

Library of Congress Control Number: 202193874
ISBN 978–1–59853–707–9

1 3 5 7 9 10 8 6 4 2

Printed in the United States of America

Molière: The Complete Richard Wilbur Translations
is published and kept in print with support from

THE FLORENCE GOULD FOUNDATION

Contents

Foreword

BY ADAM GOPNIK

Indispensable translations mark the intersection, and some-times the head-on collision, of two sensibilities, and usually two eras. In English, the King James Version of the Bible, most obviously, brings Solomon's time and Shakespeare's into direct overlap, while Alexander Pope's Homer is a still more extreme, inspired collision of archaic Greece and eighteenth-century London. Even Scott Moncrieff's version of Proust, though made close in time to the original, marks a distinct space between the severe French symbolist sounds of Proust's *fin de siècle* and the somewhat more glossily aestheticized sen-sibility of the English one—so that Proust's austere title *In Search of Lost Time* becomes the more self-consciously poetic (and Shakespearean) *Remembrance of Things Past*.

Yet for a translation of a classic to remain impressive in our minds, the original and the new version need somehow to rise from an allied point of view. Some secret concord needs to exist between the two eras for the translation to remain golden. The King James Bible triumphs because it was trans-lated into English at a time when elaborate metaphoric rhet-oric and polysyndeton, extended composition through the simple dignity of "ands," were natural to English style. Pope's Homer was united with Homer's Homer by a shared love in their audiences for large-scale poetic storytelling, and more patience than we have today for long speeches in high diction and endless-seeming lists. The same taste that could put up with all the minor dunces in *The Dunciad* was necessary to put up with all the lists of ships in *The Iliad*.

No translations mark the intersection of two authors and two ages more strikingly than do Richard Wilbur's trans-lations of ten comedies by the seventeenth-century French playwright Molière (1622–1673). Wilbur's first translation, *The Misanthrope*, published in 1955, was soon followed by his *Tartuffe* in 1963, with the last, *Lovers' Quarrels*, appearing more than a half century later, in 2009. All are now collected here by Library of America in two volumes.

Miraculously theatrical in ways that more academic translations are not, Wilbur's Molière is nonetheless miraculously authentic to the original, written in a flowing, vigilantly smooth version of Molière's rhyming couplets, instead of in the lumpy prose of previous English translations. At once readable and stage-friendly, his translations achieve the improbable end of making seventeenth-century French prosody completely playable in English, while remaining true to the essentials of French *grand siècle* style. Wilbur took Molière's Alexandrines, the eleven-syllable rhymed line of classic French theatre and turned it into a more English-friendly iambic pentameter, the ten-syllable heroic couplet of Pope. To do this, he drew on living resources in the American language of his time, particularly on the reality that American ears had become accustomed, both in the then-booming business of light verse and in ambitious musical theater—of which Wilbur himself was to write a supreme example in his lyrics for Leonard Bernstein's *Candide*—to accepting easy rhyme as an aid to emotion.

Well, a better playwright than Molière does not exist, and a better translation of a great writer's plays does not exist—but though that is nearly *that*, all that need be said, it is not quite that. The intersection of author and translator is something far more than a library or even a theatrical triumph. The overlap between Wilbur and Molière is social as much as stylistic. To put it simply—or perhaps to state it as simply as a complicated case can be put—though Molière made his life in and around courts, his role was to become the first great comic poet of the emerging and ascendant middle classes, portraying their domestic concentrations, their appetite for erudition, their constant insecurities, and their easy readiness to be wowed by fashions and trends. Wilbur came to Molière at a moment when that same bourgeoise in America was newly ascendant in another way—when a highly educated postwar GI culture had taken happy possession of a European cultural heritage then undermined on its own ground, a time when all the heritage of European culture seemed in need of American succor and American support. Clive James recalled a Wilbur visit to London in 1962, the height of the period, as offering "the epitome of cool . . . somehow it seemed plausible that the traditional high culture of Europe should be represented . . . by an American who looked like a jet jockey. . . . The internationalization of a mind like Wilbur's, its seemingly relaxed roaming in the European tradition, fitted the picture perfectly." James, writing in 1972, felt obliged to dilute his admiration with a tincture of derision; later on, he would have muted the tone. But the basic picture is sound; much of the confidence and optimism of that postwar epoch is still caught, however improbably, in Wilbur's translations. Wilbur's Molière lives both as masterpieces of the translator's art and as witness to a hopeful (and still not quite finished) American moment.

Wilbur tells us that he had first come upon the idea of translating Molière in 1948, when he saw a production of Cyrano at the Comédie-Française. Wilbur had been one of the great generations of GI aesthetes, those young boys who unthinkingly and instantly threw themselves into the draft and the war, making for a democratized experience of the military alien to post-Vietnam generations—but also meaning that the experience of the war in Europe could offer a sentimental education in European culture, if you survived. (Two great American art historians of Picasso and Rodin respectively, William Rubin and Albert Elsen, would recall in later life how they met on a troopship leaving New York, when they were the only soldiers too aesthetically fastidious to rush to the other side of the deck to look at the Statue of Liberty.) This European education could take very odd forms indeed. The great critic Randall Jarrell came away infatuated with the German romantic culture that had been to some degree causal of the worst of nationalist excess.

Wilbur, instead, became a Francophile. With his elegant

French hand-tooled on the soldiers' road to Paris, he was known as a master craftsman already, after the publication of his shimmeringly precisionist first collection of poetry, *The Beautiful Changes* (1947). But the craftsmanship was metrical and largely expressed in unrhymed verse, and so his decision to write Molière over in English rhyme was far from self-evident. English has, famously but truly, a scarcity of rhyme words, even as it lends itself almost too easily to alliteration. Anyone who dips even a big toe in versification starts to recognize the limited familiar repertory of rhyme words tumbling toward the listener: every chance will produce a romance, and then a dance. An instant, illuminating, ironic illustration of this truth about the scarcity of rhyme in English: a search for rhymes for that word, "scarcity," in English provides . . . precisely zero true rhymes. (You could toy with "ferocity" or the like, or go the Larry Hart route and rhyme it, playfully mis-stressed, with a word pair: i.e., "There's always such a scary scarcity / of honest folks here in our fair city.") The French word for scarcity, by contrast, *rareté*, has such an abundance of rhymes that it makes an English rhymester weep, with *engagé*, *écarté*, and *retardé* leading the charge and many more coming up behind. In French, as in Italian and the other Romance languages, rhyme comes so easy that it can just sneak by our attention on its way to speech. That's how Molière uses it. Not quite invisible, it simply adds the artful tone that iambs do in English.

Rhyme in its nature stylizes and distances an emotion. It's why even the most Francophile of English speakers find something puzzling in Racine: that much rhyming seems "off" for the tragic passions. A Cleopatra who says, in effect, "Give me that knife from off the shelf / Now I have to kill myself" is inescapably comic. Pope's rhetorical exercises in rhyming pathos—his "Eloisa to Abelard"—are DOA to modern readers, as much as his epistles are alive. In English, rhyme belongs almost exclusively to extravagant humor, with Gilbert and Sullivan being both the apotheosis and the cul de sac of this truth. You can't go further in that direction without becoming wholly mechanized.

Wilbur accepted this circumstance of the difficulty of English rhyme, and its inherent bend to the comic, by ingeniously underplaying it. There is not much showy rhyme in Wilbur's Molière, hardly a moment when one is self-consciously impressed by the ingenuity of the rhyme scheme. Scrolling down a random page of his version of *The School for Wives*, one finds all the standards: *care* and *there*, *bliss* and *this*, *two* and *you*, *role* and *soul*. (One rhyme alone—you would be / and nonentity—is witty, and works.)

The rhymes themselves can be commonplace, because the act of rhyming is not. Wilbur knows that whereas in French, rhyme is neutral, in English, rhyme, smoothly and consistently appliquéd, injects a rolling comic energy irresistibly into the text. Its simple presence is enough to produce an effect of ingenuity. Wilbur himself speaks of the importance of making the repetitions in Molière, which are part of the high style of aphoristic argument, land as elegance rather than irritate as overemphasis—Wilbur points out that there is scarcely a metaphor in all of Molière's writing—and that the rhymed couplet is essential to this task.

Yet if rhyming in English is inherently comic, the art and wit of rhyming in English is, as Ogden Nash understood, to land self-consciously on a "find" when you find one. Impressive on every page, Wilbur's wit is particularly so when stretched out across dialogue, so that the exchanges are both perfectly unstilted and idiomatic, and still delight with the ingenuity of each line "tag." Take, for instance, the moment when Alceste, in *The Misanthrope*, responds to the miserable sonnet of Oronte. In French, Oronte says, "Je voudrais bien, pour voir, que de votres manière / Vous en composassiez sur la même matière," and Alceste replies, "Je'n pourrais, par malheur, faire d'aussi méchants; / Mais je me garderais de les montrer aux gens." This exchange becomes, in Wilbur, "Come now, I'll lend you the subject of my sonnet / I'd like to see you try to improve upon it," with Alceste's rejoinder rendered as "I might by chance write something just as shoddy / But then I wouldn't show it to everybody." It is typical of Wilbur's skill that the translation is both nearly literal, word for word, and still inspired: Molière's unemphatic rhyme of *gens* and *méchants* is expressed as the Cole Porterish, more self-consciously inventive, "shoddy" and "everybody"—a rhyme that, it seems fair to say, has rarely, if ever, been found in English before, and gives us wit along with point.

The insistence on rhyme, particularly the play of invisible, "perfect" rhyme with marked "foregrounded" rhyme, that one finds in Wilbur's Molière was part of a larger, though still select, "return to rhyme" in American literary culture in the fifties and sixties, part of a mini-*rappel à l'ordre*, a recall to order, of the time. Ignited by the American Auden's long, neoclassical poems of the forties—particularly his wartime meditation written in Swiftian couplets, "New Year Letter," and the slightly later satiric masterpiece "Under Which Lyre"—rhyme for a period of twenty years or so seemed a vital affirmation of tradition that also, in its self-conscious artifice, had a modernist twang: it guyed the undue inaccessibility of high modernism while, with the elegant knowingness of its revivalist urge, remaining under its umbrella of self-conscious irony. Couplets were as romantic as couples. John Updike, who saw himself first as a light-verse writer, wrote in praise of rhyme, with Wilbur perhaps in the back of his mind, in the early sixties. Updike said that "by rhyming, language calls attention to its own mechanical nature and relieves the represented reality of seriousness. . . . Light verse, an isolated acolyte [isolated, that is, from the main ground of modernism], tends the thin flame of formal magic and tempers the inhuman darkness of reality with the comedy of human artifice." The composer and lyricist Stephen Sondheim, another exact contemporary of Wilbur's, insisted in a parallel way on rejecting in theatre music the increasingly slack—and differently expressive—diction of American pop music, which would lead at last to the sixties revolution in lyric writing. Bob Dylan could, eventually, win the Nobel Prize for Literature while rhyming, in one famous song, "divorced" and "force." Sondheim insisted on lyric writing in favor of true rhyme schemes, seeing in "perfect" rhyme the same kind of formal magic, imposed by the sheer obdurate resistance of rhyme to easy composition—a sign of the resistance of intelligence to kitsch. To this day Broadway circles are the last place in American culture where a prosodic distinction has religious force, with the true-rhyme/near-rhyme distinction inspiring bitter quarrels and feuds. (One major Broadway composer came away from the great and rap-based *Hamilton* indignant and unhappy at Lin Manuel Miranda's rhyme of "country" and "hungry" in the now famous line "I'm like my country / I'm young, scrappy and hungry.")

It is no accident, as the academics say, but an act of fraternity that Sondheim, in his slightly perverse way, placed Wilbur's one-time-only Broadway lyrics, for *Candide*, alongside those of Heywood Dubose, the one-time-only lyricist for *Porgy and Bess*, at the very top of the American theatrical pile. So Wilbur's is a period style in the best sense. A smooth surface of unostentatious rhyme could suggest a sensibility at once firmly modernist and still comfortably classicized, rather like the glittering windowed surfaces of fifties skyscrapers, the Seagram Building and Lever House, gleaming daughters of the Bauhaus at home among the Beaux-Arts buildings on Park Avenue.

Yet Wilbur's Molière reaches us for more profound reasons than its skillful surface. Wilbur himself has neatly articulated Molière's universality: his subject is what happens to social groups—the microsociety of a family or the larger society of a social class—when an unbalanced figure appears within it. And Molière could speak to an American audience because the moral pluses and minuses were remarkably unaltered. Having an uncomfortable truth seeker and teller in our midst provokes the same mixture of exasperation and admiration in 1952 Cambridge as it might in seventeenth-century Paris. The writer Larry David has made a brilliant career as a comedian on just this basis, as the man who will innocently say the uncomfortable truth—that a parent's death suddenly creates an all-purpose excuse for avoiding obligatory socializing. An unplugged fanatic like Tartuffe is always going to have an unsettling effect on a family—though today our fanatic may as easily be a yoga enthusiast or a New Age seer as a puritanical hypocrite. (There is no more memorable description of a modern Tartuffe than that in Michael Downing's *Shoes Outside the Door*, of the Zen roshi who, dazzling his adepts with Americanized Zen, turned out to have a lecherous interest in women students.)

Both timeless and timebound, Molière is not our contemporary in some facile and fatuous way: he is not a radical, certainly, in our sense, nor even a romantic, in the nineteenth-century sense—he is a common-sense realist, opposed to putting ideas and obsessions and *idées fixes* in place of people and relationships, and believing not in an ordered but a balanced world. What he is almost uniquely good at doing—perhaps only Jane Austen among the world's masters equals him here—is conveying the quality that Wilbur celebrates in his poetry, that quality of unschooled intelligence we call common sense. Common sense these days is condemned as a conspiracy by the privileged against the excluded; the suspicious circles of what counts as "common" are, we're told, an indictment against the sense. But Molière reaches out across the centuries to remind us that in truth common sense has legs as long as laughter itself. The model of patriarchal order in the plays is not merely impotent; the common sense of the other characters, their knowledge of actual human possibility, leaves it instantly disregarded as absurd. The plays are filled with patriarchal impositions, but the patriarchal figure is always ridiculous, and quickly shown to be completely incompetent and ineffective. In both *The School for Wives* and *The School for Husbands* the protagonists are men so terrified of femininity and the power of women's minds that they bend their worlds right out of shape in order to keep their wards or fiancées ignorant and subordinate. Molière's point, first made in *The School for Husbands* and italicized in *The School for Wives*, is that this is not only a repugnant activity but a ludicrous one, doomed to comic failure. The repressed, cloistered women are instinctively aware of their own repression, and respond to it by making their own clear-eyed choices of suitors and potential husbands. Sganarelle and Ariste, in *The School for Husbands,* are counterpoised as bad and good suitors, a grand siècle Goofus and Gallant: Sganarelle treats his intended as both prey and potential danger; Ariste treats his intended as a full human being; one relationship ends absurdly, the other happily. In *The School for Wives,* Arnolphe's paranoia about feminine choice is so extreme that it compels him to have isolated his object of desire since she was a child. Both Arnolphe and Sganarelle get schooled by the very women they thought they were schooling. The common sense of the women X-rays the patriarchal hypocrisies and then obliterates their absurdities.

Molière's great theme is the folly of fanaticism of every kind: the religious fanaticism in *Tartuffe,* where a self-seeking pseudo-holy man warps a family's life, or the social fanaticism in *The Misanthrope,* where the proudly plainspoken Alceste has to be instructed by his mistress and his friends that too much candor is egocentric and vain, not admirable. Molière is no philistine; he is the *poet* of common sense, not merely in his ridicule of the idea that life can be lived by a rule of excessive piety or in his exposure of erudition for its own sake, but by being most fully alive on the stage when dramatizing their opposite. He holds what every professor wants for a satirist: a set of positive ideas made more positive by not being ideas. Molière loves natural actions and affections, including that of lust. In *The Learned Ladies,* Molière's feminist point is not that the ladies should not be learned, but that their natural wit, all that they know already from their own experience, is more profound than what their lecherous tutors, with their extravagantly abstract ideas, wish to teach them. Molière escapes fatuity in his candor that what restores a universe unbalanced by intellectual obsession is, most often, normal erotic appetite. In Molière, sex is always the rejuvenating juice of common sense. Alceste loves Célimène, in part because she is clearly his only intellectual equal in the play, but also because he is sexually infatuated with her, and the intensity of his desire, though it makes him miserable, humanizes him. She, in turn, cannot understand his raging jealousy at the attraction she offers to other men; she is not being flirtatious—or not merely flirtatious, or "coquettish"— in her insistence that her plethora of suitors is not a sign of bad faith but exactly an extension of the same sincerity of affect that Alceste claims to admire as a virtue, and cultivates in himself. Being flirtatious with many, she is being true to herself. Tartuffe is shown as a hypocrite in his lecheries, but a human being in his appetites. It's the purpose of comedy to restore energy to sanity—to make common sense come alive to our dramatic imagination by making the pious certitudes that censure common sense look as loony as they are.

Those values are Wilbur's values, too, yet expressed in his poetry more often in an elegiac and wistfully observant key than in a satiric or wholly comic one. Molière releases Wilbur's lyricism into laughter. There's no harm in small white lies; it's egocentric to give way to undue passion; what matters in life is not hierarchical order but emotional ease. Easy does it, Molière says, and our romantic-trained minds still rebel a little against the fatuity of the injunction. But he's right. A more truly radical feminism, a better form of family piety, emerge when we recognize the folly of trying to live by maxims and morals and principles and plans, instead of by the equilibrium of actual existence.

A romantic Molière has been the desideratum of some since the romantic period began. Jean-Jacques Rousseau famously said that he could not understand why anyone laughed at Alceste, and many a modern reading of Molière tried to make him "radical" in this sense—readings in which the balancing forces are seen as pernicious and the unbalancing disruptive force benign, or subversive.

Perhaps if there is a backward blessing in this latest and hardest recent disruption, the pandemic of 2020–2021 under which these lines are written, it may be its reminder that domestic balance is in itself a good thing, to the degree it can be achieved. Once again subject to the vagaries of an untamable and vindictive-seeming Nature, we have a keener sense of the values of the circle drawn around us to keep Nature away. On stage as in mid-plague, there is nothing like a mask to regulate our passions. And nothing like high comedy in rhyme, rolling down the page and affirming the primacy of unaffected affection, to blow away our bourgeois blues.

MOLIÈRE

The Complete Richard Wilbur Translations

VOLUME I

THE BUNGLER

COMEDY IN FIVE ACTS, 1655

For my son Christopher

Introduction

The Bungler (*l'Étourdi*) was Molière's first verse comedy.
For his troupe, which had been touring the provinces for a
decade, the play's successful premiere at Lyons in 1655 was a
crucial moment in its progress toward Paris. The same play
was the first offering of Molière's company when, spon-
sored by the king's brother, it began its Parisian career at the
Petit-Bourbon in 1658. Once again, the piece was wildly successful. Molière offered it frequently thereafter, and since his
death it has been presented hundreds of times, with such
great comic actors as Coquelin in the part of Mascarille. All
of which may make one wonder why *The Bungler*—which
Victor Hugo considered the best of Molière's comedies—is
so seldom mentioned in discussions of its author's works.

The answer, I think, is that (apart from comic timing, wit
and poetic genius) the virtues of this hilarious five-acter are
not those of Molière's major phase. *The Bungler* does not
depict the manners of Molière's society. It does not create
complex characters, like Alceste and Orgon. It has no such
artful plot structure as *The Misanthrope* possesses and no
such thematic weight as we find, for instance, in *The Learned
Ladies'* consideration of the place of art and erudition in
everyday life. What *The Bungler* is, is a zestful and sustained
performance in the vein of that Italian popular comedy with
which Molière and all of mid-seventeenth-century France
were familiar. It derives from the *commedia dell'arte*, a form of
theater in which stock characters improvised within sketchy
outlines or "scenarios," and from such plays as Nicolò Barbi-
eri's *l'Inavvertito* (which was, in fact, a "scenario" elaborated
into a prose script). Molière makes plain his adaptive intentions by laying the action in Messina, by giving his characters
such Italianate names as Pandolfe and by evoking the stock

figures and situations of *commedia*: avaricious and domineering old men, young lovers separated by obstacles, cunning
servants who spin intrigues in the lovers' interest. *The Bungler*, which with vigor and invention transports all this into
the high mode of verse comedy, is the French enhancement
of an Italian genre.

As Act One begins, it is convenient to know that a beautiful young woman named Célie, who was part of a gypsy
band, has lately been given by the gypsies to a rich old man
named Trufaldin as security for a loan. It's in that sense that
she can be described as a "slave" or "captive." The play's impet-
uous young hero, Lélie, who formerly vied with a young man
named Léandre for the favor of a girl named Hippolyte, has
spied Célie and transferred his affections to her. Learning
now that Léandre, too, is smitten by Célie, and is once again
his rival, he turns for strategic help to his clever valet Mascarille, who proceeds to cook up the first of many schemes.

All of that, despite the novel feature of a pawned heroine,
feels like a standard opening situation for a comedy: we know
that it will be the business of the play to unite Lélie and his
Célie; we suspect that Célie will prove to be no gypsy, but a
girl of gentle birth; we count on Mascarille to hatch some
great intrigue whereby to win Célie for his master, though we
are not quite sure why it should take five acts for that to be
accomplished. Five acts prove to be necessary because, even
when made a part of Mascarille's cunning plots—as initially
he is not—the rash and blundering Lélie somehow manages
to torpedo them, one after another. That is the distinctive
repeated joke of *l'Étourdi*, and it does not become tiresome.
A chief delight of the play is to witness Mascarille's resilient
ability to think up ever-new devices, and to see how the plot
will arrange for them to be frustrated, again and again, by the
intended beneficiary.

An eighteenth-century French editor of *l'Étourdi* found
the play morally disquieting, and there is no question that it
toys throughout with our ambivalent feelings about deception and fraud. Mascarille, who tirelessly strives to be "the
most glorious trickster in the town," and who has the longest

part in all of Molière, is massively central to that theme, yet there is scarcely a character in the piece who does not have moments, venial or otherwise, of guileful behavior. Célie, playing the seeress in order to deceive Trufaldin, shows a natural aptitude for intrigue. Hippolyte engages Mascarille to scheme for her success in love, and a plot of Mascarille's is readily embraced by Pandolfe. Anselme achieves a sly counter-swindle in retrieving his purse. Léandre attempts to abduct Célie under cover of a masquerade. As for the hero Lélie, he begs his valet to aid him with plots and ruses, takes part in some of them, soliloquizes in extenuation of a fraud (Act Two, Scene One), and pulls a hoax of his own (Act Two, Scenes Ten and Eleven) of which he is very proud. A comedy, however, is not a court of law, and the play gives its young lovers a blanket absolution on the principle that all's fair in love. Furthermore, they all have attractive and redeeming qualities: Célie is noble and honorable, Hippolyte is magnanimous, Léandre is a good sport and the warm, naive and spontaneous Lélie is gallant in rescuing a stranger from false arrest. In Mascarille, by contrast, the main motive for duplicity is not love but *amour-propre* and a need to be the smartest of outsmarters; he is a diabolical inverter of values, who describes his chicanery as "virtue" and aspires to be the acknowledged *imperator* of rascals. Outside of this play, he would be deplorable; within its comic precincts he provides wit and irrepressibility and a tang of the sinister. One reason why his intricate and dubious plottings are purely enjoyable is that they come to nothing, and that the denouement—the disclosures, recognitions and happy pairings of the fifth act— is, after all, none of his doing.

John Dryden once freely reworked for the stage a prose translation of *l'Étourdi* by the Duke of Newcastle, adding much other material, borrowed or fresh, and some Restoration coarseness. The result, *Sir Martin Mar-All* (1667), was judged by Samuel Pepys, who saw it again and again, to be "the best comedy ever was wrote." An eighteenth-century prose rendering by Baker and Miller, like the nineteenth-century version by Charles Heron Wall, was worthy but not stageworthy, and what follows is intended as the second playable treatment of *l'Étourdi* in English. I hope also to have done a good and exact translation for the contemporary reader. I've sought to be strictly faithful to the original in all respects—in sense, in tone and in verse form—and it may amuse the reader to know of a couplet whose punning character stumped me. In Act Five, Scene Five, Mascarille has disguised himself as a German-accented Swiss landlord, in order to deceive Andrès. Lélie inopportunely appears and, in Andrès's presence, addresses his valet by name: "Well, Mascarille! No one would ever guess / That it was you in that outlandish dress." Mascarille's reply is:

> *Moi souis ein chant t'honneur, moi non point Maquerille:*
> *Chai point fentre chamais le fame ni le fille.*

That might be translated:

> Vy do you say I am a *Maquereau*?
> I sell no vimmen here, I'll haf you know.

Unfortunately, though my great Funk and Wagnalls (1913) gives "maquereau" as an English word meaning "pimp" or "procurer," the word is not to be found in any of the more recent dictionaries I have consulted. The *Shorter OED* allows "mackerel" (meaning procurer), but once again the term seems not to have much currency. For intelligibility's sake, and because Mascarille has already, in Scene Three, held forth on the propriety of his establishment, I have settled for:

> Vy do you call me Mackerel? I don't vish
> Zat you make fun of me und call me fish.

Purists may choose, in reading my translation, to substitute the "maquereau" couplet; actors will doubtless find that, for their audiences, the fish joke is clearer and funnier.

For general encouragement in my translating of Molière, I wish to thank Jacques Barzun, William Jay Smith and Sonja

Haussmann Smith. And for his specific suggestion that I undertake *The Bungler*, I am grateful to Albert Bermel. My wife Charlotte has as always given me her good and patient counsel.

—*RW*

Cummington, Massachusetts, 1999

Characters

LÉLIE (lay-LEE), Pandolfe's son

CÉLIE (say-LEE), Trufaldin's slave

MASCARILLE (mah-ska-REE), Lélie's valet

ANSELME (ahn-SELM), Hippolyte's father

HIPPOLYTE (ee-po-LEET), Anselme's daughter

TRUFALDIN (tru-fal-DAN), an old man

PANDOLFE (pahn-DOLF), Lélie's father

LÉANDRE (lay-AHN-druh), a young man of good family

ANDRÈS (ahn-DRACE), a supposed gypsy

ERGASTE (air-GHAST), a friend of Mascarille's

A MESSENGER

TWO COMPANIES OF MASQUERADERS

Place

A public square in Messina, Sicily.

A Note to Directors and Actors

The two names Albert and Horace are frequently spoken in *The Bungler*, and should be pronounced in a more or less French manner as "al-BEAR" and "o-RAHSS."

Act One
SCENE ONE

Lélie

LÉLIE
Well then, Léandre, get ready for a fray!
We'll see which one of us will win the day—
Which one will thwart the other's longing for
The heavenly creature whom we both adore.
Muster your forces, and be on your guard;
I mean to press the attack, and press it hard!

SCENE TWO

———— •••• ————

Lélie, Mascarille

LÉLIE

Ah, Mascarille!

MASCARILLE

Sir?

LÉLIE

I'm in a dreadful state;
My love life's always being spoiled by fate:
Léandre now loves Célie, so that although
I've a new love, I have the same old foe.

MASCARILLE

Léandre loves Célie!

LÉLIE

Adores her; yes.

MASCARILLE

Bad luck.

LÉLIE

It is; imagine my distress.
Yet I'd be foolish to despair or doubt;
With your help, I feel sure of winning out.
You're full of clever schemes; your canny wit
Finds no predicament too much for it;
You are, I think, a king among valets;
In all the world . . .

MASCARILLE

Whoa! No more sugary praise.
When masters need the help of us poor hinds,

They call us paragons with brilliant minds;
But let us make some slip, and in a flash
We're stupid scoundrels who deserve the lash.

LÉLIE

Ah no, you wrong me. That's not how I behave.
But let us speak now of the lovely slave.
Tell me, could any heart, however cold,
Not melt for one so charming to behold?
Given her gentle speech and perfect face,
I think that she must come of noble race,
And that some fate has made her hide within
A humble guise her lofty origin.

MASCARILLE

A fine romantic fancy, to be sure.
But will Pandolfe approve this new amour?
He is your father, sir, or so he claims.
You know how, if you cross him, it inflames
His temper—how it makes him roar and rave
Whenever, in his view, you misbehave.
His plan is for Anselme, his neighbor, to
Bestow his daughter Hippolyte on you,
Because he thinks that only marriage can
Convert a rash youth to a sober man.
Were he to find that you refuse to wed
The girl he's chosen, and pursue instead
An unknown siren whose bewitching beauty
Has caused you to forget your filial duty,
God knows what thunders would afflict your ear,
And what long sermons you would have to hear.

LÉLIE

Enough, now! No more speeches, if you please.

MASCARILLE

Enough talk, then, of schemes and strategies!
The game's not worth the candle, and you'd be wiser . . .

LÉLIE

Thank you, I have no need of an advisor.
You know I hate advice, and a valet
Who lectures me will find it doesn't pay.

MASCARILLE

(*Aside:*)
He's getting angry.
(*To Lélie:*)
                    I was but teasing, sir,
To learn how strong your amorous feelings were.
Is Mascarille some grim, censorious creature?
Am I the foe of youth and human nature?
Ah, never could you so mistake me, knowing
How jovial I am, how easygoing.
Forget the crabbèd sermons of your sire;
Be free, I say, and do as you desire.
I think that these old fogies who give tongue
To stern ideas are envious of the young;
Time having forced them to be virtuous,
They want the joys of life denied to us.
You know my gifts, sir; what would you have me do?

LÉLIE

Now, that's the talk I like to hear from you.
Well, then. My love, I find, does not despise
The passion wakened in me by her eyes.
Just now, however, Léandre said to me
That he intends to rob me of Célie:
That's why we must act quickly, now, and hatch
Some plan to make her mine with all despatch.
What trick or ruse or plot can you concoct,
Whereby my rival's purpose will be blocked?

MASCARILLE

Give me your leave to ponder that a while.
(*Aside:*)
Can I think up some useful bit of guile?

LÉLIE

Well, what's our stratagem?

MASCARILLE

I beg you, wait.
My mind can't move at such a rapid rate.
I have it: You must . . . No, you'd better not.
Still, if you went . . .

LÉLIE

Where?

MASCARILLE

No, that's a sorry plot.
But here's a notion—

LÉLIE

What?

MASCARILLE

It wouldn't do.
Perhaps—

LÉLIE

Yes?

MASCARILLE

No, that wouldn't work for you.
You might approach Anselme.

LÉLIE

Why? What could I say?

MASCARILLE

It's true, we'd only make things worse that way.
Yet we must have her. It's Trufaldin you must see.

LÉLIE

What for?

MASCARILLE

I'm not sure.

LÉLIE

                    This is too much for me;
Your dithering is more than I can stand.

MASCARILLE

Sir, if you had a well-stuffed purse in hand,
There'd be no need for us to fret and muse
On how to gain your end by some sly ruse:
We could quite simply *buy* the slave, and thus
Prevent your rival from forestalling us.
Trufaldin fears that the gypsy family
Who left her with him as security
Will cheat him, and that his loan won't be repaid.
To reimburse himself, he'll sell the maid
Gladly, for he's a miser through and through.
He'd let himself be whipped for half a sou,
And money is the god to which he kneels.
The trouble is . . .

LÉLIE

          What?

MASCARILLE

                    That your father feels
A like regard for money, so that his treasure
Is nothing you can draw on at your pleasure.
In fact, I know of no purse in the land
Likely to open up at your command.
But let us seek to talk now with Célie,
And find out what her sentiments may be.
Right there's her window.

LÉLIE
Trufaldin, night and day,
Keeps watch upon her in a hawk-like way.
Take care.

MASCARILLE
Let's hide, then, in this corner here.
But look! What luck, that she should now appear!

SCENE THREE

———— • ————

Célie, Lélie, Mascarille

LÉLIE

Ah, how I thank high Heaven, when I view
The heavenly charms it has bestowed on you!
Though by those eyes I have been all but slain,
What joy it is to see them once again!

CÉLIE

My heart, which hears your words with some alarm,
Would never wish my eyes to do men harm,
And if in some way they have made you grieve,
Please know that it was done without my leave.

LÉLIE

So sweetly have they pierced me that, I swear,
I glory in the precious wounds I bear,
And . . .

MASCARILLE

        Sir, all this is a little too high-flown;
Our business here requires a brisker tone.
Let's quickly ask, before it is too late,
How she . . .

TRUFALDIN

(*Within the house:*)
        Célie!

MASCARILLE

You see?

LÉLIE

O cruel fate!
Why must that old ape interrupt us now?

MASCARILLE

Go, hide yourself; I'll handle him somehow.

SCENE FOUR

Trufaldin, Célie, Lélie hiding in a corner, Mascarille

TRUFALDIN

(*To Célie:*)
What are you doing outside? As I recall,
I bade you speak to no one, no one at all.

CÉLIE

I met this honest fellow years ago,
And you need have no fears of him, I know.

MASCARILLE

Is this the famous Trufaldin?

CÉLIE
The same.

MASCARILLE

Sir, I rejoice to meet a man whose name
Is spoken everywhere with reverence.
Pray you, accept my humble compliments.

TRUFALDIN

Your servant.

MASCARILLE
I intrude here, I'm afraid;
But when I knew her earlier, she displayed
Great powers of divination. I hope, now, that her
Insight will help me solve a pressing matter.

TRUFALDIN

Hmm. You dabble in black magic. Is that so?

CÉLIE

My only magic is as white as snow.

MASCARILLE

Well, here's the problem. My master's heart's been captured
By a certain person; he's utterly enraptured,
And would long since have passionately expressed
To her he loves the tumult in his breast,
Did not a sharp-eyed dragon fiercely guard
That treasure, so that all approach is barred.
What's more, it's just now grieved him to discover
That a keen rival is enamored of her.
Therefore his heart, with anxious eagerness,
Asks if its love can hope for some success,
And I have come here, confident that you
Can give an answer sibylline and true.

CÉLIE

Under what star was he born, this master of yours?

MASCARILLE

The star of those whose truthful love endures.

CÉLIE

No need to name the maid who's won his heart;
I know her intimately, through my art.
She has much spirit, and though she must abide
An adverse fate, retains a noble pride;
She would not wish too freely to reveal
The secret stirrings that her heart may feel,
But I, who read her heart as well as she,
And am less proud, shall tell you what I see.

MASCARILLE

Oh, but the powers of magic art are great!

CÉLIE

If your master is as constant as you state,
And his intent is on the highest plane,
He need not fear that he will love in vain.
There's room for hope, and the fortress he would win
Consents to parley, and may indeed give in.

MASCARILLE

Ah, good. But this fortress has a commandant
Who's hard to handle.

CÉLIE

Yes, hard as adamant.

MASCARILLE

(*Aside, looking at Lélie, who has been peering around the corner:*)
The Devil take that fool, who won't stop peeking!

CÉLIE

Here's what to do, to gain the prize you're seeking.

LÉLIE

(*Coming forth and joining the others.*)
Don't let our visit disturb you, Trufaldin!
At my behest this faithful servingman
Has come to see you at your dwelling place
To bring my compliments, and discuss the case
Of this young lady, whose freedom I shall buy
If we can find a just price, you and I.

MASCARILLE

The idiot!

TRUFALDIN

Well, now! Someone's deceiving me!
The tales you've told me don't at all agree.

MASCARILLE

This gentleman's brain was damaged by a blow,
As you may have heard, sir.

TRUFALDIN

        What I know, I know.
Some sneaky business is afoot, that's clear.
(*To Célie:*)
Go in. Don't leave the house again, d'you hear?
And you, you knaves, when next I'm to be tricked,
Make certain that your stories don't conflict.

(*Exit.*)

MASCARILLE

Well done! I only wish he'd given us
A well-earned thrashing for having blundered thus.
Why did you have to show yourself, and why
Did you make a speech that gave my words the lie?

LÉLIE

I thought it the thing to say.

MASCARILLE

        You thought unwisely.
But why should any act of yours surprise me?
You know so many ways to botch and blunder
That no mistake of yours is grounds for wonder.

LÉLIE

Should a small slip be so fiercely reprehended?
Have I done such harm that matters can't be mended?
If you've no new scheme to make the lady mine,
Do at least thwart Léandre's sly design:
Don't let him buy Célie before I do.
Well, lest by some mistake I anger you,
I'll take my leave.

MASCARILLE

Good.

(*Exit Lélie.*)

Money, it is plain,
Would be a wondrous help in our campaign,
But having none, we'll find some other way.

SCENE FIVE

———— •• ————

Anselme, Mascarille

ANSELME

It's a shameful time we live in, I must say!
Never was wealth so wastefully displayed,
Yet the loans I make are grudgingly repaid.
How blithely people borrow, yet all debts
These days are like the children one begets
In pleasure, but which cost such pain to bear.
When gold flows into our purse, we're debonair,
But when we must deliver, and get it out—
Well, that's a thing to weep and groan about.
Still, this two thousand which, for two years past,
Was owed to me, has now been paid at last.
That's something.

MASCARILLE

(*Aside:*)
                        Look! Here comes some splendid game
To shoot at on the wing, and I shall aim
To bag him with some flattery and lies.
I well know on what theme to improvise . . .
(*To Anselme:*)
Anselme, I just saw . . .

ANSELME

Whom?

MASCARILLE

            Your dear Nérine.

ANSELME

What did she say of me, that bewitching queen?

MASCARILLE

She's mad for you.

ANSELME

She is?

MASCARILLE

It pains my spirit
To see such yearning.

ANSELME

I'm gratified to hear it.

MASCARILLE

She's almost dead of love, poor little thing.
"Anselme, my dear," one hears her whimpering,
"When shall you quench these flames that you've ignited,
And our two hearts in marriage be united?"

ANSELME

But why has she hid these feelings until now?
Women are very deep, I must allow.
Tell me now, Mascarille: although I'm old,
Are my looks still fairly pleasant to behold?

MASCARILLE

Though not quite handsome, your face is very striking,
And a certain fair one finds it to her liking.

ANSELME

I see.

MASCARILLE

(*Trying to seize Anselme's purse.*)
And so she's in a lovesick state,
And thinks of you as—

ANSELME
What?

MASCARILLE
                    Her future mate;
And vows to . . .

ANSELME
          What?

MASCARILLE
          To capture, come what may,
Your purse.

ANSELME
          My what?

MASCARILLE
(*Taking the purse and letting it fall to the ground.*)
                    Your heart, I meant to say.

ANSELME
Ah yes, of course. See here, when next you see
The girl, I hope that you'll speak well of me.

MASCARILLE
Gladly.

ANSELME
          Good-bye, then.

MASCARILLE
(*Aside:*)
                    Bless you! Go with God!

ANSELME
(*Coming back.*)
Heavens! I've just done something very odd,

And you must think me stingy, I'm afraid.
In my love affair, you've promised me your aid,
You've brought me welcome news for which I feel
Most grateful, and yet I didn't reward your zeal!
Here, so you won't forget me . . .

MASCARILLE

No, no, please!

ANSELME

Let me . . .

MASCARILLE

I don't expect gratuities.

ANSELME

I know, but still—

MASCARILLE

No, I'd be mortified;
I'm a man of honor, and it would hurt my pride.

ANSELME

Farewell, then.

MASCARILLE

(*Aside:*)

What a talker!

ANSELME

(*Coming back.*)
I've a notion to
Send the dear girl some gift by way of you;
I'll give you enough to buy her some small trinket—
A ring, perhaps, or a bracelet if you think it
Would please her taste.

MASCARILLE
     No, keep your money, sir:
Leave it to me; I'll take some gift to her.
I've a charming ring that someone gave me lately,
And if it fits her, you can compensate me.

ANSELME
Good. Give it in my name, then, and endeavor
To keep her love for me as strong as ever.

SCENE SIX

Lélie, Anselme, Mascarille

LÉLIE

(*Picking up the purse.*)
Whose purse is this?

ANSELME
                  I must have dropped it there!
I'd have thought a thief had taken it, I declare!
Well, thank you for the great good turn you've done me;
You've spared me much distress, and saved my money,
Which I'll take home and put away securely.

(*Exit.*)

MASCARILLE
You are the world's worst interferer, surely.

LÉLIE
Why, he'd have lost his purse, had I not seen it!

MASCARILLE
Oh, yes, you've done a wondrous deed! I mean it!
You've shown great timing, and vast mental powers;
Just keep it up, and victory will be ours.

LÉLIE
What have I done now?

MASCARILLE
                  Since you ask, I'll spell
It out. You've been a fool. F, O, O, L.
Your father will not help us, as you know;
Your rival is a formidable foe;

Yet when I try a daring ruse, and take
The risk of shame and prison for your sake . . .

LÉLIE

D'you mean? . . .

MASCARILLE
                    Yes, wastrel, that purse was to have been
A ransom for Célie. Then you barged in.

LÉLIE

In that case, I was wrong. But how could I guess?

MASCARILLE

It called, indeed, for rare perceptiveness!

LÉLIE

You should have given me some sign, instead—

MASCARILLE

Oh, yes, I should've had eyes in the back of my head.
Leave me alone, and in the name of Zeus,
Don't vex me with that sort of lame excuse.
After what's happened, another man would quit;
But I've just thought of a master stroke of wit,
A shrewd idea, and I shall now apply it,
So long as . . .

LÉLIE
                    No, I promise to keep quiet.
I'll stay away, and never interfere.

MASCARILLE

Go, then. Your presence irks me. Get out of here.

LÉLIE

For fear of Léandre, you had better hurry.

MASCARILLE

Go on, I said. I'll act at once, don't worry.
(*Exit Lélie.*)
If I can bring this off, I shall applaud
Myself as master of the art of fraud.
I'll go and . . . Good, here's just the man I'm seeking.

SCENE SEVEN

Pandolfe, Mascarille

PANDOLFE

Mascarille!

MASCARILLE

    Sir?

PANDOLFE

        I'm not pleased, frankly speaking,
By the conduct of my son.

MASCARILLE

           My master, sir?
You're not alone in that; I quite concur.
His bad behavior, by which I'm horrified,
Has caused my patience to be sorely tried.

PANDOLFE

That's odd. 'Twas my impression that you two
Saw eye to eye.

MASCARILLE

        Ah no, sir, that's not true.
He and I always have some bone to pick;
My talk of duty makes him choleric.
Just now we quarreled, because he doesn't choose
To marry Hippolyte, and dares refuse
Your wise arrangements for him. He just won't show you
The deference which a proper son would owe you.

PANDOLFE

You quarreled?

MASCARILLE
Indeed we did; we all but fought.

PANDOLFE
Then I've been much mistaken; I always thought
That you abetted him in every way.

MASCARILLE
What! I? Well, there you have the world today,
Where innocence is wronged and misconstrued!
Sir, if you only knew my rectitude,
Though I am but his servant, I think that you
Would want to pay me as his teacher, too.
Yes, you could not more earnestly advise
Your son than I do, bidding him be wise.
Often I say to him, "In Heaven's name,
Stop drifting through this world without an aim:
Do settle down; look at the worthy sire
Whom Heaven gave you, and whom all admire;
Don't grieve him by a life of foolish whim,
But be a sound and sober man like him."

PANDOLFE
Well put. What answer does he give to that?

MASCARILLE
He fends me off with a lot of silly chat.
Mind you, I know that deep within his heart
Are the values which you've striven to impart;
But, just at present, his reason is impaired.
I could suggest a method, if I dared,
Whereby his waywardness might be restrained.

PANDOLFE
Speak on.

MASCARILLE
There's a secret which I could be caned

For uttering; but I can trust in your
Discretion, sir, and so I feel secure.

PANDOLFE

You may.

MASCARILLE

Your son resists your plans, since they've
Less charm for him than has a certain slave.

PANDOLFE

So I have heard; but now that you have said it,
The story has for me a greater credit.

MASCARILLE

I'm not your son's confederate now, you'll grant.

PANDOLFE

I grant it gladly.

MASCARILLE

Meanwhile, if you want
To lead him back to the path from which he's erred,
The way . . . I hope that I'm not overheard;
If he knew what I've been saying, he'd break my neck . . .
The way, I say, to put his plans in check
Is to purchase his belovèd captive, and
Send her in secret to some far-off land.
Anselme knows Trufaldin; dispatch him, do,
This very morning, to buy the slave for you;
Then, if you care to entrust the girl to me,
I know slave traders, and can guarantee
That you'll get back whatever she may cost,
And that all traces of her will be lost.
If your son's to settle down and wed, it's clear
That this new love of his must disappear;
For, even if he willingly complied,
And took the one you've chosen as his bride,

The nearness of this other could revive
His passion, and the marriage might not thrive.

PANDOLFE

Well said. Your plan makes sense, I'm bound to say.
Here comes Anselme; I'll seek, without delay,
To gain possession of that slave, that pest,
And put her in your hands. You'll do the rest.

MASCARILLE

(*Alone:*)
Good. Now to inform my master of all this.
Long live chicanery and artifice!

SCENE EIGHT

—— •◆• ——

Hippolyte, Mascarille

HIPPOLYTE

So this is how you serve me, faithless man!
Had I not overheard your crafty plan,
I'd never have believed such treachery!
You reek of falsehood, and you've lied to me.
You promised that you'd be the champion of
My hopes to wed Léandre, whom I love,
And that you'd save me in some clever way
From having to accept as fiancé
Lélie, who is my father's favorite.
Yet now you've done the very opposite!
Well, you shall not succeed, for I know how
To block the purchase you arranged just now.
I'll go . . .

MASCARILLE

My, my! You've flown right off the handle!
Your temper's flared up like a Roman candle!
Not pausing to consider that you might
Be wrong, you've hurt me by your rage and spite.
I ought to cease my services to you,
And make your unjust accusations true.

HIPPOLYTE

Would you have me doubt my senses? How absurd!
Can you deny what I just saw and heard?

MASCARILLE

No, but the whole scenario that I planned
Was in your interest, please understand.
The bill of goods that you just heard me sell
Will dupe old Pandolfe, and Anselme as well.
When by their means the captive maid is free,

I shall at once convey her to Lélie,
And it will aggravate your father so
To see how he's been hoodwinked, and to know
That his chosen son-in-law has opted out,
He'll turn then to Léandre, without a doubt.

HIPPOLYTE

What! This great scheme, which I misunderstood,
Was all for my sake?

MASCARILLE

                    I sought to do you good.
But since my efforts earn no gratitude,
Since I must bear these violent shifts of mood,
And since, for all reward, you vilify me
As a base deceiver, a trickster low and slimy,
I shall reform at once, and be pure-hearted,
And put a stop to this intrigue I've started.

HIPPOLYTE

(*Stopping him:*)
Oh, pray don't treat me in so brusque a fashion;
Do, please, forgive my foolish burst of passion.

MASCARILLE

No, let me go. I know a way to halt
That vicious plot with which you find such fault.
You'll have no cause then to complain of me,
And you shall wed my master, wait and see.

HIPPOLYTE

Dear friend, I was an idiot to misjudge
Your good intentions; but please don't hold a grudge.
(*Taking out her purse.*)
Permit me, in some small way, to atone.
You wouldn't leave me helpless and alone?

MASCARILLE

No, no, I couldn't, even if I tried.
But your too hasty temper has hurt my pride.
For a man of noble mind, there's no worse wound
Than when his sacred honor has been impugned.

HIPPOLYTE

It's true, I said quite dreadful things; but please,
Let these gold Louis heal your injuries.

MASCARILLE

(*Taking the coins.*)
Ah, there are wrongs which gold cannot redress.
But I shall rise above all bitterness:
We must forgive our friends their little flaws.

HIPPOLYTE

Do you really think you can advance my cause
By means of this bold plot that you've devised,
And that my fond hopes may be realized?

MASCARILLE

Don't bank too much upon our present chances.
I've tricks and schemes to fit all circumstances,
And if we're luckless in my current plot,
Another will succeed where this did not.

HIPPOLYTE

Hippolyte shall be ever in your debt.

MASCARILLE

I'll serve you; but not for the gold that I may get.

HIPPOLYTE

Your master's beckoning you, and I shall go.
You'll keep on working for my cause, I know.

SCENE NINE

Lélie, Mascarille

LÉLIE

Why are you idling here? You swore that you'd
Do wonders for me. Well, what ineptitude!
If my good angel hadn't warned me, I'd
Now see my hopes defeated and denied.
Farewell to joy! Farewell to happiness!
I'd be a prey to endless dark distress.
Yes, had I not been there just now, that knave
Anselme might well have bought my precious slave;
But I made such a row, and roared so well,
That Trufaldin took fright and wouldn't sell.
She's back in his house.

MASCARILLE

        You've botched my plans once more!
That's three times, and I'm tired of keeping score.
I had arranged, fool, that Anselme would pay her
Ransom to Trufaldin, and then convey her
Without delay into my charge and care;
But you came meddling, and wrecked the whole affair.
Do you count on my keen wits to help you now?
No more! I'd rather I were a witless cow,
A goose, a lamppost, or a cabbage head,
And that Beelzebub would strike you dead.

LÉLIE

(*Alone:*)
I'd better take him to some inn that's handy,
And let him vent his fury on the brandy.

Act Two

SCENE ONE

———•———

Lélie, Mascarille

MASCARILLE

I've yielded to your pleas, although I swore
Never to serve your interests anymore,
Because I felt an itch to undertake
One final bold endeavor for your sake.
You see how pliant my heart is, and how tender;
Had Nature made me of the other gender,
Think what a passionate life I might have led!
I conjure you, however, to use your head
And not confound my present undertaking
By one of those weird blunders you've been making.
I'll beg Anselme to excuse the scene you made,
Because our new plot will require his aid;
But one more gaffe, and I shall cease to care
Whether you prosper in your love affair.

LÉLIE

No, no, you needn't worry, I promise you.
I'll watch my step.

MASCARILLE

Make certain that you do.
Now, I've devised for you a daring scheme.
Your father has been slow in the extreme
To die, and leave you with the funds you need,
And so I've killed him—in word, if not in deed.
I've spread a rumor about him, telling folk
That the old boy's had a sudden, fatal stroke.
But first, to give that lie an honest face,
I made him vanish to his country place.
I sent a man to tell him that the crew

Of workmen he'd engaged to dig a new
Foundation for his barn had just now found
A chest of treasure buried in the ground.
Well! Off to the country, in a flash, he flew,
With all his household, save for me and you,
And I could now announce his death, you see,
And promptly bury him in effigy.
There now: You have the outline of our plot.
Play your part carefully, and if I do not
Follow the script, or if I miss my cues,
Call me an ass, or any name you choose.

LÉLIE

(*Alone:*)
He's found a very strange and devious way
To make my dreams come true, I'm bound to say.
But when a girl has set one's heart on fire,
What won't one do to gain the heart's desire?
Passion, which is considered to excuse
Great crimes, should justify this little ruse,
To which my love and my envisagement
Of future joys have forced me to consent.
Good heavens; listen! Our play's about to start;
I must get in the mood to play my part.

SCENE TWO

Anselme, Mascarille

MASCARILLE
You're taken aback, I know, by news so grim.

ANSELME
What a way to die!

MASCARILLE
'Twas very wrong of him
To play us such a sudden, shocking trick.

ANSELME
He didn't even take time to be sick!

MASCARILLE
No man was ever in such haste to die.

ANSELME
How is Lélie?

MASCARILLE
Alas, he's maddened by
His grief; he beats his breast; I hear him rave
That he wants to follow his papa to the grave.
Indeed, his anguish causes me such worry
That I've had the corpse enshrouded in a hurry,
For fear that its depressing sight could lead
The poor boy to commit some fatal deed.

ANSELME
Still, you should have waited longer. —I'd have preferred
To see him again before he was interred.
It can be murder to bury a man too quickly;
Many a man looks dead when he's just sickly.

MASCARILLE

I assure you that, in the fullest sense, he's dead.
But, to return to what we earlier said,
Lélie's conceived a loving son's desire
To hold a lavish funeral for his sire,
And thus, through rites and honors, give at least
Some consolation to the dear deceased.
He has a fine inheritance, but he's
A babe in business, and thus far all he sees
Are funds tied up in distant tracts of land
And bonds he can't convert to cash in hand.
Therefore he begs you, if you can forget
His recent conduct, which fills him with regret,
To lend him what the obsequies will cost . . .

ANSELME

Yes. First, I'll go see the dear friend I have lost.

(*Exit.*)

MASCARILLE

(*Alone:*)
Our plot is launched, and goes ahead full sail;
Let's stay alert now, or our hopes may fail.
Lest, in the very port, we come to grief,
Let's steer with care 'round every rock and reef.

SCENE THREE

Anselme, Lélie, Mascarille

ANSELME
Alas, it pains me more than I can say
To see him wrapped up in that mournful way.
He was just alive, and now he's dead. How strange!

MASCARILLE
In a short time, a man can greatly change.

LÉLIE
(*Weeping:*)
Ohh!

ANSELME
He was but mortal. Even Rome, my dear Lélie,
Cannot dispense us from mortality.

LÉLIE
Ohh!

ANSELME
Death, without warning, claims all humankind.
All through our lives it stalks us, close behind.

LÉLIE
Ohh!

ANSELME
Deaf to all our prayers, that ravenous beast
Will not forgo one morsel of his feast;
He eats us all.

LÉLIE
Ohh!

MASCARILLE
Your preaching is in vain;
It can't eradicate so deep a pain.

ANSELME
If my words, Lélie, can't heal this bitter blow,
Do try, at least, to moderate your woe.

LÉLIE
Ohh!

MASCARILLE
To curb his grief just now is out of the question.

ANSELME
In any case, at your valet's suggestion,
I've brought a sum of money which should with ease
Pay for your worthy father's obsequies.

LÉLIE
Ohh! Ohh!

MASCARILLE
How that word "father" makes him cry!
At the thought of what he's lost, he longs to die.

ANSELME
When you check the dear man's books, you'll notice there
That I owe much more than this to you, his heir;
But even if I owed you nothing at all,
My fortune would be at your beck and call.
Take this; whatever I possess is yours.

LÉLIE
(*Going.*)
Ohh!

MASCARILLE

My poor master. What anguish he endures!

ANSELME

Mascarille, I think that it would be discreet
For him to dash me off a short receipt.

MASCARILLE

Ohh!

ANSELME

There are always unforeseen events.

MASCARILLE

Ohh!

ANSELME

Just the briefest of acknowledgments.

MASCARILLE

Ah, how can he write things in his present state?
Permit this stormy sorrow to abate,
And once his woes have given him some rest,
I'll have him sign the paper you request.
Farewell. My heart is bursting. I shall go
To my master's side, and let my salt tears flow.
Ohh!

ANSELME

(*Alone:*)

In this troubled world, no man can keep
From meeting daily with some cause to weep.
Yes, here below . . .

SCENE FOUR

—•—

Pandolfe, Anselme

ANSELME

Oh, God! What's this? Alack,
Pandolfe won't rest in peace; he's coming back!
Now that he's dead, how pale his cheeks appear!
No! Keep your distance! Kindly don't come near!
I just don't care to touch a man who's dead.

PANDOLFE

What is this nonsense? Are you off your head?

ANSELME

Why are you here? Stand back, and tell me why.
If you're looking for me so as to say good-bye,
You're being much too formal. Believe you me,
I could have done without this courtesy.
If your soul's in torment and in need of prayers,
I'll tend to that, but let's have no more scares!
On the word of a terrified man, I'll go full speed
To the church, and buy you all the prayers you need.
(*He kneels.*)

Ghost, ghost, go away!
So upon my knees I pray.
May your spirit be at rest,
And in Heaven be ever blest.

PANDOLFE

(*Laughing:*)
I don't know whether to laugh, or be offended.

ANSELME

You're very gay for a man whose life has ended!

PANDOLFE

Is this a joke, or have your brains decayed?
Why treat a living person as a shade?

ANSELME

I've seen your corpse. You're dead; I cannot doubt it.

PANDOLFE

What! Can a man die, and not know about it?

ANSELME

Alas, when Mascarille first let me know
The tragic news, I almost died of woe.

PANDOLFE

Enough, now. If you're asleep, it's time to waken.
Do you not see me in the flesh?

ANSELME

                              You've taken
A spectral form that's not unlike your own,
But which, in a trice, could change to shapes unknown.
I tremble lest you swell to giant size,
With a huge, ugly face and burning eyes.
For God's sake, don't become some hideous freak,
Or I shall be too horrified to speak.

PANDOLFE

At another time, Anselme, the naïveté
And droll credulity that you display
Would give me much to jest and chaff about,
And I might wish to draw the subject out:
But this reported death of mine, combined
With a fake treasure I was sent to find,
Appear to justify my strong belief
That Mascarille's a villain, knave and thief
Who has no fear or conscience, and descends
To the basest trickery to gain his ends.

ANSELME

Have I been hoodwinked? Am I a dupe, a clown?
Oh, my intelligence, how you've let me down!
Just to be sure, I'll touch him; yes, it's he.
Plague take the ass that I've turned out to be!
Don't spread this story abroad, in Heaven's name;
They'd write a farce about me; I'd die of shame.
But now, Pandolfe, I hope you'll help me to
Get back the money I lent to bury you.

PANDOLFE

Money, you say? Ah, that's the answer! There
Is the hidden motive in this whole affair:
Well, that's your worry. I'll go complain of these
Dishonest actions to the authorities,
And once they catch that Mascarille, I'll hope
To see him dangle from a hangman's rope.

ANSELME

(*Alone:*)
I've been a credulous fool, a trusting dunce,
And lost my cunning and my cash at once.
Gray hair becomes me, if I now can make
This sort of senile, doddering mistake,
And fall so readily into a snare.
But look . . .

SCENE FIVE

———— • ————

Lélie, Anselme

LÉLIE

(*Not seeing Anselme.*)
    Now, with this passport that I bear,
I know that Trufaldin will welcome me.

ANSELME

Your sorrow has left you, I am glad to see.

LÉLIE

What's that? Oh, no, sir. Woe shall never leave
This orphaned heart, which must forever grieve.

ANSELME

I hurried back to tell you that, by chance,
That purse could cause you trouble. Though at a glance
The coins look good, I fear that I mixed in,
By error, a few which are not genuine,
And I've brought honest gold to exchange for those.
Alas, these counterfeiters! Their number grows
Each year, and thanks to them it's come about
That all transactions now are tinged with doubt.
Hang all such rascals! They deserve to die.

LÉLIE

You're kind to replace the bogus coins, though I
Did not see any. They must be hard to spot.

ANSELME

I'll recognize them; here, let me have the lot.
It's all here?

LÉLIE

Yes.

ANSELME

Good. Now, you're mine once more,
Dear purse. Slip into my pocket, as before.
Young thief, you'll get no more ill-gotten wealth.
So, you bury a man when he's in perfect health!
To a poor old father-in-law, what might you have done?
To think I'd chosen you to be my son,
And wanted Hippolyte to take your name!
Be off. Go die, sir, of remorse and shame.

LÉLIE

(*Alone:*)
Well, he saw through me. But how could he be so quick
To grow suspicious of our clever trick?

SCENE SIX

Lélie, Mascarille

MASCARILLE

So, you'd gone out! I've looked for you everywhere.
Well, now! Success at last! I do declare
That I've no equal as a scheming knave.
Give me the money, and I'll go buy our slave.
Your rival's going to be thunderstruck.

LÉLIE

Ah, my dear fellow, I fear we're out of luck.
You won't believe the bitterness of my lot.

MASCARILLE

What are you saying?

LÉLIE

              Anselme divined our plot,
And, offering to replace some counterfeit
Coins in that purse, he just made off with it.

MASCARILLE

You're joking, surely?

LÉLIE

              I fear it's all too true.

MASCARILLE

You really mean it?

LÉLIE

            Unfortunately, I do.
And now, I know, you're going to be furious.

MASCARILLE

I, sir? Of course not. Anger is injurious
To health, and I let nothing trouble me.
Whether Célie's in bondage or goes free,
Whether Léandre buys her, or does not,
Are matters I don't care about one jot.

LÉLIE

Oh, don't deny me your concern and aid,
And please forgive the little slip I made!
Up to that time, you'll grant, I'd played the part
Of a grief-stricken son with wondrous art;
The sharpest eye could never have perceived
That I was not most horribly bereaved.

MASCARILLE

Go on and praise yourself I couldn't care less.

LÉLIE

Oh, well. I made a mess of it, I confess.
But if you wish me happy, I hope you will
Forget my stupid error, and help me still.

MASCARILLE

Your servant, sir. I've other things to do.

LÉLIE

Dear Mascarille!

MASCARILLE

No.

LÉLIE

Help me, I beg of you.

MASCARILLE

No, I'll do nothing.

LÉLIE
If you won't change your mind,
I'll kill myself.

MASCARILLE
Do, if you're so inclined.

LÉLIE
You won't relent?

MASCARILLE
No.

LÉLIE
You see that my sword is drawn?

MASCARILLE
Yes.

LÉLIE
I shall thrust it through my heart.

MASCARILLE
Go on.

LÉLIE
Won't you be sad to have taken my life from me?

MASCARILLE
No.

LÉLIE
Then, farewell.

MASCARILLE
Farewell, Monsieur Lélie.

LÉLIE

So! . . .

MASCARILLE
Hurry up, please; less talk, more suicide.

LÉLIE
Because you'd get my wardrobe if I died,
You'd have me play the fool and pierce my heart.

MASCARILLE
I knew that you were faking, from the start.
Men often swear to kill themselves, and yet
Few of them, nowadays, make good their threat.

SCENE SEVEN

Trufaldin, Léandre, Lélie, Mascarille
Trufaldin and Léandre confer in low voices at stage rear.

LÉLIE

Look! Léandre and Trufaldin in conversation!
He'll buy Célie! Oh, dread and trepidation!

MASCARILLE

No doubt he wants to buy her, and if he's got
Money enough, he'll get her, like as not.
Well, I'm delighted: It's the price that must be paid
For all the blundering rashness you've displayed.

LÉLIE

What can I do now, in this fearful plight?

MASCARILLE

Who knows?

LÉLIE

I know; I'll challenge him to a fight.

MASCARILLE

What good would come of that?

LÉLIE

Advise me, then:
How can I stop him?

MASCARILLE

There, there; I'll once again
Show pity and forgive you. Leave me now;
I'll keep an eye upon him, and learn somehow,
By peaceful means, how his affairs proceed.

(*Exit Lélie.*)

TRUFALDIN

(*To Léandre:*)
When the man comes, I'll deliver, as agreed.

(*Exit Trufaldin.*)

MASCARILLE

(*Aside, as he exits:*)
I must deceive him, so that he'll unveil
His plans to me, and I can make them fail.

LÉANDRE

(*Alone:*)
  Thank Heaven, my happiness is guaranteed;
What I've arranged is certain to succeed.
There's nothing now to fear, and I'm exempt
From anything my rival might attempt.

MASCARILLE

(*Utters these two lines offstage, then enters:*)
Ouch! Ouch! Help, murder! Oh, what a cruel blow!
Stop it, you brute, you monster! Oh! Oh! Oh!

LÉANDRE

What's this? What ails you? Why these cries of pain?

MASCARILLE

Two hundred blows he gave me, with his cane.

LÉANDRE

Who did?

MASCARILLE

  Lélie.

LÉANDRE

But why?

MASCARILLE

For a mere bagatelle
He's thrown me out, and beaten me as well.

LÉANDRE

That's very wrong of him.

MASCARILLE

As soon as I can,
I vow to avenge myself on that vile man.
Yes, you shall learn, you brute who've battered me,
That you can't strike me with impunity,
That, servant though I am, I have my pride,
And that my four years' service at your side
Did not deserve this harsh emolument,
Which both my honor and my back resent.
Yes, I shall be avenged! You've wished me to
Secure a certain charming slave for you,
But I'll make sure now that some other lover,
With my assistance, will deprive you of her.

LÉANDRE

Do calm your anger, Mascarille, and hear me.
I've always liked you, and have wished sincerely
That a keen, loyal fellow of your kind
Might some day be my servant. If you're inclined
To accept the post I offer, and serve me in it,
I'll take you into my employ this minute.

MASCARILLE

Sir, I accept your offer with delight,
Because, in serving you, I'll serve him right,
And shall, in my endeavors for your sake,
Punish the beast whose cane has made me ache.
I'm sure that, through my artful aid, Célie . . .

LÉANDRE

That goal's already been achieved, by me.
Charmed by that girl, who has no peer on earth,
I've just now bought her, for far less than she's worth.

MASCARILLE

Célie is yours, then?

LÉANDRE

                              You'd see her here beside me
If I had only my desires to guide me:
But Father rules my life; he lately sent
Me word that it's his wish and firm intent
That I wed Hippolyte. He'd rage, I fear,
If rumors of Célie should reach his ear.
With Trufaldin, I thought it best to claim
That I was acting in another's name;
And we agreed that he was to consign
Célie to a man who'd show this ring of mine.
But first I must devise a means whereby
To hide my charmer from the public eye,
And find for her some quiet place where she
Can dwell in comfort and in secrecy.

MASCARILLE

Not far from town, I've an old kinsman whose
Small house I could arrange for you to use.
It's most secluded; no one would be aware
That you had secretly installed her there.

LÉANDRE

You've solved my problem; it sounds like just the thing.
Go, then, to Trufaldin, and take this ring.
As soon as he sees it, he'll release the fair
Captive whom I adore into your care.
And you can take her then to that retreat
Of which you speak. But hush! Here's Hippolyte.

SCENE EIGHT

Hippolyte, Léandre, Mascarille

HIPPOLYTE

I have some news for you, Léandre—though
Whether you'll like or loathe it, I don't know.

LÉANDRE

Before I tell you what my feelings are,
I'll have to hear it.

HIPPOLYTE

        Then walk with me as far
As the church, and I shall tell you on the way.

LÉANDRE

(*To Mascarille:*)
Go, do me that small service. And hurry, pray.

MASCARILLE

(*Alone:*)
I'll serve you, sir, with a dish of humble pie.
What rascal could be luckier than I?
What joy Lélie will shortly feel! What bliss
That the girl should drop into our hands like this!
How fine that a rival, bent on our defeat,
Has handed us a victory so sweet!
After this triumph, they'll paint me with a wreath
On my heroic brow, and underneath
Will be the glorious title I've always sought for:
MASCARILLUS RASCALUM IMPERATOR.

SCENE NINE

Trufaldin, Mascarille

MASCARILLE

Ho, there!

TRUFALDIN

(*Opening his door.*)
        What do you want?

MASCARILLE

                It should be clear,
From this familiar ring, what brings me here.

TRUFALDIN

I know the ring, and I know your errand, too.
Wait here a moment; I'll fetch the slave for you.

SCENE TEN

Trufaldin, a Messenger, Mascarille

MESSENGER

(*To Trufaldin:*)
Sir, be so kind as to tell me where a man . . .

TRUFALDIN

What man?

MESSENGER

I think his name is Trufaldin.

TRUFALDIN

You're looking at him. What do you want him for?

MESSENGER

To put this letter in his hand, no more.

TRUFALDIN

(*Reading:*)

> The kindness of that Heaven which we adore
> Has lately brought the welcome news to me
> That my daughter, kidnapped at the age of four,
> Is now your slave, and bears the name "Célie."
> If you have been a father, and have known
> How deep and tender is that natural bond,
> Then pray protect, as if she were your own,
> The precious child of whom I am so fond.
> I shall set out at once to repossess
> My daughter, and give you a reward so fine,
> So opulent, that in your happiness
> You'll bless the day when you returned me mine.
> Don Pedro De Gusman,

Marquis of Montalcana,
Madrid.

(*Trufaldin continues, aside:*)
Gypsies are not renowned for speaking truly,
Yet those who brought Célie and sold her to me
Said that a rich man soon would pay her ransom,
And that the payment would be more than handsome.
Great heavens! In my doubt and my impatience,
I almost lost my golden expectations.
(*To the Messenger:*)
Your message got here with no time to spare:
I'd all but given her to that fellow there.
But now I'll keep her safe, in every way.
(*Exit the Messenger. To Mascarille:*)
You've heard, of course, what the letter had to say.
Go tell the man who sent you here that I
Can't keep our bargain. Ask him to come by
And get his money back.

MASCARILLE
Sir, he'll be nettled
By such a breach of—

TRUFALDIN
Go, the matter's settled.

MASCARILLE
(*Alone:*)
That blasted letter was bad news for us,
And fortune has indeed been treacherous!
At a fatal moment, that rogue arrived from Spain;
May he go back through thunder, hail and rain!
Never has such a fine beginning had
An ending quite so sudden or so sad.

SCENE ELEVEN

Lélie (laughing), Mascarille

MASCARILLE

Well, well. What is it that delights you so?

LÉLIE

When I've finished laughing, I shall let you know.

MASCARILLE

Laugh, by all means; it's just the time for laughter.

LÉLIE

You'll never again complain of me; hereafter,
You won't be able to scold me as the man
Whose bungling spoils your every plot and plan,
For I've just played a shrewd trick of my own.
I can be rash and hasty, as I've shown,
But when I'm in the mood I can contrive
Fine schemes as well as any man alive,
And you yourself will grant that what I've done
Displays a wit unmatched by anyone.

MASCARILLE

Well, what have you done? Don't keep me in suspense.

LÉLIE

Just now, when I saw my foe in conference
With Trufaldin, I felt a deep disquiet,
And, seeking for some way to rectify it,
Marshaled my powers and, by means of them,
Conceived and carried out a stratagem
Which, if compared to the dazzling tricks you've played,
Is brighter still, and puts them in the shade.

MASCARILLE

Exactly what? . . .

LÉLIE

Be patient, please, I wrote
And sent to Trufaldin a spurious note.
Signed by a nobleman of my invention,
Who said that Heaven had brought to his attention
The fact that his lost daughter, now called "Célie,"
Was dwelling, as a slave, with the addressee.
He conjured Trufaldin to give good care
To the girl, until her father could be there,
Adding that he was leaving Spain that day
And planned upon arrival to repay
The latter's kindness with a lavish sum.

MASCARILLE

Splendid.

LÉLIE

But wait, the best is yet to come.
The messenger who gave Trufaldin my letter
Said that its timing couldn't have been better!
A man had claimed Célie, and was about
To bear her off, but the fool was put to rout.

MASCARILLE

Did the Devil help you in this bright endeavor?

LÉLIE

Would you have dreamt that I could be so clever?
You should commend the style and expertise
With which I foiled my rival's strategies.

MASCARILLE

I fear I lack the eloquence and strength
To praise your deed with proper force and length.
My tongue is powerless to describe the bold

Exploit which I was privileged to behold,
And the workings of a wit which can "contrive
Fine schemes as well as any man alive."
I wish, indeed, that I possessed a mind
In which all art and wisdom were combined,
And so could tell you in great prose or verse
That you will always be, for better or worse,
What you have been from the hour of your birth—
That is to say, the rashest fool on earth,
A man whose reason is deranged and ill,
Whose judgment's warped, whose common sense is nil,
A blunderer, a dolt, a knucklehead,
And . . . a hundred other things I might have said.
There's a brief sample of the praise that's due you.

LÉLIE

Have I done something that's annoying to you?
Why are you angry? What can the reason be?

MASCARILLE

No, you've done nothing; but don't you follow me.

LÉLIE

I'll follow you until I get an answer.

MASCARILLE

Will you? Then run as quickly as you can, sir.
I'll give your legs a bit of exercise.

LÉLIE

(*Alone:*)
He's got away. Alas, I can't surmise
The reason for that violent tirade.
What blunder can I possibly have made?

Act Three

———◆•◆———

Mascarille

MASCARILLE

Hush, my good nature; you haven't a grain of sense,
And I'll no longer hear your arguments.
It's you, my anger, that I'll listen to.
Am I obliged forever to undo
The blunders of a clod? I should resign!
That fool has spoiled too many schemes of mine.
And yet, let's think about this matter coolly.
Were I to let my just impatience rule me,
They'd say that I'd been quick to call it quits,
And that I'd lost the vigor of my wits;
And what then would become of my renown
As the most glorious trickster in the town,
A reputation that I've earned by never
Failing to think of something wildly clever?
O Mascarille, let honor be your guide!
Persist in those great works which are your pride,
And though your master irks you, persevere
Not for his sake, but for your own career.
Yet what can you accomplish, when the force
Of a demonic head wind blocks your course,
And you're compelled to tack and tack again?
What is the use of persevering, when
His folly brings continual heavy weather,
And sinks the best schemes you can put together?
Well, out of kindness, let us give it one
Final attempt, and see what can be done;
Then, if he wrecks our chances as before,
I swear that I'll not help him anymore.
We might, in fact, accomplish our desire
If we could get our rival to retire—

If, backing off, Léandre would allow
Me one whole day for the plot I'm hatching now.
Yes, I'm now thinking out an artful plan
Which surely will succeed, if I but can
Remove the obstacle I've spoken of
He's coming: I'll test the firmness of his love.

SCENE TWO

Léandre, Mascarille

MASCARILLE
Bad news, sir; Trufaldin won't keep his word.

LÉANDRE
I've just now seen him, and that's what I heard.
I've also learned that that romantic blather
About a stolen child whose noble father
Is coming with a bag of gold from Spain
Is purest fabrication and chicane,
Whereby Lélie has kept, for a day or two,
My purchase of Célie from going through.

MASCARILLE
What a beast he is!

LÉANDRE
                    Yet Trufaldin's unable
To see that story as a silly fable,
And has so greedily swallowed all those lies
That no one can persuade him otherwise.

MASCARILLE
He'll keep her now in strictest custody;
There's nothing we can do, that I can see.

LÉANDRE
From the very first, I felt affection for her,
But now, in truth, I utterly adore her,
And there are many times when I incline
To drop all caution and to make her mine—
To change her bonds for those of wedded life,
And mend her lot by making her my wife.

MASCARILLE

You'd marry her?

LÉANDRE

Well, I'm not entirely sure;
But though her background is a bit obscure,
Her grace and virtue have, it must be said,
A power to win one's heart and turn one's head.

MASCARILLE

Her virtue? Hmm.

LÉANDRE

What? Why do you grunt when I
Make mention of her virtue? Tell me why.

MASCARILLE

Your countenance, sir, is darker than before;
I would be wise, perhaps, to say no more.

LÉANDRE

No, no, speak out.

MASCARILLE

Well then, from Christian kindness,
I shall proceed to cure you of your blindness.
That wench . . .

LÉANDRE

Go on.

MASCARILLE

Is anything but chilly.
In secret, she's a most obliging filly,
And any man who treats her well will find
That her heart isn't of the flinty kind.
She seems demure, and feigns to be a prude,

But I can speak of her with certitude.
It's part of my profession, you might say,
To know the shady games that people play.

LÉANDRE

But—

MASCARILLE

  Her modesty's the purest of pretenses;
Her virtue is a fort without defenses,
A shadow which, as many a man could tell,
The glitter of a gold piece can dispel.

LÉANDRE

What are you saying? How can I believe . . .

MASCARILLE

Do as you like, sir; you're free to be naive.
Yes, doubt my word and do as you have planned—
Purchase the wench, and offer her your hand.
The whole town will applaud you, for you'll be
The keeper of its common property.

LÉANDRE

I'm stunned.

MASCARILLE

(*Aside:*)
  Aha! This fish begins to bite,
And if I hook him well, and play him right,
We shall have one impediment the less.

LÉANDRE

I'm overcome with horror and distress.

MASCARILLE

Well, now you . . .

LÉANDRE

        Go to the post house, please, and see
If there's a letter there addressed to me.
(*Alone, having brooded for a moment or two:*)
It's true, no doubt; but how was one to tell?
Never did any face deceive so well.

SCENE THREE

Lélie, Léandre

LÉLIE

Why is it that you look so very sad?

LÉANDRE

I?

LÉLIE

You.

LÉANDRE

I have no grounds for feeling bad.

LÉLIE

Oh, yes, you do: Célie is on your mind.

LÉANDRE

My thoughts don't stoop to trifles of that kind.

LÉLIE

You had great plans for snaring her somehow,
But since they failed, you feign indifference now.

LÉANDRE

If I were fool enough to pin my dreams
On her, I'd soon make mock of all your schemes.

LÉLIE

What schemes?

LÉANDRE

Come, come! We know it all, my friend.

LÉLIE

All what?

LÉANDRE

Your whole campaign, from end to end.

LÉLIE

What can you mean? You're talking gibberish.

LÉANDRE

Claim not to understand me, if you wish.
But let me tell you something: You needn't fear
That I'll try to take away your captive dear.
I worship beauty when it's fresh and chaste,
But I can't yearn for what has been debased.

LÉLIE

Take care, Léandre!

LÉANDRE

Oh, how you've been taken in!
Go on, then; court this spotless heroine,
And boast then of your amorous success.
She has uncommon beauty, I confess,
But the rest of her, Lélie, is common stuff

LÉLIE

No more such talk, Léandre; that's enough.
Vie with me all you like, and strive to claim her,
But let's not hear you slander and defame her.
I charge myself with utter cowardice
For letting you blaspheme Célie like this,
And though I can endure it that you love her,
I cannot brook your speaking evil of her.

LÉANDRE

I've good authority for speaking so.

LÉLIE

Whoever said such things is false and low.
The girl is wholly innocent and pure;
I know her heart.

LÉANDRE

But Mascarille, I'm sure,
Is a good judge of hearts and their affairs,
And he condemns her.

LÉLIE

He?

LÉANDRE
Yes, he.

LÉLIE

He dares
Malign a blameless girl, who lives uprightly?
Does he suppose that I will take that lightly?
He'll eat his words!

LÉANDRE
I wager he will not.

LÉLIE

By God, I'd beat him senseless on the spot,
If he dared reiterate so base a lie.

LÉANDRE

I'd crop his ears if he were to deny
The things he told me. He'd better stand his ground.

SCENE FOUR

———————◦•◦———————

Lélie, Léandre, Mascarille

LÉLIE

Ah, there he is! Come here, you cursèd hound.

MASCARILLE

What?

LÉLIE

Yes, you monster of duplicity,
How could you sink your fangs into Célie,
Blackening the virtue of the brightest maid
Ever to dwell within misfortune's shade?

MASCARILLE

(*Sotto voce, to Lélie:*)
Calm down, sir; it's just part of a little hoax.

LÉLIE

No, none of your winking; none of your merry jokes;
I'm blind and deaf to all you do and say.
Were you my brother, there'd still be Hell to pay,
For anyone who speaks a calumny
Of her I love has deeply wounded me.
Stop making faces! Now, what did you say, you scum?

MASCARILLE

I'm going, sir, lest our talk grow quarrelsome.

LÉLIE

No, you shall stay.

MASCARILLE

Ouch!

LÉLIE

Out with it, now! Confess.

MASCARILLE

(*Sotto voce, to Lélie:*)
'Twas just a bit of intrigue—no more, no less.

LÉLIE

Enough, now. Tell me, what did you say of her?

MASCARILLE

(*Sotto voce, to Lélie:*)
I said what I said; don't lose your temper, sir.

LÉLIE

(*Drawing his sword.*)
You'll change your tune, by Heaven, before I'm through!

LÉANDRE

(*Stopping him.*)
Don't let your anger run away with you.

MASCARILLE

(*Aside:*)
In all the world, was there ever a brain so dim?

LÉLIE

Come, let me wreak my righteous wrath on him.

LÉANDRE

If you struck him in my presence, I'd take offense.

LÉLIE

Can't I punish my own servant? That makes no sense.

LÉANDRE

Your servant?

MASCARILLE

(*Aside:*)
> Ohh! He'll soon see through my plot.

LÉLIE

If I want to beat him to death, why should I not?
He is, after all, my man.

LÉANDRE
> He's my man now.

LÉLIE

That's most amusing. Kindly tell me how
He comes to be yours.

MASCARILLE

(*Sotto voce, to Lélie:*)
> Take care.

LÉLIE
>> What's that you say?

MASCARILLE

(*Aside:*)
What a dolt! He's bound to give the game away.
He sees my signals, but he pays no heed.

LÉLIE

Léandre, you have strange ideas indeed.
He's not my man, eh?

LÉANDRE
> Wasn't he shown the door
Because of some small thing you blamed him for?

LÉLIE

That's news to me.

LÉANDRE

And didn't you bestow
A savage beating when you bade him go?

LÉLIE

What! I discharge my man? And thrash him too?
You're having fun with me . . . or he with you.

MASCARILLE

(*Aside:*)
Go on, fool: You're your own worst adversary.

LÉANDRE

(*To Mascarille:*)
So, that fierce beating was imaginary!

MASCARILLE

It's slipped his mind. His memory's—

LÉANDRE

No, no,
As all the evidence now seems to show,
You've played me a crafty trick, which I'll forgive
Because the ruse was so imaginative.
It's enough for me that I now know the facts,
And know the motive for your cunning acts,
And that, considering how hard I fell
For your deceits, I've come off pretty well.
Henceforth I'll be more cautious, thanks to you.
Your humble servant, dear Lélie. Adieu.

(*Exit Léandre.*)

MASCARILLE

Courage, my boy; our cause must never yield.
Let's draw our swords and bravely take the field;
We'll sweep to victory like Huns or Vandals!

LÉLIE

He said that you were spreading filthy scandals
About . . .

MASCARILLE

Why wouldn't you go along with my
Deceptions, which he'd swallowed, and whereby
I'd all but killed his feelings for Célie?
But no, my master wouldn't lie, not he!
I win his rival's confidence, and the dunce
Gives me a chance to steal Célie at once;
My master ruins everything, however,
By a note from Spain which frustrates my endeavor.
I undermine his rival's passion, but then
My master comes and props it up again,
Ignores my winks and whispers, and refuses
To stop till he's dismantled all my ruses.
Rare work by one who says he can "contrive
Fine schemes as well as any man alive"!
Such art as you have shown should hang, say I,
In the king's gorgeous palace at Versailles.

LÉLIE

It isn't *my* fault that I sometimes mar
Your plans; if you don't tell me what they are,
I'm bound to do so.

MASCARILLE

So much the worse for you.

LÉLIE

You'd have a right to chide me if I knew
A bit about the plots you were devising;
But since you tell me nothing, it's not surprising
That I am made to seem a blundering fool.

MASCARILLE

You really ought to run a fencing school.

How well you avoid the point! And your deflection
Of my attack is something like perfection.

LÉLIE

What's done is done; let's let the subject drop.
My rival, in any case, can't put a stop
To our endeavors, and I rely on you . . .

MASCARILLE

If you don't mind, let's drop that subject, too.
My anger's not so easily mollified,
And if you want my temper to subside,
You must do me a service first. I'll ponder then
Whether to run your love campaigns again.

LÉLIE

Whatever you ask, I'll happily accord.
Do you need my good right arm, my trusty sword?

MASCARILLE

What brutal fancies occupy his mind!
You sound like some swashbuckler of the kind
That's always readier to draw a blade
Than draw his purse and give a poor man aid.

LÉLIE

What, then, can I do for you?

MASCARILLE

                                Go see your sire;
Do everything you can to appease his ire.

LÉLIE

I've gained his pardon.

MASCARILLE

                                Well, I have not. I spread
A rumor, for your sake, that he was dead,

And it upset him greatly. One gets no thanks
From agèd men for playing them such pranks,
And causing them to contemplate with fear
The melancholy end that's drawing near.
The old boy's still in love with life, and he
Sees nothing funny in mortality;
He's furious and, according to report,
It's his intent to haul me into court.
I fear that, if I took up residence
In prison, living at the king's expense,
It might be long before I was at large.
I've been accused of many an unjust charge,
For virtue's hated in these wicked times,
And persecuted like the worst of crimes.
Go. Make him forgive me.

LÉLIE
I'll do so; count on me.

But promise me in return . . .

MASCARILLE
Yes, yes. We'll see.

(*Exit Lélie.*)
Now I'll relax, and yield to my fatigue.
No plots for a while, no dodges, no intrigue,
No more behaving like a man possessed.
Léandre can't act against our interest,
Because Célie is under lock and key . . .

SCENE FIVE

Ergaste, Mascarille

ERGASTE

Ah! I've been looking for you, Mascarille.
There's a secret matter of which I've just got word.

MASCARILLE

What is it, Ergaste?

ERGASTE

We won't be overheard?

MASCARILLE

No.

ERGASTE

As your bosom friend, I'm well aware
Of the part you play in your master's love affair.
Well, be on your guard. Léandre has a plan
To steal Célie away from Trufaldin
This very night. He, having understood
That certain ladies of the neighborhood
Go visiting in masks this time of year,
Has planned his own sly masquerade, I hear.

MASCARILLE

Is that so? Well, he's not yet won the day.
I just might fool him, and rob him of his prey.
Yes, I'll turn his tricks against him! It won't be hard
To hoist the fellow with his own petard.
He doesn't know my gifts, Ergaste. Adieu;
When next we meet, we'll drain a glass or two.
(*Exit Ergaste.*)
I'll borrow our rival's plan, converting it
Adroitly to my master's benefit,

And thus, by a maneuver bold yet wise,
Avoid all risk, yet carry off the prize.
If I don a mask, and get there first, then I'll
Be sure at least to cramp Léandre's style;
And if I manage to achieve our aim
And steal Célie, it's he who'll get the blame!
Since word of his scheme's already gotten out,
It's he who'd be accused, beyond a doubt,
And so I undertake this dangerous mission
Without a qualm, and fearless of suspicion.
This is called being subtle, shrewd and cool,
And using someone as a pawn, or tool.
Well, I must hurry and enlist the aid
Of a few comrades for this masquerade;
I have connections, and I can supply
Both men and gear in the twinkling of an eye.
'Twill be a brilliant coup, believe you me;
The Lord endowed me with rascality,
And I am not the thankless sort of knave
Who hides beneath a bushel what Heaven gave.

SCENE SIX

Lélie, Ergaste

LÉLIE

So, he'll gain entry as a masquer, then,
And carry her off?

ERGASTE

    Exactly. One of his men
Told me as much, and I ran instantly
To break the whole affair to Mascarille,
Who left at once to foil Léandre's plot
By some device he'd thought of on the spot.
Soon afterward, I met by chance with you,
And thought it best, sir, to inform you, too.

LÉLIE

For this intelligence, I'm in your debt.
Go. What you've done for me, I shan't forget.
(*Exit Ergaste.*)
My knave will play them some fine trick, I know;
But I'm moved to help him, and somehow strike a blow.
It's wrong, in matters which concern me most,
That I should stand by like a stump or post.
Night's falling. They'll be surprised to see me there.
I should have brought my musket, I declare.
But let who will attack me! By the Lord,
I've two good pistols and a good sharp sword.
Ho there, inside!

SCENE SEVEN

Trufaldin (at his window), Lélie

TRUFALDIN
Who called me, and what for?

LÉLIE
Make sure, this evening, that you've locked the door.

TRUFALDIN
Why?

LÉLIE
There's a merry troupe of masquers coming,
Who mean to treat you to some curious mumming;
They plan to abduct Célie.

TRUFALDIN
They do? Oh, dear!

LÉLIE
I have no doubt that they will soon be here.
Stay at your window, and you'll see the show.
There now, they're coming! Didn't I tell you so?
Hush! I'll confront them, and we'll have some fun
With these impostors, unless they cut and run.

SCENE EIGHT

*Lélie, Trufaldin, Mascarille and his company
(masked and in dresses)*

TRUFALDIN
Rogues! It takes more to fool me than a mask!

LÉLIE
Well, ladies! Where are you off to, may I ask?
Let them in, Trufaldin; they'll dance and sing.
(*To Mascarille, disguised as a woman:*)
My, what a charmer; what a sweet young thing!
Why are you muttering so? Fairest of creatures,
Let me remove your mask and see your features!

TRUFALDIN
Be off, you vicious knaves! Get out of my sight,
You wretches! And you, sir, thank you and good night.

(*Exit Trufaldin.*)

LÉLIE
(*Having unmasked Mascarille.*)
Mascarille, is it you?

MASCARILLE
No, it's someone else entirely.

LÉLIE
What a shock! Alas, fate's treated me most direly.
Since you'd told me nothing, how could I surmise
That you were hidden under that disguise?
Poor botcher that I am, it makes me sick
Unwittingly to have played you such a trick.
So angry am I that I'd like to whack
Myself a thousand times across my back.

MASCARILLE

Farewell, fine schemer, cleverest of men.

LÉLIE

If you're too enraged to help me ever again,
Then who will guide me?

MASCARILLE

Satan will do that for you.

LÉLIE

Oh, if you don't yet hate me, I implore you
Once more to pardon my stupidities!
If I must kiss your feet, or clasp your knees,
I'll gladly . . .

MASCARILLE

Nonsense. Come, my lads, I hear
Another band of revelers drawing near.

SCENE NINE

—•—

Léandre and his company (masked),
Trufaldin (at his window)

LÉANDRE

No noise, now; let's be proper and polite.

TRUFALDIN

What! Throngs of masquers at my door all night?
Don't catch a cold for nothing, sirs; take care;
You're going to have a good long wait out there.
It's a little late for carrying off Célie,
Who offers her regrets, by way of me.
She's gone to bed, and cannot see you now,
But, wishing to express her thanks somehow
For all your kind solicitude and pains,
She sends you what this fragrant pot contains.

LÉANDRE

Oh no, I'm soaked! And what an awful stink!
Let's go, my friends; they're on to us, I think.

Act Four

SCENE ONE

Lélie (disguised as an Armenian), Mascarille

MASCARILLE

In that weird garb, you're the prettiest thing alive.

LÉLIE

Your new scheme makes my fainting hopes revive.

MASCARILLE

I can't stay angry; my wrath is quickly spent.
I rage, and then, as always, I relent.

LÉLIE

My friend, if ever I come into my own,
My gratitude will lavishly be shown.
And while I have one crust of bread to share—

MASCARILLE

Enough. You have a part, now, to prepare.
This time, you have a role to memorize,
And can't claim to be taken by surprise
If you should blunder, and spoil another plan.

LÉLIE

You're living now, you say, with Trufaldin?

MASCARILLE

Yes. I feigned a deep concern for the old duffer,
And warned him to be careful lest he suffer
From plots and strategies his foes were hatching.
Two parties, so I said, were bent on snatching
The slave regarding whom he'd just received
A letter too absurd to be believed.

They had, I said, attempted to enlist
My aid, but it was easy to resist,
Because I loved him so, and would not hurt him,
And felt it was my duty to alert him.
I then held forth on how deceit and fraud,
In these dark days, walk brazenly abroad;
How I'd grown weary of the worldly life
And, wishing to withdraw from sin and strife
So as to mend my soul, had formed a plan
To dwell beneath the roof of some good man.
I added that, if he were willing, I'd
Rejoice to live with him until I died;
That my devotion to him was so fervent
That I'd expect no wages as his servant;
That I'd entrust to his wise custody
My savings and my father's legacy;
And that, if Heaven called me to my rest,
He would inherit all that I possessed.
That last thought won his heart, needless to say.
My aim in all this was to find a way
For you and your beloved to rendezvous
In secret, and determine what to do;
But I was led to think how you might be
Admitted to her house quite openly,
When, speaking of a long-lost son, he said
That he'd seen him, in a dream, rise from the dead.
Now, here's the history which he then related,
And on which our new hoax is predicated.

LÉLIE

I know all that; you've told me twice before.

MASCARILLE

Yes, yes; and though I tell it all once more,
It may be that your great mind still will fail
To recollect some critical detail.

LÉLIE

I cannot bear to stand around and stall.

MASCARILLE

Let's not be hasty, or we may trip and fall.
Your brain, sir, is a little thick and slow;
Learn your part cold, and then we'll have our show.
'Twas from Naples, you'll recall, that Trufaldin came.
Zanobio Ruberti was then his name.
It was suspected (though he's not the sort
To topple governments) that he'd lent support
To some insurgents of the left or right,
And so he had to flee the town by night.
His wife and infant daughter were left behind,
And he soon heard, with great distress of mind,
That they were dead. Alone and much cast down,
He wished to take his wealth to some new town
And buy a house, and live there with his one
Remaining child—Horace, a dear young son.
He wrote a letter to Bologna, where
The boy was being schooled by one Albert,
And sadly waited while, for two years' space,
None came to the appointed meeting place.
At last he judged that they were dead, and so
Moved to this city, and took the name we know,
And has in twelve years had no word, alas,
Of this Albert or of the son, Horace.
There's the tale, retold in a manner brief and broad,
To help you grasp the groundwork of our fraud.
Now, you're an Armenian merchant, and you're to tell
Of seeing those two in Turkey—alive and well,
As Trufaldin predicted in his dream.
I chose that fiction for our little scheme,
Since folk are often, in romantic works,
Kidnapped at sea by buccaneering Turks,
Are thought to be dead for fifteen years or more,
Then turn up smiling at their kinfolks' door.
I've read a hundred stories in that vein.

Let's steal the plot; 'twill save us mental strain.
So—you're to tell how the two men had been sold
As slaves; and how you ransomed them with gold;
And how, when you left because of urgent news,
Horace asked you to see his father, whose
Address he'd lately learned, and linger here
For a few days until they should appear.
Have you followed that long-winded exposition?

LÉLIE

It's pointless, all this boring repetition.
I understood it all the first time through.

MASCARILLE

Then I'll go in, and prepare the way for you.

LÉLIE

Wait, Mascarille. There's one small thing, just one:
What if he asks me to describe his son?

MASCARILLE

Why should that be a problem? After all,
His son, when last he saw him, was very small.
And can we not assume, in any case,
That time and slavery have transformed his face?

LÉLIE

That's true. But . . . if he remembers seeing me,
What shall I do?

MASCARILLE

Have you no memory?
I've said already that your features can
Have made no real impression on Trufaldin,
Since you so briefly passed before his eyes.
What's more, your beard and clothes are a fine disguise.

LÉLIE

All right . . . But where, in Turkey, shall I claim . . . ?

MASCARILLE

Turkey or Barbary, it's all the same.

LÉLIE

But where did I see them? What's the name of the town?

MASCARILLE

Tunis! He'll keep me here till the sun goes down.
He says my repetitions are a bore,
But he's made me name that town ten times or more.

LÉLIE

Go in, then, and prepare the way; I'm ready.

MASCARILLE

Now, do act prudently; be staid and steady.
None of your Spanish inspirations, please.

LÉLIE

Don't worry. You have such strange anxieties!

MASCARILLE

Horace—schooled in Bologna. Trufaldin—
Zanobio Ruberti in Naples, where he began—
Albert the tutor . . .

LÉLIE

It sounds like grammar school
When you drill me so; do you take me for a fool?

MASCARILLE

No, just a little retarded, so to speak.

LÉLIE

(*Alone:*)
When I don't require his help, he's mild and meek,
But when he knows I need him, as at present,
His tongue grows disrespectful and unpleasant.
Ah, soon she'll turn those radiant eyes on me
Which hold me in such sweet captivity;
Soon I'll be free to let that fair one know,
In burning words, what pains I undergo,
And learn from her my fate . . . But here they are.

SCENE TWO

Trufaldin, Lélie, Mascarille

TRUFALDIN

Praise be to Heaven, and to my lucky star!

MASCARILLE

You're good at "seeing visions and dreaming dreams,"
Since what you dream about comes true, it seems.

TRUFALDIN

(*To Lélie:*)
For these good tidings, how can I thank you, sir?
You seem to me a heavenly messenger.

LÉLIE

Spare me such compliments, I beg of you.

TRUFALDIN

(*To Mascarille:*)
I don't know where, but I've seen someone who
Resembles this Armenian.

MASCARILLE

It's the same with me:
It's eerie how alike some men can be.

TRUFALDIN

So you've seen the son on whom my fond hopes rest?

LÉLIE

Oh, yes, signor, he's hale and full of zest.

TRUFALDIN

Did he speak of me, when he told you of his fate?

LÉLIE

Oh, a thousand times!

MASCARILLE

(*Aside to Lélie:*)

Let's not exaggerate.

LÉLIE

He described you to me, just as I see you now:
Your face, your bearing . . .

TRUFALDIN

He did? I don't see how.
He was but seven when he saw me last.
Even his tutor, since so much time has passed,
Would find it hard to recognize my face.

MASCARILLE

From a son's deep memory, nothing can erase
His father's image, and in that sense bereave him;
My own dear father . . .

TRUFALDIN

Enough.

(*To Lélie:*)
Where did you leave him?

LÉLIE

At Turin, in Turkey.

TRUFALDIN

Turin? But that town
Is in Piedmont, surely?

MASCARILLE

(*Aside:*)

Oh, that brainless clown!

(*To Trufaldin:*)
You misunderstand, sir; *Tunis*, he means to say.
That's where he left your son the other day.
Armenians have some odd pronunciations
Which jar upon the ears of other nations:
They voice the syllable *nis* as *rin*, and thus
When they say "Tunis," it sounds like "Turin" to us.

TRUFALDIN

Such a curious fact was more than I could guess.
(*To Lélie:*)
How did you find me? Did he give you my address?

MASCARILLE

(*Aside:*)
Will the idiot never answer?
(*Mascarille makes urgent signals to Lélie, and when this is
noticed by Trufaldin, pretends to be fencing.*)
             I was just
Rehearsing a little bit of cut and thrust.
I used to be a champion at that sport,
And shone in fencing bouts of every sort.

TRUFALDIN

(*To Mascarille:*)
Fencing is not my present interest.
(*To Lélie:*)
What other name did he say I had possessed?

MASCARILLE

Ah, Signor Zanobio Ruberti, what a joy
That Heaven's restored to you your cherished boy!

LÉLIE

That's your real name; the other's a pseudonym.

TRUFALDIN

And where was he born? Did you learn that, too, from him?

MASCARILLE

Naples would seem a charming place to live,
Though your memories must be dark and negative.

TRUFALDIN

Can't you be still and let us talk, my man?

LÉLIE

It was in Naples that his life began.

TRUFALDIN

Where was he sent as a child, and in whose care?

MASCARILLE

You should think highly of the good Albert;
After Bologna, he stayed at your son's side,
Still serving as his guardian and his guide.

TRUFALDIN

Humph!

MASCARILLE

(*Aside:*)
            If this goes on much longer, we're undone.

TRUFALDIN

Tell me what happened to him and to my son;
When Fate surprised them, what vessel were they on?

MASCARILLE

It's strange, I can't do anything but yawn.
Come, Signor Trufaldin, don't you think it meet
That your foreign guest be given a bite to eat?
It's growing late.

LÉLIE

No thank you; nothing for me.

MASCARILLE

You're hungrier than you think, sir. Wait and see.

TRUFALDIN

Come in, then.

LÉLIE

After you.

MASCARILLE

In Armenia, sir,
The host goes in before the visitor.
(*To Lélie, after Trufaldin has gone into the house:*)
You poor thing! Can't you speak?

LÉLIE

I was at first
Flustered, and so forgot what we'd rehearsed.
But now, don't worry, I shall talk a lot . . .

MASCARILLE

Here comes your rival, who doesn't suspect our plot.

SCENE THREE

—◆—●—

Anselme, Léandre

ANSELME

Wait, Léandre. I've some counsels to impart
That have your honor and peace of mind at heart.
I don't come as the father of Hippolyte,
To urge you for our sake to be discreet;
Rather I speak as your dear father would,
If he gave you frank advice for your own good,
Or as I'd wish some man, with kindly suasion,
To advise my own son, were there a like occasion.
D'you know what the town's been saying since last night,
When this amour of yours first came to light?—
To what coarse gossip, sneers and winking eyes
Your last night's escapade has given rise?—
What people think of your capricious taste
In choosing for your lady an unchaste
Gypsy, a woman of the streets, a jade
Whose noblest calling is the beggar's trade?
I blush for you; and for myself no less,
Who am involved in this opprobrious mess:
For if my daughter, whom you courted, were
Forsaken, 'twould insult both me and her.
Léandre, my boy, put all of this behind you!
Don't let infatuation further blind you.
No man is always wise; we've all transgressed;
But the shortest errors always are the best.
When a wife brings only beauty as her dower,
One's marriage soon grows needy, cold and sour,
And the wife's pretty face cannot contend
With the gloom in which such hasty matches end.
No, I repeat, these rash and starry-eyed

Weddings, these ardent unions, can provide
A few sweet nights of passion, to be sure;
But such felicities do not endure.
Once it is gratified, desire decays,
And those sweet nights give way to bitter days—
To cares and miseries, to frets and bothers,
And sons cut off by their indignant fathers.

LÉANDRE

In what you've said, there's nothing I've not heard
From my own conscience, almost word for word.
For the honor you would do me, I'm your debtor,
And I shall strive, sir, to deserve it better.
Though passion still would blind me, I now see
Your daughter's worth and virtue beckoning me,
And I'm determined—

ANSELME

          That door is opening! Come,
Let's get away from here, for fear that some
Black magic from that house will seize your soul.

SCENE FOUR

Lélie, Mascarille

MASCARILLE

If you keep on making dumb mistakes, our whole
Conspiracy will crumble in our hands.

LÉLIE

Why must I hear these endless reprimands?
What have I done? Didn't I get things right
Once we had gone inside the house?

MASCARILLE

Not quite.
You said that the Turks are heretics, and swore
With utter certainty that they adore
The sun and moon as their ancestral gods.
Well, let that pass. What's crazier, by all odds,
Is the moonstruck way you act around Célie.
Your love is like a simmering fricassee,
Which, when the fire beneath it gets too hot,
Comes bubbling up and overflows the pot.

LÉLIE

My coolness and restraint were infinite!
I hardly spoke to her, you must admit.

MASCARILLE

You hardly spoke, but how you did behave!
During our brief repast, your actions gave
More reason for suspicion than, I fear,
Another man could give in half a year.

LÉLIE

How so?

MASCARILLE

How so? When Trufaldin asked Célie
To join us at the table, all could see
How your enchanted gaze was fixed on her.
Blushing and mute and lovesick as you were,
You left your food untouched, and had no thirst,
Unless she took a sip of claret first;
Then you would seize her glass with eager will,
Not letting any drop of liquid spill,
And drink whatever wine remained within,
Placing your lips where her two lips had been.
Each scrap of bread that she had touched or bitten
You pounced upon as quickly as a kitten
That seeks to pin a mouse beneath its paw,
And popped them all into your greedy maw.
Under the table, furthermore, your feet
Kept up a jittery annoying beat
And Trufaldin, whom you twice kicked in the shins,
Punished two blameless puppies for your sins,
Because they couldn't speak and clear their name.
Was all this wise behavior, as you claim?
Watching you made me twist and squirm and get,
Despite the season, into a burning sweat.
I watched you as a man who plays at bowls
Studies his ball's trajectory as it rolls,
And, like that man, I writhed and twitched, as though
I could control your folly by doing so.

LÉLIE

My passionate acts are easy to condemn,
Since you're not in love with what occasions them!
Still, for your sake, I'll try now to subdue
The amorous seizures that I'm subject to.
I'll . . .

SCENE FIVE

Trufaldin, Lélie, Mascarille

MASCARILLE
We were speaking of your son's adversities.

TRUFALDIN
That's kind of you.
(*To Lélie:*)
Will you permit me, please,
To have a private word with Mascarille?

LÉLIE
I'll gladly do you, sir, that courtesy.

(*Lélie goes into Trufaldin's house.*)

TRUFALDIN
Now, listen: Do you know what I've just done?

MASCARILLE
I don't, sir; but the odds are ten to one
That you'll soon tell me.

TRUFALDIN
            From a great oak, tall and strong,
Whose mighty life is now two centuries long,
I cut a handsome branch, selecting it
Because it had the largeness requisite.
Of it I fashioned, with much skill and quickness,
(*Holding out his arm.*)
A cudgel of . . . let's see . . . about this thickness,
Though tapered at one end. A single whack
From it's worth fifty lashes on the back,
Because it's heavy, and full of knots as well.

MASCARILLE

For whose sake have you done all this, pray tell?

TRUFALDIN

For you, first; then for that most pious brother
Who'd foist one person on me, and filch another—
That rascal in Armenian disguise
Who took me in with a damned pack of lies.

MASCARILLE

What! You don't think . . .

TRUFALDIN

There's nothing you can say,
For he himself has given the game away:
He whispered to Célie, squeezing her hand,
That for her sake his wicked hoax was planned—
Not knowing that Jeannette, my godchild, heard
The whole confession, missing not a word.
He didn't mention you, but I've no doubt
That you were in cahoots with him throughout.

MASCARILLE

Oh, sir, you wrong me. If he imposed on you,
He fooled me first. I thought his tale was true.

TRUFALDIN

If you want to prove to me that you're sincere,
Then help me throw that scoundrel out of here.
Once we have banged and battered him a little,
I shall bestow on you a full acquittal.

MASCARILLE

I'll gladly thrash him, and prove that I did not
Have any part in this distasteful plot.
(*Aside:*)
Yes, you Armenian ass, you're going to pay
For this last bungle!

SCENE SIX

——◆——

Lélie, Trufaldin, Mascarille

TRUFALDIN
(*To Lélie, having knocked at his door:*)
                    Come out and join us, pray.
So, you impostor! Do you dare deceive
An honest man with cruel make-believe . . .

MASCARILLE
Pretending to have seen his son abroad,
So as to get into his house by fraud?

TRUFALDIN
(*Beating Lélie.*)
Be off, this minute!

LÉLIE
(*To Mascarille, who is also beating him:*)
                    Ah, you knave!

MASCARILLE
                              It's thus
That tricksters . . .

LÉLIE
Villain!

MASCARILLE
      Are chastised by us.
Take that!

LÉLIE
        Shall a gentleman be knocked about . . . ?

MASCARILLE

I'll knock your head off, if you don't clear out.

TRUFALDIN

Well done. Come, let's go in. I'm satisfied.

LÉLIE

(*Returning.*)
Thrashed by my own valet! I'm mortified.
Who would have thought the flunky could betray
His master in so insolent a way?

MASCARILLE

(*From Trufaldin's window.*)
If you don't mind my asking, how's your back?

LÉLIE

You dare address me, after that base attack?

MASCARILLE

I've no apologies. It's what you get
For babbling, and not noticing Jeannette.
But I won't rage against you now. For once
I shan't blow up and curse you for a dunce;
Though what you did was rash and asinine,
I've taken out my anger on your spine.

LÉLIE

I'll have revenge for that disloyal act!

MASCARILLE

You brought that beating on yourself, in fact.

LÉLIE

I? How?

MASCARILLE

If you had used your wits in there,

When you were talking with your lady fair,
You would have seen the young Jeannette draw near
And drink in all you said with eager ear.

LÉLIE

That I was overheard, I can't conceive.

MASCARILLE

Why, then, were you so brusquely asked to leave?
No, no, your loose tongue gave our game away.
I'd hate to see you try to play piquet:
You'd show your hand and lose, again and again.

LÉLIE

Oh, I'm the most unfortunate of men!
But why did you join our host in beating me?

MASCARILLE

It was the brainy thing to do, lest he
Suspect that I had framed our plot, or deem
That I'd been your accomplice in the scheme.

LÉLIE

You could at least have beaten me more gently.

MASCARILLE

No. Trufaldin was watching me intently:
Besides, I rather relished an excuse
To turn my anger and frustration loose.
But now, what's done is done. If you will state
Your solemn promise not to retaliate—
Either directly or more roundaboutly—
For the blows I rained upon your back so stoutly,
I shall exploit my situation here,
And in two days gain for you your captive dear.

LÉLIE

My back still feels resentful, but you've made me
An offer which is certain to persuade me!

MASCARILLE

You give your word, then?

LÉLIE

Yes, I promise you.

MASCARILLE

Promise me, too, that in whatever I do
You will no longer interfere and blunder.

LÉLIE

Agreed.

MASCARILLE

You'd better keep your word, by thunder!

LÉLIE

Keep yours and help me win the best of maids.

MASCARILLE

Go rub some ointment on your shoulder blades.

LÉLIE

(*Alone:*)
Why is it that misfortune dogs me so?
Why am I visited by woe on woe?

MASCARILLE

(*Emerging from Trufaldin's house.*)
What! Haven't you gone? Be off now, in a hurry.
Leave everything to me; it's not your worry.
I shall be working for you, and you must never
Attempt to help in any way whatever.
Go home; do nothing.

LÉLIE

(*Leaving.*)

All right, then. Count on me.

MASCARILLE

Now to conceive a brand-new strategy.

SCENE SEVEN

Ergaste, Mascarille

ERGASTE

Wait, Mascarille. I have some news that seems
A bitter setback for your hopes and schemes.
Even as I speak, a fine young gypsy man,
Well bred and fair, is seeking Trufaldin,
Accompanied by a crone with trembling chin.
He's come to buy that slave you'd hoped to win,
And speaks of her in tones of anxious love.

MASCARILLE

No doubt, he's the swain Célie has told me of.
In this affair, what endless trials we face!
When one threat fades, another takes its place.
What matter that Léandre, so they claim,
Will now give up Célie and quit the game;
That his father's come to town, has judged it meet
And proper that his son wed Hippolyte,
And has so moved Léandre to obey
That the marriage contract's to be signed today?
One rival's gone; but another far more dire
Has come to rob us of our heart's desire.
However, by a bit of brilliant guile
I shall prevent their leaving for a while,
And thus allow myself some time to spend
On bringing things to a triumphant end.
There've been some unsolved robberies of late;
Theft is a crime that gypsies perpetrate;
I'll cleverly arrange that on a frail
Suspicion, this fellow shall be thrown in jail.
I know some officers, full of zeal and zest,
Who're always glad to make a false arrest;
They find it a most profitable sport,

Because of the little bribes they can extort;
The suspect may be innocent, but they
Regard his purse as guilty, and make it pay.

Act Five

SCENE ONE

———————•◦•———————

Mascarille, Ergaste

MASCARILLE

You ape! You ox! You blockhead! Must you forever
Subvert my every project and endeavor?

ERGASTE

Your friends the officers did their duty well,
And nabbed the gypsy. He'd now be in a cell,
Had not your master, happening on the scene,
Been furiously moved to intervene.
"To see a gentleman so abused," he cried,
"Is a shameful thing which I shall not abide.
Release him! I'm prepared to stand his bail."
When still they sought to drag their prey to jail,
Your master fell upon those paladins
So fiercely that they ran to save their skins.
No doubt they're running yet, and each one feels
That a wild Lélie is close upon his heels.

MASCARILLE

He doesn't know, poor fool, that the gypsy's there
Inside, about to steal his lady fair.

ERGASTE

I'm off. A bit of pressing business calls me.

MASCARILLE

(*Alone:*)
Alas, this latest feat of his appalls me.
It might be said (and I might well attest)
That the meddling imp by which he is possessed
Delights in balking me, and prompting him

To do whatever makes our chances dim.
Still, I shall not abandon our campaign.
We'll see who wins—his devil, or my brain.
Célie is rather fond of him, and so
Is far from feeling a desire to go.
I'll seek to take advantage of that fact.
But now they're coming, and it's time to act.
That house across the way is mine to use,
For our good cause, in any way I choose.
I'm the custodian, and I keep the key.
All will be well, if fortune favors me.
Oh, my! What a busy day or two I've spent!
How many tricks a scoundrel must invent!

SCENE TWO

Célie, Andrès

ANDRÈS

I have done everything a man could do,
Célie, to prove my ardent love to you.
When I dwelt in Venice, in my younger days,
My courage as a soldier won me praise,
And, not to boast, I might have had a very
Distinguished future in the military.
But that, and everything, I could dismiss
When, in a sudden metamorphosis,
I came to be your rapt adorer, and
A fellow wanderer in your gypsy band,
Who followed you in spite of strange events
And adverse fates, and your indifference.
Of late, when we by chance were separated
For a longer time than I'd anticipated,
I spared no pains to learn where you had flown;
At last a gypsy woman, an ancient crone,
Relieved my anxious heart by telling me
That you'd been left here as security
For monies that your band had had to borrow
To save themselves from penury and sorrow.
I've hastened here to free you, and I stand
In readiness to obey your least command,
Though disappointed that your eyes express
A pensive gloom instead of happiness.
If you would like a settled life, then come—
I can support us both in Venice, from
My portion of the spoils we took in war;
Or if you wish to wander, as before,
I'll gladly follow; my heart's one craving, now,
Is to be near to you, no matter how.

CÉLIE

Your kindly zeal is most apparent to me;
I'd be ungrateful if it made me gloomy.
The fact is that my face does not reveal,
At the present moment, what I truly feel.
It's a fierce headache that makes me frown this way;
And if I can command you, as you say,
I'd like our voyage hence to be suspended,
For a few days, until this pain is ended.

ANDRÈS

We'll put it off as long as you require.
To please you is the one thing I desire.
Let's find a place where you can stay and rest.
That house, it seems, will take a paying guest.

(*He points to a* ROOMS TO LET *sign which Mascarille has just
put in the window.*)

SCENE THREE

—•◦•—

Célie, Andrès, Mascarille (disguised as a Swiss)

ANDRÈS
Ah, the landlord. You are Swiss, sir, one presumes.

MASCARILLE
Ja, at your serfice.

ANDRÈS
May we engage some rooms?

MASCARILLE
For strainchers, I haf goot accomodations,
But not for doze mit vicked reputations.

ANDRÈS
Your house is free, I'm sure, of wickedness.

MASCARILLE
You vas a straincher in diss city, yes?

ANDRÈS
Yes.

MASCARILLE
De mattam, she iss married to de mister?

ANDRÈS
What?

MASCARILLE
She iss your vife, or maype iss your schvister?

ANDRÈS
No.

MASCARILLE

Ach, she iss pooty. You come on piziness, eh?
Maype you bring a zoot in court today?
Lawzoot is one bad sing, it cost zo much.
De lawyer iss a tief, zo iss de jutch.

ANDRÈS

We have no lawsuit.

MASCARILLE

                    Den you bring her here mit you
To valk aroundt de city, und zee de fiew?

ANDRÈS

Yes, yes.
(*To Célie:*)
I'll let you rest a bit, my dear,
While I bring the ancient gypsy woman here,
And countermand the carriage that I hired.

MASCARILLE

She's not vell?

ANDRÈS

                    She has a headache, and is tired.

MASCARILLE

I haf goot vine, also I haf goot cheece.
Enter my little dvellink, if you pleece.

(*Célie, Andrès and Mascarille go into the house.*)

SCENE FOUR

Lélie, Andrès

LÉLIE

(*Alone:*)
Impatient as my heart may be, I swore
That I would take no action anymore.
My man shall act alone, and I must wait
To see how Heaven will decide my fate.
(*To Andrès, who is coming out of the house:*)
Were you seeking someone in that building, pray?

ANDRÈS

No, it's an inn, where I've arranged to stay.

LÉLIE

What! My father owns that house, and the fact is
That my man sleeps there, and guards the premises.

ANDRÈS

Well, that placard plainly offers rooms for rent.
Read it.

LÉLIE

It does! I'm filled with wonderment.
Who in the deuce would put it there, and why?
Ah! I've a notion where the truth may lie!
There's just one answer to this mystery.

ANDRÈS

May I presume to ask what that may be?

LÉLIE

From all but you, I'd guard this secret well.
But you're not involved, and I know you wouldn't tell.
I have no doubt that the placard you behold—

At least, I think so—is another bold
Prank by the man of whom I just made mention;
Part of some deft intrigue of his invention,
Designed to put me in possession of
A gypsy girl whom I intensely love.
We've not yet gained her, though we've tried no end.

ANDRÈS

What's her name?

LÉLIE

Célie.

ANDRÈS

     If you'd told me earlier, friend,
I could have spared you all the pains it took
To think up this deceit, and bait the hook.

LÉLIE

How so? Do you know her?

ANDRÈS

                    'Twas I who just now bought
Her freedom.

LÉLIE

     You did? I'm staggered by the thought.

ANDRÈS

She wasn't well enough to travel, and thus
I'd just engaged—in there—some rooms for us.
Well, I'm delighted that you've told me, sir,
Of your intentions with regard to her.

LÉLIE

What! Will you cause my cup to overflow
By helping me to gain her?

ANDRÈS

(*Knocking on the door.*)

You soon shall know.

LÉLIE

How can I ever thank you for this kind . . .

ANDRÈS

No, no, let's have no thanks, if you don't mind.

SCENE FIVE

———— • ————

Lélie, Andrès, Mascarille

MASCARILLE

(*Aside:*)
Ohh! What do I see but my demented master?
Now, I am sure, we'll have some new disaster.

LÉLIE

Well, Mascarille! No one would ever guess
That it was you in that outlandish dress.

MASCARILLE

Vy do you call me Mackerel? I don't vish
Zat you make fun of me und call me fish.

LÉLIE

Ha! What delightful gibberish you talk!

MASCARILLE

Schtop laughing at me; go take yourself a valk.

LÉLIE

Come, I'm your master; let's play this game no more.

MASCARILLE

By Himmel, I neffer zee your face before.

LÉLIE

It's all been settled; drop all these droll pretenses.

MASCARILLE

If you von't go, I knock you from your senses.

LÉLIE

Stop talking German, I tell you; there's no need.

This generous man and I are fully agreed.
I am to have the thing I hold most dear,
And you've no grounds for diffidence or fear.

MASCARILLE

If you're so happily agreed, I'll then
De-Swiss myself, and be myself again.

ANDRÈS

Your man has served you with great zeal and wit.
I'll soon rejoin you; kindly wait a bit.

(*Andrès goes into the house.*)

LÉLIE

Well! What do you say?

MASCARILLE

                    I say that I'm completely
Happy to see our labors end so sweetly.

LÉLIE

You were rather slow to shed your Swiss disguise,
And you heard my glorious news with doubtful eyes.

MASCARILLE

Knowing you as I do, I felt uneasy,
And your blithe report still leaves me feeling queasy.

LÉLIE

Oh, come! Confess that I have done great things:
This makes up for my former blunderings,
And crowns with victory our joint campaign.

MASCARILLE

You may be right: With luck, who needs a brain?

SCENE SIX

———— • • ————

Célie, Andrès, Lélie, Mascarille

ANDRÈS
Is this the lady of whom you spoke, of late?

LÉLIE
What bliss so sweet as mine, what joy so great!

ANDRÈS
I owe you thanks for a gallant deed, I know;
Not to acknowledge it would be base and low:
Yet it would be too harsh a recompense
If I repaid you at my heart's expense.
Without this beautiful lady, I'd be lost.
Would you have me pay my debt at such a cost?
No, you're too generous. Farewell. Our plans
Are to spend a day or two at Trufaldin's.

(*He exits with Célie.*)

MASCARILLE
(*After singing for some time.*)
I laugh and sing, but in truth I feel no glee.
You're "fully agreed"! He's giving you Célie!
Well, I needn't say it.

LÉLIE
                          This is too much! I'm through
Begging your aid, and botching all you do.
I'm an oaf, a ninny, a bumbling blatherskite,
Unworthy of help, unable to do things right.
Go; cease to serve a fool who hates success,
And fends off every chance of happiness.

After my mad mistakes in word and deed,
Death is the only helper that I need.

(*Exit.*)

MASCARILLE

(*Alone:*)
Yes, that would be a perfect finishing touch;
Nothing adorns a foolish life so much
As a good suicide in the finale.
But I won't let his rage at his own folly
Lead him to throw my services away.
In spite of him, I'll serve him. Come what may,
I'll best the devil that makes him blunder so.
It's noble to confront so stubborn a foe,
And all one's trials are but handmaids who
Adorn one's virtue in high Heaven's view.

SCENE SEVEN

Célie, Mascarille

CÉLIE
(*To Mascarille, who has been whispering to her:*)
Whatever anyone may do or say,
Little, I think, will come of this delay.
By what just happened, we can see how far
From any compromise the two men are,
And, as I've told you, I couldn't bear to make
One man unhappy for the other's sake.
To each of them, for different reasons, I
Feel bound by a profound and potent tie.
Lélie has by the power of love subdued
My heart, but Andrès has my gratitude,
Which bars me, even in my secret mind,
From any course which he would think unkind.
Yes, if I cannot grant his heart's desire,
And meet his ardor with an answering fire,
I can at least, in view of all he's done,
Refuse to give my hand to anyone,
And let my amorous wishes be suppressed
As painfully as those that he's professed.
You see what honor forces me to do,
And what faint hopes I can hold out to you.

MASCARILLE
The hopes you give are faint indeed, that's clear,
And I don't deal in miracles, I fear.
But I'll make use of every skill I've learned—
Move earth and Heaven, leave no stone unturned—
To find some exit from this cul-de-sac.
As soon as I've news to bring you, I'll be back.

SCENE EIGHT

Hippolyte, Célie

HIPPOLYTE

Since you came here, madam, the ladies of these parts
Have learned to fear your eyes, which steal men's hearts;
Their cherished conquests have been lost to you;
Their lovers, one and all, are now untrue.
There is no man, it seems, who stands a chance
Before the lovely arrows of your glance,
And, every day, our losses are your gains,
As free men, by the score, put on your chains.
As for myself, I would have seen no harm
In the sovereign power of your wondrous charm
If, when you took my lovers from me, you'd
Spared me just one to warm my solitude;
But since you inhumanely left me none,
I feel I must complain of what you've done.

CÉLIE

Madam, how charmingly you chaff and tease;
But do have pity on me, if you please.
Your own eyes know their power far too well
To fear that such as I could break their spell;
They are too conscious of their loveliness
To harbor such alarms as you express.

HIPPOLYTE

Yet when I said that you purloin our beaus,
I only said what everybody knows;
Léandre and Lélie, to name but two,
Are well known to have lost their hearts to you.

CÉLIE

If there is truth in that report about them,
I'm sure that you will gladly do without them,

For any errant lover who has shown
Such wretched taste can hardly please your own.

HIPPOLYTE

Ah, no. Indeed, I feel quite otherwise.
Your beauty is so stunning in my eyes
That I can see good reason to acquit
A straying lover who's been stunned by it.
I cannot blame Léandre who, when he
Beheld your face, forgot his vows to me,
And I'll receive him without rancor when,
At his sire's insistence, he is mine again.

SCENE NINE

Célie, Hippolyte, Mascarille

MASCARILLE

Great news! Good tidings! Harken to my voice,
And I shall give you reason to rejoice!

CÉLIE

Quick! Tell us!

MASCARILLE

Hear me; this is going to be . . .

CÉLIE

What?

MASCARILLE

Like the ending of a comedy.
Just now, that ancient gypsy woman . . .

CÉLIE

Yes! Hurry!

MASCARILLE

Was strolling through the square, without a worry,
When another hag, who had been keeping pace
With her, and closely studying her face,
Burst into loud reproaches, screamed and swore,
And gave the signal for a bloody war.
'Twas not with sword or musket that they fought,
But with four withered claws, whereby they sought
To pick each other clean, those scrawny crones,
Of the little flesh still clinging to their bones.
Such words as "slut" and "vixen" filled the air.
Their bonnets soon flew off, and thus laid bare
A couple of bald heads, so that the twosome

Composed a battle scene both droll and gruesome.
Andrès and Trufaldin, who were in the van
Of a crowd that gathered when the fray began,
Found it no easy task to separate
Two combatants whose anger was so great.
When the storm abated, and each of them had sped
To cover up the bareness of her head,
And the crowd was asking what had caused the brawl,
The strange old woman who'd begun it all,
Though still much agitated and inflamed,
Looked fixedly at Trufaldin, and exclaimed:
"It's you, sir, of whom I heard not long ago
That you were living here *incognito*!
Yes, yes, it's you! O wondrous circumstance!
Signor Zanobio Ruberti, by happy chance
I've found you just when I'd begun to take
A vigorous course of action for your sake.
When you left Naples and your family,
I was your little daughter's nurse, and she
At four possessed a charm and grace which were
Remarkable, as you'll remember, sir.
The vile hag whom you see there wormed her way
Into our household till, one bitter day,
She stole my precious charge. Alas, your wife
Was seized by deepest sorrow, and her life
Was shortened by a loss she could not bear.
Since the child had been abducted from my care,
I feared your wrath, and had you notified
That both the mother and the child had died.
But let's compel this woman, now that I've caught her,
To tell us what has happened to your daughter."
At the name "Zanobio Ruberti," which occurred
A number of times in the long speech we heard,
Andrès turned pale, and then at last began
This speech to the astonished Trufaldin:
"Thank Heaven, which has helped me to regain
The sire whom, until now, I sought in vain!
How strange that, seeing you, I was unseeing,

And did not know the author of my being!
Yes, Father, I am Horace, your long-lost son.
When Albert died, who'd been my guardian,
A restless mood came over me, and I
Forsook Bologna, put my studies by,
And, driven by my curiosity,
Wandered for six years over land and sea,
Until, in time, I felt a secret yen
To see my kindred and my home again.
Alas, in Naples, Father, I could not find you,
And since you'd gone, and left no trail behind you,
I ceased my wanderings and my fruitless quest,
Settled in Venice, and was a while at rest.
From that time to the present, I have known
Nought of our family but the name alone."
I leave you to imagine with what bliss
Trufaldin lent an ear to all of this.
But to be brief—since you can learn with ease
Whatever further history you may please—
Trufaldin, having heard the gypsy crone
Confess, has recognized you as his own;
Andrès, then, is your brother; and since a brother
And sister cannot marry one another,
He would repay an act of chivalry
By yielding you in marriage to Lélie.
My master's father, who was there, concurred,
And gave his warm consent—then, feeling stirred
To make a grand occasion still more grand,
Gave the new-found Horace his daughter's hand.
Was there ever such a blizzard of events?

CÉLIE

I'm overwhelmed by these developments.

MASCARILLE

Everyone's bound this way, save those two hags,
Who need to rest from battle, and mend their rags.

(*To Hippolyte:*)
Léandre's coming, and your father as well.
As for myself, I'll go in haste and tell
My downcast master that his luck in love
Has been restored, as if by Heaven above.

(*Exit.*)

HIPPOLYTE

I'm overcome with joy, and couldn't be
More joyous if these things had happened to me.
But here they come.

SCENE TEN

Trufaldin, Anselme, Pandolfe, Célie, Hippolyte,
Léandre, Andrès

TRUFALDIN

My daughter!

CÉLIE

Father dear!

TRUFALDIN

Has the news of all our blessings reached you here?

CÉLIE

Yes, the whole astounding story has been told.

HIPPOLYTE

(To Léandre, gesturing toward Célie:)
No need to excuse yourself; my eyes behold
What might make any heart a renegade.

LÉANDRE

I beg your kind forgiveness for having strayed.
Believe me, it's not the urging of my sire
That brings me back to you, but my own desire.

ANDRÈS

(To Célie:)
Who would have thought that Nature could condemn
My fervor and my love, and banish them?
Yet since in them the purest honor reigned,
They shall, with slight adjustments, be retained.

CÉLIE

I long felt guilty, because I couldn't seem
To look on you with more than deep esteem.

I knew not what great obstacle kept my feet
From the path of love, so dangerous and sweet,
And warned me to deny the wild appeal
Of what my senses wished my heart to feel.

TRUFALDIN

(*To Célie:*)
Now that I've got you back, what would you say
If I thought at once of giving you away—
(*Gesturing to Pandolfe.*)
In marriage, to this gentleman's son? What say you?

CÉLIE

I'd say that I was bound, sir, to obey you.

SCENE ELEVEN

———— ✦•✦ ————

Trufaldin, Anselme, Pandolfe, Célie, Hippolyte,
Lélie, Léandre, Andrès, Mascarille

MASCARILLE

(*To Lélie:*)
Let's see if your inner devil can destroy
A surefire prospect of delight and joy,
And if you will invent some more "fine schemes"
To block the realization of your dreams.
A wondrous turn of fortune now ensures
Your future happiness, and Célie is yours.

LÉLIE

Is it true? Has Heaven graciously decreed . . . ?

TRUFALDIN

It's true, my son-in-law.

PANDOLFE

We're all agreed.

ANDRÈS

In this, I gladly pay the debt I owe you.

LÉLIE

(*To Mascarille:*)
I'll give you a thousand hugs, dear man, to show you
My gratitude.

MASCARILLE

Oof! Please! Let go of me!
I'm suffocated. I fear for poor Célie
If, in your ardor, you embrace her so.
Such hugs as that I'm happy to forgo.

TRUFALDIN

(*To Lélie:*)
You know how Heaven has blessed me; but, my boy,
Since this one day has filled us all with joy,
Let's spend the rest together, and invite
Léandre's father to feast with us tonight.

MASCARILLE

So, you're all provided for. Is there no girl
Who'd like to give poor Mascarille a whirl?
Seeing these happy he's and she's converge
Has given me a sudden marrying urge.

ANSELME

I've a girl for you.

MASCARILLE

Then let's go—and through Heaven's graces
May all our children have their father's faces!

Lovers' Quarrels

COMEDY IN FIVE ACTS, 1656

Introduction

Lovers' Quarrels (*Le Dépit amoureux*) was Molière's second verse comedy and had its premiere in 1656, at Béziers in Languedoc, with the author playing the role of the irascible Albert. Two years later, when Molière's players returned to Paris and were installed in the Petit-Bourbon, they initially displeased the public by attempting a number of Corneille's tragedies, but salvaged that first season with two Molière farces. *The Bungler* (*L'Étourdi*) was successfully offered in November 1658, and Lovers' Quarrels, which followed in December, did quite as well. Together, the two plays brought in some money and created a following. Le Boulanger de Chalussay, in a dramatic satire against Molière (1670), was forced to concede that the latter play had drawn "ahs" from its audience:

> On all sides there were cheers, and everyone
> Cried, "That's how plays should be conceived and done!"

George Saintsbury wrote of Lovers' Quarrels that "nothing so good had yet been seen on the French stage, as the quarrels and reconciliations of the quartet of master, mistress, valet and soubrette." The scenes in question, involving Éraste, Lucile, Gros-René and Marinette, are in Molière's liveliest vein, and their tone and theme might put us in mind of Michael Drayton's famous sonnet "Since there's no help, come let us kiss and part," while for Molière's contemporaries they might have recalled a charming dialogic ode of Horace's (Act Three, Scene Nine) in which two lovers reunite. The quarrel-and-reconciliation scenes have long been excerpted and combined, in France, to constitute a pleasing short version of the play. In the original text, however, they are ably interwoven with plot borrowings from such Italian sources as Nicolo Secchi's *L'Interesse*, to make a comedy of error, misunderstanding and intrigue.

Though the persons of the play are well provided with qualities (Éraste is jealous, Valère is rash, Mascarille is cowardly), it is plot, rather than character, in which the play's complexities lie. These are traceable, as we gradually discover, to something that happened some twenty years in the past. At that time a rich kinsman promised an inheritance to Albert and his family, provided that the child Albert's wife was carrying proved to be male; if that condition was not met, the money would go to Polidore, the father of Valère. When Albert's wife bore a girl child, Albert secretly and dishonestly exchanged it for the illegitimate male child of Ignès the flower girl. To his newly acquired son, Albert gave the name of Ascagne, and Ignès meanwhile placed her new daughter in the care of Frosine's mother, a wet nurse. Not long afterward, when Albert was out of town on business, the boy Ascagne died; the wife, fearing a violent reaction from Albert, then secretly retrieved her daughter from the wet nurse, transferred to her the name of Ascagne, and dressed her as a boy.

A score of years later, we find Ascagne still in male attire, and passing now for a young man; however, as she tells her confidante Frosine in Act Two, Scene One, Cupid has penetrated her disguise and filled her woman's heart with love for Valère, who has vainly been courting her sister, Lucile. Pretending to be Lucile, Ascagne has had a succession of rendezvous with Valère, meeting him in a black veil and in the dark of night. On a fifth or sixth such occasion, she has deceived him into a secret marriage, in the darkling presence of a notary, a tailor and Valère's valet, Mascarille.

What now develops, in the play's present time, is an imbroglio or general mixup, deriving from past deceptions. The characters are entangled in a web of misapprehensions, and it is these that generate the atmosphere of the play and drive its action. Ascagne believes that her hoaxing marriage to Valère has made her his wife. Valère understandably believes that the same rite has wedded him secretly to Lucile. Éraste,

who has won the favor of Lucile, is troubled by the compla-
cent air of his defeated rival, and presses his jealous inqui-
ries until Mascarille—honestly, but mistakenly—gives him
seeming grounds for a breach which is not repaired until the
fourth act. The falling-out and reconciliation of Éraste and
Lucile is mirrored in the behavior of their servants, Gros-
René and Marinette. Meanwhile, Valère mortally offends
Lucile and her father by claiming to have married her, and
might well incur a bloodier duel than the jesting one which
awaits him in the final act. Nor are these all of the mistakings
and confusions that animate the skits and comic turns of the
play: Albert, quite incredibly, believes after twenty years of
family life that his child Ascagne is male. That is made plain
at the beginning of his scene with the tutor Métaphraste,
which (like the later scene with Polidore) is a frenzy of mutual
incomprehension.

Throughout *Lovers' Quarrels*, the caroming encounters
of the characters lead to further complication, rather than
understanding and resolution, and Frosine, who from the
first has some of the answers, shares her knowledge with
Ascagne alone. Her breakneck expository speech in Act Five,
Scene Four informs Ascagne that the work of disentangle-
ment has been accomplished offstage by her and by Ignès,
and such matters as Albert's long defrauding of Polidore are
dismissed as settled. The play then proceeds to give us not
leisurely explanations and rapprochements but yet another
hoax, in which Valère must be fooled and then enlightened
as to the sex of his dueling opponent.

It would be churlish to ask of a madcap play like *Lovers'*
Quarrels that its every event seem probable, but more than
one critic has questioned the suddenness with which Valère,
on finding that Ascagne is a woman, is seized with wonder,
love and pleasure. Sir John Vanbrugh's *The Mistake* (1706),
a spirited prose adaptation of *Le Dépit amoureux* which re-
situates the play in Spain, seeks to improve the final scene
by a stage direction in which Camillo (i.e., Ascagne) "*kneels,*
and lets her periwig fall off." This revelation of her sex and
comeliness fills Lorenzo (i.e., Valère) with amazement; it

also causes Lopez (Mascarille) to exclaim that she is indeed a "pretty one," and Isabel (Frosine) to make such mention of her "virtue, beauty, wit and love" that Lorenzo might seem to love her by acclamation. But perhaps it suffices that Molière's Valère has been portrayed throughout as impulsive, fiery and bold. In any case, I and whatever audiences may see this translation played will agree with Vanbrugh that Ascagne's feminine beauty must be revealed. I don't know whether, after Albert's, "Let her go and change," there may be time for her to change costume and return to the scene; but I am certain that, for the curtain call, she must be in woman's dress and irresistible.

—*RW*
Cummington, Massachusetts, 2005

Characters

ÉRASTE (ay-RAHST), in love with Lucile

ALBERT (ahl-BEAR), father of Lucile and Ascagne

GROS-RENÉ (grow-re-NAY), Éraste's valet

VALÈRE (vah-LARE), son of Polidore

LUCILE (loo-SEAL), daughter of Albert

MARINETTE (mah-ree-NET), Lucile's maid

POLIDORE (po-lee-DORE), father of Valère

FROSINE (fro-SEEN), confidante to Ascagne

MASCARILLE (mah-ska-REE), Valère's valet

MÉTAPHRASTE (may-ta-FRAST), a pedant

LA RAPIÈRE (lah-rah-PIERRE), a bravo

ASCAGNE (ah-SKAHN-ya), Albert's daughter, disguised
as a man

PLACE
A city street.

Act One

SCENE ONE

———◦━◦———

Éraste, Gros-René

ÉRASTE

Well, if you want to know, I feel oppressed
By nagging doubts which give my mind no rest.
I fear my amorous hopes have been betrayed,
Whatever you say. At times I'm even afraid
That my rival's purse has bought your loyalty,
Or that my love deceives both you and me.

GROS-RENÉ

With all respect, sir, for your troubled heart,
Your fear that I might play a traitor's part
Is wounding to my pride and honesty,
And shows no grasp of physiognomy.
Men of my round proportions, sir, are not
Regarded as the type to scheme and plot—
Which good opinion I shall not gainsay:
I'm a solid citizen in every way.
That I have been deceived could well be so;
It's possible; I don't believe it, though.
Try as I will, I cannot figure out
What grounds you have for being racked by doubt.
Lucile is clearly fond of you, I'd say,
And welcomes you at any hour of day,
Whereas Valère, the source of your anxiety,
Is now but rarely seen in her society.

ÉRASTE

Such logic doesn't comfort me; good Lord,
He who's most seen may not be most adored,
And a woman's sugared words may serve to cover
Her warmer feelings for another lover.

Valère, moreover, shows too little pain
To be a recently discarded swain;
Hearing the lady speaking fondly to me,
He's blithe, and cool, and anything but gloomy—
Which spoils my sense of triumph, mars my bliss,
Stirs up those doubts you urge me to dismiss,
Makes me mistrust my happiness, and feel
Unsure of the sincerity of Lucile.
How it would simplify my life if he,
My rival, were consumed with jealousy!
If he would show a normal gloom and grief,
T'would ease my mind and give my thoughts relief.
Don't you, too, think it strange that he can be
So blithe about a rival's victory?
Do you not see, then, why I brood upon
The matter, and try to guess what's going on?

GROS-RENÉ

Perhaps he found a new love when the old
Rejected him, and so feels quite consoled.

ÉRASTE

A man who's been rejected would not pay
Blithe visits to the lady every day.
No, after a rebuff so grave and sore,
He could not wait upon her anymore.
One can't be cool when in the presence of
The heartless person whom one used to love:
Either one feels a sullen anger, or
One's jilted passion flares up as before.
However well an old flame's been suppressed,
There's still some jealousy in the lover's breast,
So that he can't look on without chagrin
While a rival claims the prize he couldn't win.

GROS-RENÉ

Such theorizing, sir, is not for me:
I put my trust in what my eyes can see,

And I'm not so fond of misery that I
Will fret and mope without good reasons why.
Why deal in dire conjectures, and rehearse
Dark arguments that make my mood the worse?
Why yield to baseless doubt and mere suspicion?
Don't look for trouble, say I. That's my position.
Grief, in my judgment, is a sorry state;
Without good cause, I want none on my plate,
And even when good causes can be had,
It goes against my nature to be sad.
In love, sir, our two destinies intertwine:
Your amorous fortune will determine mine,
For if the lady broke her faith to you,
Her lady's maid would send me packing, too.
I do my best, though, not to think about it.
If she says, "I love you," I refuse to doubt it,
Nor shall I judge the happiness of my lot
By whether Mascarille is glum or not.
So long as Marinette will be so kind
As to kiss and hug me when I'm so inclined,
My rival's free to laugh his head off, while
I match him laugh for laugh in the same style,
And we shall see whose laugh sounds more sincere.

ÉRASTE

Well, that's your nature.

GROS-RENÉ
But look, she's drawing near.

SCENE TWO

Éraste, Marinette, Gros-René

GROS-RENÉ

Psst! Marinette!

MARINETTE

Ooh! What are you doing there?

GROS-RENÉ

We were discussing you, my lady fair.

MARINETTE

(*To Éraste:*)
So you're here, too, sir! You've made me run about
Like a headless chicken, and I'm tuckered out.

ÉRASTE

Oh? Why?

MARINETTE

I've covered miles and miles of ground,
And I guarantee you . . .

ÉRASTE
What?

MARINETTE

That you can't be found
At home, or church, or plaza, or café.

GROS-RENÉ

Well, that's a safe conclusion.

ÉRASTE
But tell me, pray,
Who sent you looking for me?

MARINETTE
Someone who
Is far from being ill-disposed toward you;
In short, my mistress.

ÉRASTE
Marinette, my dear,
If you're her heart's true oracle and seer,
Keep no dark secrets from me, I implore you.
Tell me—it won't affect my feelings for you—
Could your lovely mistress so deceive my zeal
As to pretend a love she doesn't feel?

MARINETTE
Lord! How can you dream up such silly stuff?
Hasn't she made her sentiments clear enough?
What more assurance could your heart require?
What do you want?

GROS-RENÉ
He'd have his heart's desire
If Valère would hang himself from the nearest tree.

MARINETTE
Why so?

GROS-RENÉ
He's jealous to the nth degree.

MARINETTE
What, of Valère? That notion is insane,
And must have issued from a feverish brain.

(*To Éraste:*)
I've always thought you sensible, and till now
I've sensed an intellect behind that brow,
But it appears that I was much misled.
(*To Gros-René:*)
Do you, too, have a fever in your head?

GROS-RENÉ

Me, jealous? God forbid that such a state
Of foolish grief should cause me to lose weight!
I trust in your fidelity, and my
Opinion of myself, love, is so high,
I'm sure I have no equal on this earth.
Where could you find a man of greater worth?

MARINETTE

Well said: A lover ought to talk that way—
None of these doubts that jealous men display!
All that one gains by them's a loss of face
That lets your rival pass you in the race.
Envy will often open a mistress' eyes
To the merits of the man with whom one vies,
And I know one such man, whose happy fate
Owes everything to a rival's jealous hate.
In matters of the heart, no man of sense
Ever displays a lack of confidence.
Don't make yourself unhappy, sir, for naught.
Those are some truths I felt you should be taught.

ÉRASTE

Enough, now. Tell me what you've come to tell.

MARINETTE

Sir, you deserve to suffer for a spell,
And I should punish you by some delay
In giving you the news I've brought today.
But come, take this, and banish doubt and fear.
Read it aloud: There's none but us to hear.

ÉRASTE

(*Reading:*)
"You told me that there was no task
Your love would not perform at my command.
Pray, prove your love this very day, and ask
My father for his daughter's hand.
Tell him my heart is ready to
Be yours, as I now give you leave to say.
If then he orders me to marry you,
I promise you that I'll obey."
Oh, joy! You are a heavenly messenger,
For bringing me these loving words from her.

GROS-RENÉ

I told you all was well, but you wouldn't be shaken.
It isn't often, sir, that I'm mistaken.

ÉRASTE

(*Reading again:*)
"Tell him my heart is ready to
Be yours, as I now give you leave to say.
If he orders me to marry you,
I promise you that I'll obey."

MARINETTE

If I told her of your dark suspicions, she
Would disavow those words, believe you me.

ÉRASTE

Oh, pray don't tell her of my passing mood
Of foolish worry and incertitude:
Or if you tell her, kindly add that I'm
Prepared to die to expiate that crime—
That if I have offended her, I desire
To sacrifice my life to her just ire.

MARINETTE

Well, let's not talk of dying; it's early yet.

ÉRASTE

In any case, I'm greatly in your debt,
And I assure you that I'll soon repay
My pretty messenger in some handsome way.

MARINETTE

Ah, that reminds me. There was another scene
Where I looked for you just now.

ÉRASTE
Eh?

MARINETTE
The place I mean
Is near the market.

ÉRASTE
Oh?

MARINETTE
The shop, you know,
Where you so kindly promised, a month ago,
To buy a ring for me.

ÉRASTE
Ah, yes! Quite true.

GROS-RENÉ

Sly wench!

ÉRASTE
I've been too slow in giving you
The little gift I promised to confer.
But . . .

MARINETTE
Heavens! I didn't mean to press you, sir.

GROS-RENÉ

Oh, *no!*

ÉRASTE

(*Giving her his own ring:*)
If this ring pleases you, why not
Take it in place of the one that I forgot?

MARINETTE

Oh, sir, I'd be ashamed to take your ring.

GROS-RENÉ

Go on and take it, you poor shamefaced thing.
Only a fool declines a gift, say I.

MARINETTE

I'll wear it to recall your kindness by.

ÉRASTE

When may I see my angel, my future bride?

MARINETTE

First, you must get her father on your side.

ÉRASTE

But what if he rejects me?

MARINETTE

Then we'll do
Whatever it takes to gain her hand for you.
She must be yours, and to achieve that aim
You'll do your utmost, and we'll do the same.

ÉRASTE

Farewell: By sundown, then, we'll know our fate.

(*Éraste rereads the letter, sotto voce.*)

MARINETTE

(*To Gros-René:*)
Well, what about *our* love? What say you, mate?
You haven't yet proposed.

GROS-RENÉ
For folks like us,
Marriage can be arranged without a fuss.
I want you; will you marry me?

MARINETTE
With pleasure.

GROS-RENÉ

Let's shake.

MARINETTE
Farewell then, Gros-René, my treasure.

GROS-RENÉ

Farewell, my star.

MARINETTE
Farewell, my cupid's dart.

GROS-RENÉ

Farewell, sweet comet, rainbow of my heart.
(*Exit Marinette.*)
Thank Heaven! We both have reason for good cheer.
Albert will not refuse you, never fear.

ÉRASTE

Here comes Valère, now.

GROS-RENÉ
Knowing what we know,
I pity the poor wretch.

SCENE THREE

Valère, Éraste, Gros-René

ÉRASTE

Well, Valère! Hello!

VALÈRE

Well, well, Éraste!

ÉRASTE

How goes your love life, eh?

VALÈRE

How's your tender passion?

ÉRASTE

Stronger every day.

VALÈRE

Mine too grows stronger.

ÉRASTE

For Lucile?

VALÈRE

Why, yes.

ÉRASTE

Well you're a paragon of doggedness,
I'm forced to say.

VALÈRE

Your stubborn constancy
Should be a model to posterity.

ÉRASTE

I'm not, myself, the sort of lover who
Will settle for a friendly smile or two,
And my devotion isn't strong enough
To overlook rejection and rebuff:
In short, I like to see my love requited.

VALÈRE

Why, so do I. In that we stand united.
However fair she is, I cannot burn
For one who doesn't love me in return.

ÉRASTE

And yet Lucile—

VALÈRE

Lucile, whom I adore,
Has given me all my heart could wish, and more.

ÉRASTE

You don't ask much, in other words.

VALÈRE

Oh, yes,
Far more than you suppose.

ÉRASTE

I, nonetheless,
Have grounds for feeling that I've won her heart.

VALÈRE

In which, dear fellow, I play the leading part.

ÉRASTE

Come, don't deceive yourself.

VALÈRE
Come, come. You'll find
That credulous desire has made you blind.

ÉRASTE
If I dared show you proof of her complete
Devotion . . . But no, your heart would cease to beat.

VALÈRE
If I dared disclose a certain fact . . . But no,
I mustn't tell; you couldn't bear the blow.

ÉRASTE
Really, you go too far in mocking me.
I'm forced to puncture your complacency.
Read this,

VALÈRE
(*Having read the letter:*)
How sweet.

ÉRASTE
You recognize the hand?

VALÈRE
Yes, it's Lucile's.

ÉRASTE
Well! Now you understand—

VALÈRE
(*Laughing as he leaves.*)
Farewell, Éraste.

GROS-RENÉ
He's mad, beyond a doubt.
What can the fellow see to laugh about?

ÉRASTE

I'm stunned by his behavior; baffled by it.
Some devilish mystery must underlie it.

GROS-RENÉ

Here comes his servant.

ÉRASTE

     Let's trick him, and discover
Some clue to his master's conduct as a lover.

SCENE FOUR

———— •• ————

Éraste, Mascarille, Gros-René

MASCARILLE

(*Aside:*)
Yes, to serve a young man who is daft with love
Is a thankless job that one gets weary of.

GROS-RENÉ

Hello.

MASCARILLE

Hello.

GROS-RENÉ

What's Mascarille doing today?
Is he coming back? Is he going? Or will he stay?

MASCARILLE

I can't come back, for I've not yet been there. Nor
Am I going, for I've stopped to talk. What's more,
I cannot stay, because this instant I
Must take my leave of you.

ÉRASTE

A neat reply.
Wait, Mascarille.

MASCARILLE

Ah. Yes, sir. At your service.

ÉRASTE

My, how you scampered off! Do I make you nervous?

MASCARILLE

I need not fear a gentleman so kind.

ÉRASTE

Shake, then. Let's put old jealousies out of mind.
We're friends, now. I concede the lady to
Your master, and wish all joy to him and you.

MASCARILLE

You mean it?

ÉRASTE

I've a brand-new passion. Ask Gros-René.

GROS-RENÉ

That's so. Marinette is yours now, needless to say.

MASCARILLE

Never mind that. Our little rivalry
Is not the battle of the century.
But you, sir, have you truly ceased to court
The lady, or did you merely speak in sport?

ÉRASTE

When I saw success would crown your master's suit,
I felt it would be foolish to dispute
The prize of her affections anymore.

MASCARILLE

I'm much relieved by what you say. Though for
A time we rather feared that you might win,
It's very wise that you should now give in.
Yes, you do well to leave a lady whose
Fond treatment of yourself was but a ruse:
A thousand times, sir, knowing what I knew,
I grieved to see false hopes aroused in you.
So to deceive a good man is a shame.
But how on earth did you see through their game?
When they exchanged their vows, no one was by
Save darkest night, two witnesses, and I,

And, until now, their nuptials seemed to be
Enshrouded in a perfect secrecy.

ÉRASTE

What are you saying?

MASCARILLE

That I am much surprised,
And cannot guess by whom you were advised
That, under false pretenses which misled
Both you and everyone, they chose to wed
In secret, so intense their passions were.

ÉRASTE

You lie!

MASCARILLE

Quite so. Whatever you prefer.

ÉRASTE

You're a scoundrel.

MASCARILLE

So I am.

ÉRASTE

What you deserve
Is a hundred lashes for this bit of nerve.

MASCARILLE

Do what you will.

ÉRASTE

Ah, Gros-René

GROS-RENÉ

I'm here.

ÉRASTE

The lie he told me may be true, I fear.
(*To Mascarille:*)
Don't try to run.

MASCARILLE

No.

ÉRASTE

Lucile is married, you say—

MASCARILLE

No, I was joking, sir.

ÉRASTE

You were joking, eh?

MASCARILLE

No, I wasn't joking.

ÉRASTE

Then it's true?

MASCARILLE

No, no!
I don't say that.

ÉRASTE

What *do* you say?

MASCARILLE

Oh, woe!
I shall say nothing, and play it safe.

ÉRASTE

Decide
Whether it's true, or whether you have lied.

MASCARILLE

Sir, have it any way you like. I dare
Not differ with you.

ÉRASTE

(*Drawing his sword:*)
                    Tell me, or I swear
That I shall loosen up your tongue with this.

MASCARILLE

If I spoke again, I'd only speak amiss.
I beg you, sir, to take a stick and give
Me twenty thumps as an alternative,
And let me then get out of here intact.

ÉRASTE

Tell me the truth, the plain and simple fact,
Or you shall die.

MASCARILLE

                    Oh, dear! I shall obey you,
But don't be angry with me, sir, I pray you.

ÉRASTE

Speak. But be very careful what you do,
If you utter just one word that isn't true.
Nothing shall save you from my righteous fury.

MASCARILLE

You may break my bones, sir, or as judge and jury,
Condemn me to be stabbed until I'm dead,
If there's the least untruth in what I've said.

ÉRASTE

Then they're really married?

MASCARILLE

                    I spoke unguardedly

In that connection, as I've come to see:
But yes, the fact is, sir, that you are right.
After five days in which they met each night
And you were used as cover for their plot,
Day before yesterday they tied the knot.
Lucile has taken care to hide thereafter
Her powerful affection for my master,
Knowing that he would sensibly construe
The warmth and favor she might show to you
As a bit of prudent camouflage, whereby
To keep their secret from the general eye.
If you don't believe me, sir, let Gros-René
Accompany me some night. I'll lead the way
And show him how my master, in the shady
Hours, has free access to the lady.

ÉRASTE

Get out of my sight, you swine!

MASCARILLE

(*Going.*)

                                        Sir, I'm not loath
To take my leave.

ÉRASTE

              Well, well.

GROS-RENÉ

                        Well, sir, we've both
Been taken in, if he can be believed.

ÉRASTE

Alas, it's all too true. I've been deceived.
His tale makes sense of everything, God knows.
Valère's reaction to this letter shows
How he and that false girl are hand in glove.
This letter's just some trick to hide their love.

SCENE FIVE

Éraste, Marinette, Gros-René

MARINETTE

My mistress tells me that toward evening, sir,
She will be in her garden. Pray call on her.

ÉRASTE

You two-faced creature! How dare you speak to me?
Go, go; and let your mistress know that she
Need bother me no more with billets-doux.
Here's what I think of them, and her, and you.

(*He tears up the letter and exits.*)

MARINETTE

Well, Gros-René! What's eating him? Tell me what—

GROS-RENÉ

How dare you speak to me, you wicked slut?
You crocodile, whose treachery has outdone
The savage, man-devouring Laestrygon!
Go, go to your mistress now, and say that we,
Despite her cunning and duplicity,
Are duped by her no longer, and that the pair
Of you may go to Hell, for all we care.

MARINETTE

(*Alone:*)
Poor Marinette! If I've not been dreaming, then
What awful demon has possessed these men?
When I tell my mistress, how it will upset her!
What a rude answer to a loving letter!

Act Two

SCENE ONE

———◆●◆———

Ascagne, Frosine

FROSINE

Ascagne, confide in me. I'll be discreet.

ASCAGNE

Is it safe to broach such matters in the street?
We must take care lest curious folk come near us,
Or someone at a window overhear us.

FROSINE

Even at home, we're not so safe as this:
There's nothing round us that our eyes could miss.
Here, we may talk in perfect privacy.

ASCAGNE

Ah, where to begin? This is so hard for me.

FROSINE

Your secret is a weighty one, I judge.

ASCAGNE

Indeed it is; it's one that I begrudge
Even to you, and would not tell you now
Unless I had to.

FROSINE

　　　　　How you wrong me! How
Can you hesitate to open up your heart
To one who's kept your secrets from the start,
To one who grew up at your side, and who
Was ever reticent concerning you,
Who knows why . . .

ASCAGNE

Yes, you know the strange, complex
Reasons why I must hide my birth and sex.
You know that in our household I was bred
To replace the boy Ascagne, who was dead,
And by that ruse retain a legacy
Which others would inherit, but for me.
Because you know these things, I'm free to share
My thoughts with you, and lay my feelings bare.
But first, Frosine, do let me have your view
Of a question which I find no answer to.
Was Albert no party to the fairy tale
That he's my father, and that my sex is male?

FROSINE

To tell the truth, this question that you raise
Is one I've never fathomed; it's like a maze
That leads me nowhere; I'm bewildered by it,
Nor could my mother help me clarify it.
Here's all I know: The dear son of Albert,
Even before his birth, had been made heir
To a large fortune, left him by a late
Uncle whose wealth and properties were great.
When that son died, his mother kept it back
From her absent husband, fearing a heart attack
If he saw the hoped-for legacy miscarry
And pass to another beneficiary.
To hide her child's death, she decided to
Replace him with another, and soon found you
At my family's house, where you'd been put to nurse.
Your mother, doubtless for a generous purse,
Agreed to the hoax, and promised not to tell,
And others, I believe, were bribed as well.
We never told Albert. His wife confined
The truth for twelve years in her secret mind,
Then died so suddenly that there was not
A chance for her to tell him of the plot.

However, he has kept in touch, I gather,
With a woman whom I know to be your mother,
And evidently helps her on the sly.
If he does so, there must be a reason why.
On the other hand, he wishes you to marry
A girl he's chosen, and that's extraordinary.
Do you think he knows that you replaced his son,
Yet doesn't know your gender? Well, let's be done
With this digression; I've rambled on, I fear.
Tell me your secret, which I long to hear.

ASCAGNE

Cupid, my dear, can't be deceived. His eyes
Have penetrated this, my male disguise,
And through these garments sent his subtle dart
Into a maiden's vulnerable heart,
I am in love.

FROSINE

In love!

ASCAGNE

Frosine, don't let
Yourself give in to wonderment just yet;
Be still, and let my trembling heart advise you
Of something that will even more surprise you.

FROSINE

What is it?

ASCAGNE

I love Valère.

FROSINE

Good Lord! You love
A man whose family has been cheated of
A fortune by your male disguise, and who,

If he divined the truth regarding you,
Would claim that legacy without delay!
This is indeed astounding, I must say.

ASCAGNE

But I've something still more wondrous to confess:
I am his wife.

FROSINE

His wife? Do you mean it?

ASCAGNE

Yes.

FROSINE

Oh! That's a shock I wasn't ready for.
My head is reeling.

ASCAGNE

Wait; there's something more.

FROSINE

There's more?

ASCAGNE

I am indeed his wife, but he
Knows nothing of my true identity.

FROSINE

Well, I give up. I'm overcome. You win.
All these surprises cause my head to spin,
And such a riddle's too much for my brain.

ASCAGNE

Then listen patiently, and I'll explain.
When Valère came suing for my sister's hand,
He seemed to be a worthy suitor, and,

Seeing his passionate appeals denied,
My sympathies were all upon his side.
I wished Lucile would fall beneath his spell;
I thought her cold, and pled his cause so well
That helplessly my heart began to stir
With the feelings he could not arouse in her.
When he spoke to her, 'twas my heart that was captured;
When he sighed in vain, 'twas I who was enraptured,
And those professions she could not return
Conquered my soul and made my spirit yearn.
You see, Frosine, how my frail heart was hit
By amorous darts which were not meant for it,
How love's deflected arrows pierced my breast
And I returned that love with interest.
After a time, my dear, the moment came
When I spoke my love, though in another's name.
Pretending, one dark night, to be Lucile,
I told Valère what I had come to feel,
And feigned so well that he did not see through
The part I played in that dark interview,
Thus, speaking as Lucile, I pleased his ear
By whispering in it that I held him dear,
But that my father favored an alliance
With someone else, and I must feign compliance;
That we must therefore hide our love from sight,
Letting our only witness be the night,
And that, lest we should give ourselves away,
We must avoid all private talk by day;
That, as before this meeting, I would be
Cool and indifferent in his company,
And that, on both our parts, no act or word
Should lead the world to guess what had occurred.
Well, not to dwell on every calculation
Which forwarded my bold impersonation,
It worked so well at last that I acquired,
As I have said, the husband I desired.

FROSINE

My, my! What hidden talents you possess!
From your cool exterior, one would never guess.
But isn't it rather rash, the thing you've done?
Although your plot's successfully begun,
How can it possibly end? Have you thought about
What soon must happen, when the truth comes out?

ASCAGNE

When love is strong enough, the lover's soul
Will stop at nothing to attain its goal,
And, once it has achieved that happy end,
It doesn't care what else the Fates may send.
There now, I've told you everything, my dear.
Advise me. Ah, but look! My husband's here.

SCENE TWO

Valère, Ascagne, Frosine

VALÈRE

My friends, if by my presence I would balk
Your wish to have a confidential talk,
I shan't disturb you.

ASCAGNE

Oh, by all means do,
For what we were discussing, sir, was you.

VALÈRE

Me?

ASCAGNE

You.

VALÈRE

Well!

ASCAGNE

I was saying that Valère,
Were I a woman, could teach my heart to care,
And that if he were fond of me, he'd find
How very quickly I'd respond in kind.

VALÈRE

Such flattering things are easy enough to say
When such an obstacle is in the way;
But if you had a magic change of gender,
I doubt your feelings would be quite so tender.

ASCAGNE

Oh yes, they would! And if you'd have me, then
I'd make you, sir, the happiest of men.

VALÈRE

If you want to make me happy, will you aid me
By interceding with a certain lady?

ASCAGNE

I fear I couldn't make myself do that.

VALÈRE

Hmm. Your refusal's rather brusque and flat.

ASCAGNE

Come! What did you expect of me, Valère?
Were I a woman, and loved you, would it be fair
To make me promise that I'd do my part
To help you win another woman's heart?
No, that's a painful task I could not do.

VALÈRE

But since you're not a woman . . .

ASCAGNE

                      What I said to you
Was spoken as a woman, and must be
So understood.

VALÈRE

             Well then, Ascagne, I see
That I can't appeal to your goodwill unless
Heaven alters you, and bids you wear a dress.
Unless you're a woman, your feelings for me fade,
And you see no cause to offer me your aid.

ASCAGNE

I'm most particular, and it doesn't suit me
When those who love don't do so absolutely,
With all their hearts. I tell you quite sincerely
That I shan't help you unless you very clearly

State, in a manner simple, frank and true,
That you're as fond of me as I of you,
That you return my friendship very strongly,
And that, were I a woman, you'd never wrong me
By wishing for another woman's hand.

VALÈRE

I've never heard so jealous a demand!
But since I value your affection, I
Shall swear to all the things you specify.

ASCAGNE

Sincerely?

VALÈRE

Yes, sincerely.

ASCAGNE

In that case, I'm
Prepared to serve you, friend, at any time.

VALÈRE

I've a great secret which I'll soon confide
To you, and I shall need you on my side.

ASCAGNE

And I've a secret, too, which when confessed
Will put your feelings for me to the test.

VALÈRE

Hmm. What's this mystery that you must conceal?

ASCAGNE

That I'm in love—with whom, I can't reveal;
And that, through your great influence with this
Belovèd of mine, you might secure my bliss.

VALÈRE

Who is it, Ascagne? I'll do what I must do
To bring you happiness, I promise you.

ASCAGNE

Ah, what a fatal promise you have made!

VALÈRE

Come, tell me what belovèd I must persuade.

ASCAGNE

No, it's too soon to tell. The person, though,
Is close to you.

VALÈRE

How wonderful; if so,
I pray that it's my sister . . .

ASCAGNE

I can't yet say.

VALÈRE

Why not?

ASCAGNE

I have my reasons for delay.
When you tell your secret, I'll tell mine to you.

VALÈRE

I can't, unless another permits me to.

ASCAGNE

Then get permission, and once each secret's heard,
We'll see which one can better keep his word.

VALÈRE

Farewell, then. We are agreed.

ASCAGNE
Agreed, Valère.

FROSINE
He wants your brotherly help, I do declare.

SCENE THREE

———— •—• ————

Lucile, Ascagne, Frosine, Marinette

LUCILE

(*Speaking the first three lines to Marinette:*)
Yes, yes, that's how I shall retaliate;
The joy of giving pain to one I hate
Is all I hope to gain by this decision.
Brother, my plans have undergone revision.
Valère, though I long took no notice of him,
Attracts me now, and I propose to love him.

ASCAGNE

Good heavens, Sister! Why this sudden change?
Your inconsistency is very strange.

LUCILE

And yours, I must say, puzzles me still more.
You were Valère's great advocate before;
You strongly pled his cause, accusing me
Of pride, caprice, injustice, cruelty:
But now, when I would love him, you protest,
And speak to me against his interest!

ASCAGNE

It's in *your* interest that I speak. I know
That someone else now has his heart in tow.
I fear that your proud feelings would be bruised
If you sought to lure him back, and he refused.

LUCILE

If that's your only worry, never fear.
To me, his heart's desires are very clear,
And his fond looks can easily be read;
Yes, you may safely tell him what I've said;
Or if you won't, I'll tell him on my own

That I'm touched by the devotion he has shown.
Speak, Brother. Can my decision so dismay you?

ASCAGNE

Oh, Sister, if I've any power to sway you,
If you will harken to a brother's prayer,
Forget this notion, and do not steal Valère
From a young girl whose cause is dear to me,
And who, in truth, deserves your sympathy.
The poor thing loves him madly, and has made known
The secrets of her heart to me alone,
With such warm feeling as might melt the pride
Of any rival, and make her step aside.
Yes, you'd take pity on her if you knew
What grief this whim of yours could drive her to;
And I, who know her heart, can testify,
Dear Sister, that the girl will surely die
If the man whom she adores is stolen by you.
Éraste's the swain who ought to satisfy you;
Your mutual fondness . . .

LUCILE

          Brother, say no more.
I don't know who it is you're pleading for,
But do, please, let this declamation cease,
And leave me to collect my thoughts in peace.

ASCAGNE

Ah, cruel Sister! If, in this affair,
You do as you have threatened, I shall despair.

SCENE FOUR

Lucile, Marinette

MARINETTE
Well! Your decision, madam, was quick indeed.

LUCILE
A heart that has been wronged reacts with speed:
It hastens to get even, and assuage
By any means its bitterness and rage.
The monster! How could he insult me so?

MARINETTE
That question baffles me; I just don't know.
I brood and brood upon the mystery,
But his strange behavior still is Greek to me.
I've never seen a man so overjoyed
By happy news; his bliss was unalloyed;
He read your note with purest happiness
And called me a "heavenly messenger," no less.
But when I brought your second message, who'd
Have dreamt that he could be so harsh and rude?
I cannot guess what happened in between
Those messages to make him turn so mean.

LUCILE
Whatever happened can't extenuate
His actions, or defend him from my hate.
Why seek some explanation other than
The viciousness and baseness of the man?
After that gracious letter which I sent,
What could excuse a wrath so violent?

MARINETTE
You're right, of course. His unprovoked attack
Was simple treason; he's stabbed you in the back.

Madam, we've both been had: Shall we allow
These scurvy rascals to deceive us now
With pretty words, and take advantage of us?
Shall we allow these dogs to say they love us,
And in our weakness yield to them again?
No, no! Enough of folly! Enough of men!

LUCILE

Well, let him boast of how he's done me wrong;
I shall not let him smirk and gloat for long.
He'll see how shallow fickleness is borne
By a noble heart, and brushed aside with scorn.

MARINETTE

In our position, one can at least be glad
Not to be in the power of some cad.
I used my head, one night, when I declined
To do the things that someone had in mind.
Another girl, in hopes of marriage, might
Have yielded to temptation on that night,
But I said *nescio vos*.

LUCILE

Be serious, please.
This is no time for trivialities.
Listen to me: My heart is racked with pain,
And should it happen that this faithless swain,
Through a happy turn of fortune which I would
Be foolish, now, to think a likelihood
(Since Heaven too much enjoys my persecution
To let me have the joy of retribution):
If ever, I say, the Fates should lead him to
Grovel before me, as he ought to do,
And groan that he does not deserve to live,
Don't plead for him and urge me to forgive.
No, no, I'd have you zealously remind me
That he has used me basely and unkindly,
And even if I'm tempted to relent

And let that scoundrel play the penitent,
Bid me preserve my hatred and my pride,
And not allow my anger to subside.

MARINETTE

Count on me, madam; I fully share your view,
I am at least as furious as you,
And I had rather die a virgin than
Be reconciled with that fat, treacherous man.
If he dared . . .

SCENE FIVE

Albert, Lucile, Marinette

ALBERT
Lucile, go tell the tutor, dear,
That I wish to have a word with him out here.
Since he's Ascagne's master, perhaps he'll know
Why my son's spirits seem to be so low.
(*Alone:*)
One guilty deed, and life becomes a sea
Of dread, and worry, and anxiety!
Since I brought up a stranger's child, pretending
That he was mine, my cares have been unending.
Greed made me do it, and it's brought such woe,
I wish I'd never thought of doing so.
Sometimes I fear the fraud will be detected,
Leaving my household poor and unrespected.
Sometimes my son, whom I must shield from harm,
Seems ringed with dangers, and I feel alarm.
If I leave town on business for a day,
I fear that folk, when I return, will say,
"Alas! You haven't heard? Your son's in bed
With a chill, or a broken leg, or a bandaged head."
In short, I lead a life of strain and tension,
Where every moment's full of apprehension.
Ah!

SCENE SIX

———— •◆• ————

Albert, Métaphraste

MÉTAPHRASTE
Mandatum tuum curo diligenter.

ALBERT
Master . . .

MÉTAPHRASTE
The root of "Master" is *magister*,
Which means "three times as great."

ALBERT
                                        That's news to me,
I'm bound to say. However, let it be.
Now, Master . . .

MÉTAPHRASTE
                Proceed.

ALBERT
                        I mean to, never fear.
But don't proceed to interrupt me, hear?
Now, once more, Master (this is my third try),
I'm worried about my son; you know how I
Have cherished him, and brought him up to be . . .

MÉTAPHRASTE
Quite so: *Filio non potest praeferri*
Nisi filius.

ALBERT
                When we talk, Master, I wish
That you'd spare me all that pointless gibberish.
You're a fine Latin scholar, your learning's great,

Or so I have been told, at any rate,
But in our conversation here today
Don't put your erudition on display
And shower me with verbiage, as if you
Were in some pulpit, and I were in a pew.
My father was a clever man of affairs,
But he taught me nothing save my Latin prayers,
Which I have said for fifty years without
The least idea of what they're all about.
So set aside your fancy lore, and please
Adjust your speech to my deficiencies.

MÉTAPHRASTE

So be it.

ALBERT

My son displays no interest
In marriage; whatever match I may suggest,
He's strangely cold, and disinclined to wed.

MÉTAPHRASTE

Perhaps what Marcus Tullius' brother said
To Atticus applies, sir, to your son;
The Greeks, moreover, say *Athanaton* . . .

ALBERT

Incorrigible pedant! Will you please
Forget these Greeks, Albanians, Portuguese,
And all your other tribes and populations.
What has my son to do with foreign nations?

MÉTAPHRASTE

Very well, then. Your son . . .

ALBERT

His looks suggest
That a secret flame may burn within his breast:
There's something on his mind, it's safe to say;

Unmarked by him, I saw him yesterday
In a part of the woods where folk are seldom seen.

MÉTAPHRASTE

"A remote place in the woods," is what you mean,
"A secluded spot." The Latin is *secessus*.
As Virgil put it, *est in secessu locus*.

ALBERT

How could this Virgil say a thing like that?
Those woods were lonely, and I'll eat my hat
If anyone was there except us two.

MÉTAPHRASTE

I mentioned Virgil as a poet who
Employed a phrase beside which yours was crude,
Not as a witness of the scene you viewed.

ALBERT

And what I say to you is: What in blazes
Do I want with poets, witnesses and phrases?
One witness is enough. Don't be absurd.

MÉTAPHRASTE

Yet it is wise to use the terms preferred
By the best authors. *Tu vivendo bonos,*
As the saying goes, *scribendo sequare peritos.*

ALBERT

The fiend won't listen! He's stubborn as an ox.

MÉTAPHRASTE

That was Quintilian's teaching, sir.

ALBERT

                              A pox
Upon this chatterer!

MÉTAPHRASTE
He also wrote,
On the same theme, a jest which I shall quote
For your delight.

ALBERT
It would delight me, knave,
To hurl you down to Hades. How I crave
To put a gag upon that ugly snout!

MÉTAPHRASTE
What is it that you're so upset about?
What do you want?

ALBERT
I want to be listened to,
As I've told you twenty times.

MÉTAPHRASTE
Of course you do,
And if that's all, your wish is my command:
I'm silent.

ALBERT
You had better be.

MÉTAPHRASTE
Here I stand,
Ready to listen.

ALBERT
Good.

MÉTAPHRASTE
May I expire
If I say one word!

ALBERT
God grant you that desire!

MÉTAPHRASTE
You'll be no longer troubled by my prating.

ALBERT
So be it!

MÉTAPHRASTE
Speak when you wish, sir.

ALBERT
I've been waiting . . .

MÉTAPHRASTE
And I won't interrupt you, never fear,

ALBERT
Enough.

MÉTAPHRASTE
My promise to you was sincere.

ALBERT
No doubt.

MÉTAPHRASTE
I told you that I would be still.

ALBERT
Yes.

MÉTAPHRASTE
Henceforth I'll be mute.

ALBERT
I'm sure you will.

MÉTAPHRASTE

Take heart, now; speak; I'm all attention, sir.
You can't say now that I'm a jabberer:
I'll make no sound, not even a cough or sneeze.

ALBERT

(*Aside:*)
The villain!

MÉTAPHRASTE

But don't be too long-winded, please.
I've listened all this time, and it's only right
That I should speak a while.

ALBERT

Damned blatherskite!

MÉTAPHRASTE

What! Must I listen to you forever? No,
Let's share the talking, sir, or I shall go.

ALBERT

My patience is . . .

MÉTAPHRASTE

Good God! Still talking, is he?
When will it end? His chatter makes me dizzy!

ALBERT

I haven't said . . .

MÉTAPHRASTE

Ah! Has he no remorse?
Nothing can stem the flood of his discourse!

ALBERT

This is too much!

MÉTAPHRASTE

What torture! Please, no more.
Come, let me speak a little, I implore.
Unless he speaks, a wise man might as well
Be foolish.

ALBERT

I'm going to silence him, by Hell.

(*Exit.*)

MÉTAPHRASTE

A great philosopher said long ago,
"Speak, that you may be known." That's apropos,
And I would think it better to have ceased
To be a man, and changed into a beast,
Than to be cheated of my right to speak.
Oh, I shall have a headache for a week . . .
How I detest these babbling fools! My word!
Yes, if the sage and learnèd are not heard,
If the wise man can't impart what he has learned,
The order of the world is overturned:
The fox shall be devoured by the hen;
Children shall be the teachers of old men;
The lamb shall crush the wolf between its jaws;
Women shall fight, and madmen make the laws;
Denounced by crooks, the judges shall be tried,
And boys at school shall tan the master's hide;
The sick shall give the well their medicine;
The timid hare . . .
(*Albert reenters, clangs a large cowbell in Métaphraste's ear, and drives him off.*)
No! No! Help; what a din!

Act Three
SCENE ONE

———◆◆———

Mascarille

MASCARILLE

Fate sometimes favors boldness, and a man
Must save his neck in any way he can.
Once I had slipped, and given away the show,
The one trick I could think of was to go
Posthaste to our old master Polidore
And fill him in on what had gone before.
His son's a violent man whose rage I dread,
And if his rival told him what I've said,
Good God! How I'd be knocked about, and mauled!
However, such a scene could be forestalled
If these old gentlemen would talk, and see
Their way to calm the waters and agree.
That's why I'm here. I've come to ask Albert
To meet with Polidore on this affair.

(*He knocks on Albert's door.*)

SCENE TWO

————— •◆• —————

Albert, Mascarille

ALBERT

Who knocks?

MASCARILLE

A friend.

ALBERT

What brings you here today,

Mascarille?

MASCARILLE

I've come here, sir, to say
Good morning . . .

ALBERT

You're good to take the trouble. I
Too say good morning.

(*Goes back inside.*)

MASCARILLE

Well, there's a brusque reply.

What a rude man!

(*Knocks.*)

ALBERT

Still here?

MASCARILLE

I wasn't through.

ALBERT

Didn't you say good morning?

MASCARILLE

Yes, that's true.

ALBERT

Well then, good morning.

(*He turns to go; Mascarille detains him.*)

MASCARILLE

Yes, but I also came
From Polidore, to greet you in his name.

ALBERT

Ah! Your master sent you, then? You were assigned
To bring me his good wishes?

MASCARILLE

Yes.

ALBERT

How kind.
Tell him I wish him joys of all varieties.

(*Goes back inside.*)

MASCARILLE

This man defies all manners and proprieties.
(*He knocks.*)
Please, sir: I've almost finished with my task.
There's an urgent favor that he'd like to ask.

ALBERT

I'm at his service, whenever he may call.

MASCARILLE

(*Detaining him:*)
Wait; two words more, and I'll have said it all.
He'd like to drop by briefly, and confer
With you upon a weighty matter, sir.

ALBERT

And what, if I may ask, is this affair
Which we must ponder?

MASCARILLE

           He's just become aware
Of a great secret which, without a doubt,
Both of you will be much concerned about.
There: That's my message.

SCENE THREE

Albert

ALBERT
          Just Heaven! I quake with fear:
We seldom see each other; what brings him here?
My schemes, no doubt, are known; their doom is sealed.
This "secret's" one I dread to see revealed.
Someone's betrayed me in the hope of gain,
And now my honor bears a lasting stain.
My fraud's discovered. Alas, the cleverest crime
Can't hide the truth for any length of time,
And how much better for my name and soul
If I had let my conscience take control:
Its voice advised me twenty times and more
To give his rightful wealth to Polidore,
And, settling matters in a quiet way,
Avoid the shame which threatens me today.
But no, I've lost my chance; it's now too late.
The wealth that fraud brought into my estate
Must now depart from me, and once it's flown
I shall have lost a fair part of my own.

SCENE FOUR

———•—•———

Albert, Polidore

POLIDORE
(*Saying the first four lines before seeing Albert:*)
To wed in secret, letting no one know!
How will it end, if our children flout us so?
I wish I knew. And I fear the young girl's sire
Both for his wealth and his paternal ire.
But there he is.

ALBERT
Gods! Polidore draws near.

POLIDORE
I cannot face him.

ALBERT
I am held back by fear.

POLIDORE
How am I to begin?

ALBERT
What shall I say?

POLIDORE
He looks upset.

ALBERT
His face is drawn and gray.

POLIDORE
Judging by your expression, you're aware
Of what has brought me here, Monsieur Albert.

ALBERT

Alas, I am.

POLIDORE

Well may you crease your brow.
I couldn't believe what I was told just now.

ALBERT

I should be blushing for chagrin and shame.

POLIDORE

An action of the kind is much to blame,
And there is no excusing it, I hold.

ALBERT

God's merciful to sinners, we are told.

POLIDORE

What shall we be, then—merciful, or just?

ALBERT

We must be Christian.

POLIDORE

Yes indeed, we must.

ALBERT

In the name of God, forgive me, Polidore!

POLIDORE

That's what *I* ask. Forgive me, I implore.

ALBERT

Upon my knees I utter my appeal.

(*Kneels.*)

POLIDORE

What! *I*, not you, should be the one to kneel.

(*Kneels.*)

ALBERT

Look with some pity on my sorry case.

POLIDORE

I supplicate you in my deep disgrace.

ALBERT

The goodness of your heart amazes me.

POLIDORE

I'm overwhelmed by your humility.

ALBERT

Once more, forgive me!

POLIDORE

Pardon *me*, once more!

ALBERT

What has occurred I utterly deplore.

POLIDORE

Your grief could not be greater than my own.

ALBERT

I beg you not to let this thing be known.

POLIDORE

Monsieur Albert, I feel the same as you.

ALBERT

Preserve my honor.

POLIDORE
That, sir, I shall do.

ALBERT
Now, as for money, please say what you require.

POLIDORE
I ask no money; do as you desire.
In all such matters, I wish you to decide,
And if you're happy, I'll be satisfied.

ALBERT
How good you are! What godlike traits you show!

POLIDORE
You, too, are godlike, after such a blow!

ALBERT
May all go well with you, through Heaven's grace!

POLIDORE
God bless you!

ALBERT
Come; a brotherly embrace.

POLIDORE
With all my heart, and I am glad indeed
That we can end thus happily agreed.

ALBERT
Yes, thank the Lord.

(*They rise from their knees.*)

POLIDORE
When I learned, sir, what my son
And your Lucile had so unwisely done,

I frankly feared your anger, and expected
That you, so well-to-do and well connected . . .

ALBERT

What's this about Lucile, and being unwise?

POLIDORE

If that offends you, I'll apologize.
My son's done wrong, I'll readily admit,
And if it will relieve your grief a bit,
I'll even say that he *alone* did wrong;
That your daughter's virtue was too pure and strong
To let her go astray or gravely err,
Had not a wicked tempter prompted her;
That the villain took advantage of her trust
And so reduced your hopes for her to dust.
Yet since the thing is done, and since we find
Ourselves, thank Heaven, attuned in heart and mind,
Let's pardon all, and let all wrongs be righted
When, in the church, our children are united.

ALBERT

(*Aside:*)
So, I was wrong! But now this news! Perplexed,
I go from one great worry to the next,
And, doubly muddled, don't know what to say.
If I speak, I fear I'll give myself away.

POLIDORE

What's on your mind, sir?

ALBERT

                        Nothing. I think that I'll
Suspend our conversation for a while.
I suddenly feel sick, and must depart.

SCENE FIVE

—◆ ● ◆—

Polidore

POLIDORE
I know his feelings, and can read his heart.
Reason has said to him *forgive, forget,*
But his deep anger's not appeased as yet.
His sense of wrong revives, and so he flees,
To hide from me his turmoil and unease.
His sorrow touches me, I share his grief.
Patience and time must bring his heart relief.
A woe too soon suppressed will but redouble.
Well, here's the foolish cause of all our trouble.

SCENE SIX

Polidore, Valère

POLIDORE

So, my fine fellow! Your antics, it appears,
Will fill with grief your father's latter years;
Must I, each day, be forced to hear reports
Of freaks and follies of a hundred sorts?

VALÈRE

To what incessant crimes do you refer?
How have I earned my father's fury, sir?

POLIDORE

Ah, yes! I'm a strange man, and a testy one,
To criticize so wise and good a son!
Just look! His life is saintly, and he stays
At home all day upon his knees, and prays!
Has he ever twisted Nature's laws awry
By turning night to day? No, that's a lie!
Has he, in scores of cases, failed to show
Due deference to his father? Heavens, no!
And did he lately, in a secret rite,
Marry the daughter of Albert by night,
Reckless of consequences grave and bad?
No, that was someone else; this innocent lad
Has no idea of what those charges meant.
Wretch, sent by Heaven as my punishment,
Shall you be willful always? Shall not I
See you act wisely once before I die?

VALÈRE

(*Alone:*)
What caused this outburst? It appears to me
That the only answer could be Mascarille.

The rogue would never admit it. Therefore I'm
Forced to use trickery, and for a time
Conceal my anger.

SCENE SEVEN

Valère, Mascarille

VALÈRE
My father is aware,
Good Mascarille, of the secret which we share.

MASCARILLE
He is?

VALÈRE
Yes.

MASCARILLE
Who in the Devil let him know?

VALÈRE
I cannot guess who would betray us so.
Still, his reaction has amazed me quite,
And given me every reason for delight.
He showed no anger, and in a gentle voice
Forgave my trespass and approved my choice.
I wish I knew who's prompted him to be
So loving, and to show such leniency.
Someone has helped to lift my spirits high.

MASCARILLE
And what, sir, would you say if it were I
Who was the cause of your glad frame of mind?

VALÈRE
Come, come: Let's have no nonsense of that kind.

MASCARILLE
'Twas I, sir, I—as your father could relate—
Who brought about your present cheerful state.

VALÈRE

Truly? No jokes, now.

MASCARILLE

The Devil take me, sir,
If I'm a jester or a perjurer.

VALÈRE

(*Drawing his sword:*)
The Devil take me, too, if I do not
Give you your just deserts upon the spot!

MASCARILLE

Sir, I'm astonished. What would you kill me for?

VALÈRE

Is this the loyalty which once you swore?
If I hadn't tricked you, you'd never have confessed
To a guilty fact which I'd already guessed.
Those babbling lips of yours, which never tire,
Have brought on me the fury of my sire.
You've ruined me and, therefore, be prepared
To die.

MASCARILLE

No, no. Not yet. Let me be spared.
My soul's not ready for it. I beg you, wait
And see how all this will eventuate.
I had the best of reasons to reveal
A marriage you yourself could scarce conceal:
It was a master stroke, and you shall see
That you are wrong to be enraged at me.
What ground is there for anger, so long as through
My efforts all your wishes can come true,
And you be free of secrecy and strain?

VALÈRE

And what if all your talk proves false and vain?

MASCARILLE

Then you'll be free to kill me, as before.
But that won't happen. I have schemes galore,
And in the end you'll think me heaven-sent,
And thank me for my brilliant management.

VALÈRE

We'll see. Lucile, now . . .

MASCARILLE

Wait! Her father's here.

SCENE EIGHT

———————•❖•———————

Albert, Valère, Mascarille

ALBERT

(*Saying the first five lines before seeing Valère:*)
Recovering from my earlier shock and fear,
I marvel that so strange a tale misled
My anxious mind and filled my heart with dread.
Lucile assures me that there's nothing in it,
And I don't doubt her statement for a minute.
Ah, sir! Are you the brazen youth who glories
In slandering people with your untrue stories?

MASCARILLE

Monsieur Albert, don't fly into a passion.
Do treat your son-in-law in gentler fashion.

ALBERT

What son-in-law? Rascal, you look to me
Like the mainspring of some conspiracy
Of which you were the chief inventor, too.

MASCARILLE

I don't see what can be upsetting you.

ALBERT

You think it splendid, do you, to defame
My daughter, and besmirch our family name?

MASCARILLE

This gentleman is yours, sir, to command.

ALBERT

Let him tell the truth, then. That's my sole demand,
If he was partial to Lucile, he could
Have sought her hand as a proper suitor would;

That is, he could have been obedient
To custom, and applied for my consent,
Rather than be perverse, and give offense
To decency by this absurd pretense.

MASCARILLE

Pretense? Was Lucile not wedded secretly
To my master?

ALBERT

No, rogue, and she'll never be.

MASCARILLE

But if in fact a secret knot was tied,
Would you give your blessing to the groom and bride?

ALBERT

And if it's proved that there was no such wedding,
Would you rather die by hanging or beheading?

VALÈRE

Sir, if you'll let me, I can prove to you
That he's told the truth.

ALBERT

Well! Here's a master who
Deserves this flunky. Two liars in a row!

MASCARILLE

On my word of honor, what I say is so.

VALÈRE

Why should we wish to fool you, Monsieur Albert?

ALBERT

(*Aside:*)
They work together, like card sharks at a fair.

MASCARILLE

But come, let's cut this quarrel short, say I:
Bring out Lucile, and let her testify.

ALBERT

And what if she declares your tale untrue?

MASCARILLE

That, sir, is something that she cannot do.
Just promise to give their union your consent,
And I'll accept the direst punishment
If she does not confess to us a great
Love for my master and for her wedded state.

ALBERT

Well, we shall see.

(*He goes and knocks on his door.*)

MASCARILLE

(*To Valère:*)
          Don't worry. Be of good cheer.

ALBERT

Come out, Lucile!

VALÈRE

(*To Mascarille:*)
          I fear . . .

MASCARILLE

          Ah, never fear.

SCENE NINE

Lucile, Albert, Valère, Mascarille

MASCARILLE

Monsieur Albert, be still, please. Madam, this
Is a moment which could bring you perfect bliss.
Your sire, informed now of your love, allows
Your choice of husband and approves your vows,
Provided that, unforced and unafraid,
You will confirm the statements we have made.

LUCILE

What is this saucy villain trying to say?

MASCARILLE

Good! We begin with compliments, right away.

LUCILE

Do tell me, sir; what clever brain created
This tale that's now so widely circulated?

VALÈRE

Forgive me; 'twas my man who dared reveal
The secret of our marriage, dear Lucile.

LUCILE

Our marriage?

VALÈRE

Yes, it's all come out, my dear,
And nothing can be hidden now, I fear.

LUCILE

So: Out of ardent love I've made you mine?

VALÈRE

All men must envy me a fate so fine:
Yet I ascribe my amorous success
Less to your ardor than to kindliness.
I know your temper must be sorely tried:
Our vows were something that you wished to hide,
And I have curbed all signs of rapture, lest
I violate the wish you had expressed.
But . . .

MASCARILLE

Yes, I did it; and what harm was done?

LUCILE

Was there ever a bolder falsehood under the sun?
You keep on lying, even to my face.
Do you think to gain me by a means so base?
Ah, what a noble lover! Because you lack
My love, it is my honor you attack,
In hopes that Father, shaken by your claim,
Will force on me a marriage full of shame!
No, even if all things were to take your part—
The Fates, my father, the wishes of my heart—
I'd still resist, with an indignant ire,
The Fates, my father, and my heart's desire,
And die before I married a complete
Scoundrel who sought to win me by deceit.
Enough, sir. If decorum did not ban
My sex from doing violence to a man,
I'd teach you what it means to treat me thus.

VALÈRE

(*To Mascarille:*)
Nothing will soothe her now. She's furious.

MASCARILLE

Sir, let me speak to her. Madam, if you please,
What is the point of these perversities?

What can you mean? What curious whim requires
That you take arms against your own desires?
If your sire were of the harsh, forbidding kind,
I'd understand; but he has an open mind,
And he has promised me that in confessing
Your secret to him, you shall gain his blessing.
No doubt 'twill make you feel a little shy
To admit the yearning you've been mastered by,
But if that flame now gives you sleepless nights,
A happy marriage will set all to rights;
And passion such as yours, though much decried,
Is not so grave a sin as homicide.
The flesh is weak, as men have always known,
And a girl, moreover, isn't made of stone.
You're not the first, as the old saying goes,
And you won't be the last one, Heaven knows.

LUCILE

Can you listen, Father, to such words as these,
And not reprove their gross indignities?

ALBERT

What would you have me say, dear? I'm afraid
Rage makes me speechless.

MASCARILLE

          Madam, you should have made
A frank confession, and so closed the case.

LUCILE

What is there to confess?

MASCARILLE

          Why, what took place
Between my master and you! You're teasing me.

LUCILE

And what, you monster of effrontery,
Took place between your master and me?

MASCARILLE

You ought
To know far better than I, I should have thought,
And you cannot have forgotten the delight
Which you experienced on a certain night.

LUCILE

Father, this lackey has forgot his place.

(*She gives Mascarille a slap in the face.*)

SCENE TEN

Albert, Valère, Mascarille

MASCARILLE

I do believe she's slapped me in the face.

ALBERT

Begone, you villain. What she did, by God,
I, as her father, heartily applaud.

MASCARILLE

Nevertheless, if anything I've said
Was not the truth, may Heaven strike me dead.

ALBERT

Nevertheless, may both my ears be cropped
If your brash chatter isn't quickly stopped.

MASCARILLE

Shall I bring two witnesses who'll prove me true?

ALBERT

Shall I call two men to whack and cudgel you?

MASCARILLE

They'll validate my story, every bit.

ALBERT

Their brawn will make up for my lack of it.

MASCARILLE

Lucile behaved so out of bashfulness.

ALBERT

For *your* behavior I shall have redress.

MASCARILLE

Do you know Ormin? He's that notary, plump and witty.

ALBERT

Do you know Grimpant, the hangman of this city?

MASCARILLE

And Simon the tailor, renowned for formal wear?

ALBERT

And the gallows tree, set up in the market square?

MASCARILLE

Those two were good friends of the bride and groom.

ALBERT

Those two will drag you off to meet your doom.

MASCARILLE

For witnesses, the couple chose those two.

ALBERT

Those two will witness my revenge on you.

MASCARILLE

They saw the nuptials of the happy pair.

ALBERT

And they shall see you dancing in the air.

MASCARILLE

A black veil hid the features of the bride.

ALBERT

They'll hoist the black flag for you, once you've died.

MASCARILLE

You old, pig-headed man!

ALBERT
Accursèd faker!
I'm old, and you had better thank your Maker
That I can't repay your insolence just now.
But I shall, don't worry. That's my solemn vow.

SCENE ELEVEN

Valère, Mascarille

VALÈRE

Well, well. The happy outcome that you planned . . .

MASCARILLE

No need to say it, sir; I understand:
All's turned against me; on all sides I see
Cudgels and swords and gallows threatening me.
I shall escape this nightmare only if
I hurl myself head foremost from a cliff,
And that's what I shall do, so long as I
Can find a cliff that's adequately high.
Farewell, sir.

VALÈRE

No, no; don't you try to flee.
Your death is something that I want to see.

MASCARILLE

I cannot die, sir, under someone's eyes.
You force me to postpone my sad demise.

VALÈRE

Come, lest my vexed belovèd make you pay
For the insults you have given her today.

MASCARILLE

(*Alone:*)
Poor Mascarille, what worries and chagrins
Are heaped on you through other people's sins!

Act Four

SCENE ONE

Ascagne, Frosine

FROSINE

It's a troubling turn of events.

ASCAGNE

                      Frosine, dear friend,
Fate has decreed for me a dismal end.
Things have now gone so far, in this affair,
That matters can't conceivably stop there;
Lucile, and my Valère, astonished by
These late events, will seek to clarify
The mystery which made them disagree,
And that will ruin both my schemes and me.
For—whether Albert was privy to deceit
Or taken in, like others, by the cheat—
If ever the truth about me should be known,
And all that wealth he's added to his own
Be taken away, think how he'd then regard me!
Unless I bring him wealth, he will discard me.
No more affection. And however my
Imposture looked then to my lover's eye,
Would he respect a wife who could not claim
A fortune, and who had no family name?

FROSINE

That is a clear and cool analysis,
But you should have made it earlier than this.
What hid the truth from you until this hour?
One didn't have to have prophetic power
To see, when first you schemed to catch Valère,
The risks of which you've now become aware.

'Twas in the cards; from the start I've understood
That your trickery couldn't come to any good.

ASCAGNE

I'm desperate, Frosine. Pretend that you
Are in my place, and tell me what to do.

FROSINE

If I put myself in your place, it will be
Your office, then, to lend advice to me,
For I shall then be you, and you'll be I:
"Frosine, you see how all has gone awry;
Tell me, I pray, what steps I ought to take."

ASCAGNE

Oh, don't make fun of me, for mercy's sake!
It's wrong of you, when I am so distressed,
To treat my situation as a jest.

FROSINE

I share your heartsick feelings, rest assured,
And I'd give anything to see them cured.
But what can I do? Alas, I don't see how
Your amorous wishes can be furthered now.

ASCAGNE

If there's no hope for me, then I must die.

FROSINE

Don't hurry, please, to bid the world good-bye.
Death's a fine remedy, but it's the sort
One should use only as a last resort.

ASCAGNE

Frosine, I mean it: If I cannot be led,
By your kind help, through all that looms ahead,
I'll let despair possess me altogether.

FROSINE

I've just now thought of something. I wonder whether . . .
But here's Éraste, who might disrupt our talk.
Let us discuss this matter while we walk.
Come, come, let's vanish.

SCENE TWO

Éraste, Gros-René

ÉRASTE
So. Rebuffed once more?

GROS-RENÉ
There never was, sir, an ambassador
So coldly treated. I'd hardly said how you
Hoped that she'd grant a moment's interview,
When she broke in and in a haughty style
Said, "Go! Both you and he are low and vile.
Tell him to keep his distance." Having sent
That charming message, she turned her back and went.
Then Marinette got on her high horse, too,
And said to me, "Be off, you lackey, you,"
And left me standing there. Your luck and mine
Are much the same: We're no one's valentine.

ÉRASTE
The thankless woman! To scorn a heart which for
Good cause was vexed, yet now is hers once more!
What! If it seems his trust has been abused,
Ought not a lover's rage to be excused?
And could my heart, at that dark moment, be
Indifferent to a rival's victory?
Who wouldn't have raged like me, as things then were,
Loath though I was to think the worst of her?
Was I slow to set aside my just suspicions?
Did I trouble her for oaths and depositions?
No; at a time when all is still unsure,
I raise to her a worship deep and pure,
And ask her pardon. Yet she makes little of
My homage, and the grandeur of my love.
Alas, she will not cure my heart of quaking
With fears and envies of my rival's making;

She dooms me to be jealous, and dares refuse
All notes, all messages, all interviews!
Clearly her love was never very strong
If it could die of such a trivial wrong;
In her abrupt severity I see
Too plainly what, in truth, she feels for me,
And just how highly I should now esteem
Those flighty charms which led my heart to dream.
No, I'll no more be at the beck and call
Of one whose feeling for me is so small;
And since she can so coldly spurn her lover,
I'll do the same, and be unburdened of her.

GROS-RENÉ

I'll do that, too, sir. Let our loves be classed
With ancient sins, and errors of the past.
Let's teach those fickle women to behave,
And let them know that we're still tough and brave.
If a man's afraid of hens, then he'll be pecked.
If men were only to demand respect,
The women wouldn't talk so big and loud.
It's our own fault that they've become so proud:
I'm hanged if I don't think that all their sex
Would soon be shyly clinging to our necks
If it were not for all the silly ways
That most men spoil the creatures nowadays.

ÉRASTE

For me, disdain's a thing that can't be borne;
And I propose to match her scorn for scorn
By giving my affection to another.

GROS-RENÉ

For me, a woman isn't worth the bother;
I shall renounce them all, and it's my view
That you'd do well to do without them, too.
For, sir, a woman is, without a doubt,
An animal that's hard to figure out,

Whose nature has been wicked since the Fall:
And since an animal's an animal,
And never shall be otherwise, although
It live a hundred thousand years, just so.
Woman is always woman, and shall stay
A woman even to the Judgment Day.
Whence a wise Greek observed that woman's head
Is like a quicksand. Listen to what he said
In this most cogent train of reasoning:
Just as the head is like the body's king,
And the body without the king becomes a brute,
If the king and the head get into a dispute,
So that the compass wavers from its course,
Certain confusions then arise, perforce;
The brutal part would gain the mastery
Over the rational; the one cries "gee,"
The other, "haw"; the one would have it slow,
The other fast, and all is touch and go.
Which goes to show, interpreters explain,
That a woman's head is like a weathervane
Up on the roof, which the least breeze can turn;
And that's why Aristotle, as we learn,
Said women are like the sea, a thought which gave
Our tongue the saying, "steady as a wave."
So, by comparison (for comparing brings
A vividness into our reasonings,
And scholars like myself prefer a shrewd
Comparison to a mere similitude):
Well, by comparison, Master, if I may:
As when the sea is stormy, and the spray
Begins to fly, the winds to shriek and squall,
Waves to collide and make a dreadful brawl,
And the ship, for all the steersman's art, is tossed
Twixt cellar and attic, and is all but lost,
So, when a woman lets that head of hers
Fill up with wild ideas, a storm occurs
In which the witch opinionates and raves,
Until the . . . tide, you know . . . or else the waves . . .

Or, so to speak, a sandbar . . . or a reef . . .
Oh, women are nothing but a lot of grief.

ÉRASTE

Well argued.

GROS-RENÉ

It wasn't bad, I'm glad to say.
But look, I see the two of them bound this way.
Stand firm, sir.

ÉRASTE

Don't you worry.

GROS-RENÉ

I fear that her
Bright eyes may once more take you prisoner.

SCENE THREE

Lucile, Éraste, Marinette, Gros-René

MARINETTE

I see that he's still here; now, don't relent.

LUCILE

Don't worry; I'm not weak to that extent.

MARINETTE

He's coming towards us.

ÉRASTE

     No, no, madam, I'm
Not here to court you yet another time.
That's over; my heart is healing, and I now see
How little of your own you gave to me.
Your lasting anger at my slight offense
Shows all too clearly your indifference;
And scorn, as I shall make you well aware,
Is what a noble spirit cannot bear.
I once discovered in your eyes, I own,
A charm and beauty which were yours alone,
And, as your ardent slave, preferred my chain
To any scepter that I might obtain.
Yes, I adored you in the deepest way;
You were my life; and I am forced to say
That after all, however much offended,
I'll find it painful that my suit is ended,
That my hurt soul, though it intends to heal,
May bleed a long time from the wound I feel,
And that, though freed from a yoke I gladly bore,
It must resolve itself to love no more.
But what's the good of talking? Since you decline
So hatefully each overture of mine,

This is the last time I shall trouble you
With the anguished feelings I am going through.

LUCILE

As for *my* feelings, sir, I'd be elated
If this last speech of yours were terminated.

ÉRASTE

Well then, my lady, cross me off your list!
I'll break with you forever, as you insist;
Yes, yes, I'll break with you, and I shan't try
To speak with you again; I'd rather die.

LUCILE

So much the better.

ÉRASTE

No, no, you'd be wrong
To think that I'll back down. Though I'm not strong
Enough to bar your image from my heart,
Yet I assure you now that, when we part,
I shan't come back.

LUCILE

To do so would be vain.

ÉRASTE

I'd hack myself to bits before I'd deign
To stoop so low as to revisit one
Who'd so mistreated me as you have done.

LUCILE

So be it. Let's say no more about it.

ÉRASTE

Yes,
Let's put an end to all this wordiness,
And let me give you solid proof that I've

Determined to escape your toils alive.
I shall keep nothing by me which could set
My heart to mourning what it must forget.
Here is your portrait: It delights the eye
With all the charms you are attended by,
And yet they hide a hundred faults from view:
It's an impostor I return to you.

GROS-RENÉ

Good!

LUCILE

Since you are returning everything,
I'll do the same: Take back your diamond ring.

MARINETTE

Well done!

ÉRASTE

This lock of hair is yours once more.

LUCILE

Your agate seal I hasten to restore.

ÉRASTE

(*Reading:*)
"You say your love is limitless, Éraste.
Though I'm not sure that mine is quite so vast,
    This I can say with certainty:
    I love it that Éraste loves me.
                    Lucile"
Those warm words gave me leave to pay you court,
But you deceived me. This is my retort.

(*He tears up the letter.*)

LUCILE

(*Reading:*)
"I don't know what will be my passion's fate,
Or for how long my longing heart must wait;
        But I know this—that I shall feel
        Eternal love for you, Lucile.
                        Éraste"
This says you'll love me through eternity.
You and this letter both have lied to me.

(*She tears up the letter.*)

GROS-RENÉ

Go on.

ÉRASTE

(*Tearing up a letter:*)
        This one's from you. It, too, shall go.

MARINETTE

(*To Lucile:*)
Steady.

LUCILE

And so shall these, I'll have him know.

GROS-RENÉ

(*To Éraste:*)
Be firm. Resist her.

MARINETTE

(*To Lucile:*)
                Don't break down. Stand fast.

LUCILE

(*Tearing up letters:*)
Here go the rest.

ÉRASTE
Thank Heaven! Free at last!
May I die, if I go back on what I said!

LUCILE
If I break my word, may Heaven strike me dead!

ÉRASTE
Farewell, then.

LUCILE
Yes, farewell.

MARINETTE
(*To Lucile:*)
You did just right.

GROS-RENÉ
(*To Éraste:*)
You got the best of it.

MARINETTE
(*To Lucile:*)
Let's get out of sight.

GROS-RENÉ
(*To Éraste:*)
You've battled bravely; now you must come away.

MARINETTE
(*To Lucile:*)
Why are you waiting?

GROS-RENÉ
(*To Éraste:*)
Why must you delay?

ÉRASTE

Lucile, Lucile, I know you'll grieve and pine,
Remembering that you lost a heart like mine.

LUCILE

Éraste, Éraste, a heart like yours is found
Quite easily; one has but to look around.

ÉRASTE

No, no, search everywhere and you'll find none
That could adore you as my heart has done.
I don't speak now in hopes that you'll relent:
In such a cause, my words would be misspent.
All my devotion could not move or win you;
You broke with me; my hopes cannot continue.
But after me, though others swoon and sigh,
None will so truly cherish you as I.

LUCILE

When we love someone, we treat that person kindly,
And never would accuse that person blindly.

ÉRASTE

When we love someone, appearances may be
Conducive to a fit of jealousy,
But a true lover could not send away
The one she loves, as you have done today.

LUCILE

Jealousy need not slander and abuse.

ÉRASTE

A passionate error's easy to excuse.

LUCILE

Ah no, Éraste, you do not truly love me.

ÉRASTE

Lucile, you've never been enamored of me.

LUCILE

Ha! I don't think that greatly troubles you.
Perhaps the wisest thing for me to do
Was never . . . But let us drop this idle chatter:
I've nothing more to say about the matter.

ÉRASTE

Why not?

LUCILE

Because we two are separating,
And have no time for bickering and debating.

ÉRASTE

We're parting?

LUCILE

Yes: Is there any cause to doubt it?

ÉRASTE

How can you sound so matter-of-fact about it?

LUCILE

You sound the same.

ÉRASTE

I?

LUCILE

Yes; one hates to show
How much it hurts to let somebody go.

ÉRASTE

But, cruel one, 'twas you who wanted it,

LUCILE

I? Not at all. 'Twas you, you must admit.

ÉRASTE

I thought you'd be made happy by the break.

LUCILE

Not so. You wished it for your own sweet sake.

ÉRASTE

But what if, yearning for captivity,
My sad heart begged you now to pardon me?

LUCILE

No, no, you mustn't: I'm weak, and I'm afraid
I'd grant too quickly the request you made.

ÉRASTE

Ah, no! You could not pardon me too soon,
Or I too quickly ask you for that boon:
Pray grant it, madam; this great love of mine
Must never cease to worship at your shrine.
Again I ask it; will you not confer
Your gracious pardon?

LUCILE

Take me home now, sir.

SCENE FOUR

———————•━•———————

Marinette, Gros-René

MARINETTE

Oh, the spineless creature!

GROS-RENÉ

What a craven quitter.

MARINETTE

I blush for her.

GROS-RENÉ

I'm furious and bitter.
Don't think that I'll give in to you that way.

MARINETTE

You won't fool me like that, try as you may.

GROS-RENÉ

Don't stir me up, or I'll go through the ceiling.

MARINETTE

Remember who I am, now; you're not dealing
With my foolish mistress. Look at that pretty mug!
My, how it makes me want to kiss him. Ugh!
Do you think I'd fall in love with such a face,
And let myself be squeezed in your embrace—
A girl like me?

GROS-RENÉ

We're quits then, it appears.
Well, not to hem and haw about it, here's
The cap you gave me, with its plume of red.
It will no longer crown my noble head.

MARINETTE

To show my scorn for you in the same way,
Here is that paper of pins which yesterday
You gave me with a philanthropic air.

GROS-RENÉ

Take back your knife; it's an object rich and rare.
It must have cost you twenty cents, that's plain.

MARINETTE

Take back your scissors and their copper chain.

GROS-RENÉ

Here's that piece of cheese you gave me. If I could
Give back the soup you gave me then, I would,
For then I'd owe you not a thing, my dear.

MARINETTE

I don't have all your letters with me here,
But when they burn, they'll make a lovely flame.

GROS-RENÉ

And what do you think I'll do with yours? The same.

MARINETTE

Do you think I'm going to take you back? No, never!

GROS-RENÉ
(*Picking up a straw:*)
The way to stay unreconciled forever
Is to break a straw in two, for it's a token
Of separation when a straw is broken.
Now, don't make eyes. I want to be irate.

MARINETTE

Don't wink at me. I'm in a furious state.

GROS-RENÉ

Come, break the straw now, so we can't back down.
You witch, you're laughing!

MARINETTE

You made me laugh, you clown.

GROS-RENÉ

Plague take your laughing: My rage has all abated.
Well, what do you say? Shall we be separated,
Or shall we not?

MARINETTE

You say.

GROS-RENÉ

You say.

MARINETTE

No, you.

GROS-RENÉ

Shall there be no more love between us two?

MARINETTE

Just as you wish.

GROS-RENÉ

What's *your* wish? Don't be shy.

MARINETTE

I shall say nothing.

GROS-RENÉ

Neither shall I.

MARINETTE

Nor I.

GROS-RENÉ

Oh, let's stop all this nonsense, for Heaven's sake.
Shake hands; I pardon you.

MARINETTE

I forgive you. Shake.

GROS-RENÉ

My, how she charms me! More than I can say!

MARINETTE

How Marinette adores her Gros-René!

Act Five

SCENE ONE

———— •◦• ————

Mascarille

MASCARILLE

"When darkness falls," he said, "I mean to steal
Into the residence of my dear Lucile.
Go home now, and make ready with great speed
Some arms, and the dark lantern we shall need."
When he said those words, I felt as if he'd said,
"Get ready to be hanged until you're dead."
Come now, my Master; because your order sent
Me reeling backwards in astonishment,
I hadn't time to question or debate;
But now I wish to speak, and set you straight:
Defend yourself; let's reason equably.
You wish, you say, to go tonight and see
Lucile? "Yes, Mascarille." What shall you do?
"What a true lover is expected to."
What a true idiot would do, who takes
A needless risk, and plays for mortal stakes.
"But you know what my motive is, my spur:
Lucile is angry." So much the worse for her.
"But love has bade me soothe her troubled heart."
But love's an ass; he isn't very smart.
If we met an angry brother, sire or rival,
Just how would love assure us of survival?
"Do you think that any of those would cause a brawl?"
Indeed I do; your rival, most of all.
"Don't worry, Mascarille; we'll go well armed,
And if we're challenged we shall not be harmed;
We'll fight them off." We will? That's just the sort
Of thing I don't regard as healthy sport.
I, fight? Good Lord! Am I some Roland, then,
Or some Achilles? Master, think again.

When I, who hold myself so dear, reflect
That an inch or two of steel can so affect
The body as to put one in the grave,
I'm shocked, and feel no impulse to be brave.
"But you'll be armored, head to foot." Then I'd
Be heavy, and couldn't run away and hide.
And furthermore, there's always some loose joint
Through which a sword can thrust its wicked point.
"They'll call you a coward." I don't care if they do,
So long as I can move my jaws and chew.
At table I can do the work of four,
But I'm a zero, sir, in fight or war.
Though the other world may seem to you a treat,
I find the air of this one very sweet,
And death's a thing that I'm not wild about.
If you choose to play the fool, just count me out.

SCENE TWO

—•◦•—

Valère, Mascarille

VALÈRE

I've never lived through such a tedious day.
The sun in Heaven seems to stay and stay,
And has so long a course to cover yet
Before it can pull in its rays and set,
I doubt its journey ever will be done.
It maddens me, the slowness of the sun.

MASCARILLE

Why yearn to plunge into the dark, intent
On figuring in some gruesome incident? . . .
Lucile's rebuffs have been both firm and plain . . .

VALÈRE

Spare me such talk. It's bothersome and vain.
I'd fight a hundred foes, could I appease
Her wrath, which has my soul in agonies;
And if I cannot melt her heart, I'll die.
My mind's made up.

MASCARILLE

        Sir, we see eye to eye.
But when we go in there, shouldn't we be
Unnoticed?

VALÈRE

    Yes.

MASCARILLE

Then something worries me.

VALÈRE

What's that?

MASCARILLE
I have a most tormenting cough,
The sound of which could tip their servants off.
(*He coughs.*)
I've never had a cough so bad as this.

VALÈRE
Well, it will pass. Just chew some licorice.

MASCARILLE
I don't believe, sir, that this cough will pass.
I wish I could go with you but, alas,
Think what regret I'd suffer if it were
My fault that something happened to you, sir.

SCENE THREE

———— • ————

Valère, La Rapière, Mascarille

LA RAPIÈRE

I've just had word, sir, from an honest source
That Éraste's enraged, and may resort to force;
Meanwhile, Albert declares that he will slaughter
Your Mascarille for slandering his daughter.

MASCARILLE

I? I? All this has nothing to do with me.
Do I deserve this talk of butchery?
Am I in charge of the virginities
Of all the girls in town? Just tell me, please:
Can I prevent temptation? And if they
Give in to it, what can I do or say?

VALÈRE

(*To La Rapière:*)
Our foes are not so fierce as you've been told;
And, though his passion may have made him bold,
Éraste will find that scaring us is hard.

LA RAPIÈRE

If you have need, sir, of a bodyguard,
I'll serve you in all weathers, foul or fair.

VALÈRE

You're kind to offer me such aid and care.

LA RAPIÈRE

I have two friends I'll bring you if I can,
Tough fellows who will draw on any man,
And who could guarantee your peace of mind.

MASCARILLE

We'd better hire them, sir.

VALÈRE

Sir, you're too kind.

LA RAPIÈRE

And little Gille, as well, could lend his aid,
But for the fatal slip he lately made.
What a shame! An able man! Perhaps you saw
What a scurvy trick was played him by the law;
He died like Caesar. Breaking him on the wheel,
The executioner couldn't make him squeal.

VALÈRE

A man like that is a great loss, indeed;
But as for your good offer, we shall not need
Protection.

LA RAPIÈRE

As you like, but don't forget
That he's looking for you, and may find you yet.

VALÈRE

Well, just to prove to you that I'm undaunted,
If it's me he wants, I'll give him what is wanted.
I'll walk all through this town with fearless stride,
And none but this one servant at my side.

MASCARILLE

Oh, sir, you're tempting Heaven: How rash of you!
You know what threats are made against us two.
Oh!

VALÈRE

What are you looking at? Something sinister?

MASCARILLE

I smell a cudgel in the offing, sir.
But now, I beg you, let us be discreet
And not stand obstinately in the street;
Let's hide somewhere.

VALÈRE

                Hide? Can you to my face
Propose—you knave!—that I do a thing so base?
Follow me now, and no more jabbering.

MASCARILLE

Dear Master, living is a lovely thing!
We have but one death, and it lasts so long! . . .

VALÈRE

If you speak again, I'll beat you like a gong.
Ascagne is coming. It's not yet clear to me
What side he takes in all this enmity.
Meanwhile, we shall go home and get our gear
For tonight's brave venture.

MASCARILLE

                All I feel is fear.
A plague on love, and on these girls who taste
Love's fruit, and then act militantly chaste!

SCENE FOUR

———————•◆•———————

Ascagne, Frosine

ASCAGNE

Then it's true, Frosine, all true beyond a doubt?
Pray tell the story, leaving nothing out.

FROSINE

You shall in time know all the facts, don't worry—
Since, as a rule, so wonderful a story
Is told, retold, and then repeated still.
All you need know is this: After that will
Had specified a male child as its heir,
Albert's wife was so luckless as to bear
A girl child. You, my dear. Albert then spun
A sly plot, taking as his own the son
Of Ignès the flower girl, who in reverse
Took you, and placed you in our house to nurse.
Some ten months later, when the boy fell prey
To a fatal chill, Albert being then away,
His wife, too, hatched a plot, by reason of
Her husband's temper and her mother love.
She took you back in secret then, to be
Once more a member of your family,
Her absent husband being notified
That his daughter, not his borrowed son, had died.
So! There's the secret of your birth revealed,
Which your feigned mother had till now concealed;
For that she's given her reasons, though I've guessed
That some weren't wholly in your interest.
In any case, my talk with her has brought
More blessings than we ever could have thought.
Ignès no longer claims you; thanks to Valère,
The time has come to lay your secret bare,
And she and I have let your father know
What his wife's diary proves to have been so;

Then, pressing our persuasions farther yet,
We've had the luck and cleverness to get
Albert and Polidore into a mood
Of tolerance, and a pliant attitude,
Telling the latter all these strange events
So gently that he did not take offense,
And, step by step, so leading him at last
To make adjustments and forgive the past
That he is quite as eager as your sire
To see you wed the husband you desire.

ASCAGNE

Frosine, my dear, what joy your words beget . . .
For all you've done, how great must be my debt!

FROSINE

One last thing: Polidore's in the mood for fun,
And bids us to say nothing to his son.

SCENE FIVE

———•-———

Polidore, Ascagne, Frosine

POLIDORE

Come, Daughter, as I may call you now; for I
Now know the secret that your clothes belie.
You've done a daring deed, in which I find
Such spirit and such cleverness of mind,
I know how much my dear son will rejoice
When he finds out who's the lady of his choice.
He'll treasure you, and I shall do the same.
But here he comes; let's play a little game.
Go bring your people here.

ASCAGNE

        Sir, I'll obey you,
As a sign of that respect I'll always pay you.

SCENE SIX

Polidore, Valère, Mascarille

MASCARILLE

(*To Valère:*)
Heaven sometimes warns us of an ill-starred thing.
I dreamt last night, sir, of a broken string
Of pearls, and broken eggs. Dark omens, eh?

VALÈRE

Coward!

POLIDORE

Valère, you face a test today
Where all your courage will be necessary.
Prepare to meet a potent adversary.

MASCARILLE

Will no one intervene, sir, and prevent
These foes from mutual dismemberment?
It's not my place to do so; but if through
Some dreadful chance your son is lost to you,
Don't blame me for it.

POLIDORE

No, no; in this case
I urge my son to face what he must face.

MASCARILLE

Unnatural father!

VALÈRE

Sir, in those words I hear
A brave man speaking, and one whom I revere.
I know that I've offended you; I repent
Of all I've done without your wise consent.

And yet, however angry you might be,
You've never ceased to hope the best of me,
And you do well to urge me not to let
Éraste's ill-tempered challenge go unmet.

POLIDORE

I worried about his anger until lately,
But now the state of things has altered greatly;
A stronger foe, from whom you cannot fly,
Will soon attack you.

MASCARILLE

Why all this fighting? Why?

VALÈRE

I fly, sir? God forbid. Bur who is my foe?

POLIDORE

Ascagne.

VALÈRE

Ascagne?

POLIDORE

He'll soon be here, I know.

VALÈRE

Strange! His good will toward me was so intense.

POLIDORE

Yes, it is he to whom you've given offense.
He asks you to the field of honor, where
In single fight you'll settle the affair.

MASCARILLE

He's a sterling man, who knows it's wrong to make
Others risk dying for his quarrel's sake.

POLIDORE

They charge you with imposture, and I have found
Their anger understandable and sound.
Albert and I, moreover, are agreed
That you must face Ascagne for that misdeed—
Both publicly, and promptly, if you please,
And with the usual formalities.

VALÈRE

How, Father, can Lucile continue to . . . ?

POLIDORE

She's marrying Éraste, and says that you
Have slandered her; and to disprove your lies,
She wants to say her vows before your eyes.

VALÈRE

Good God, what shamelessness, what impudence!
Can she have lost all honor, faith and sense?

SCENE SEVEN

Albert, Polidore, Lucile, Éraste, Valère, Mascarille

ALBERT

Well, time for combat! Our man is close behind.
Have you got yours in a fighting frame of mind?

VALÈRE

Yes, yes, I'm ready, since you'd have me fight,
And if my wrath, at first, was slow to ignite,
A lingering devotion made it so,
And not the strength and valor of my foe;
But this, now, is too much; I feel no more
Devotion, and my thoughts are full of gore,
Faced as I am with perfidy so great
That my heart hungers to retaliate.
(*To Lucile:*)
Not that my heart desires you, at this stage:
All of its fires have changed to burning rage,
And once I've told the world your infamy,
Your guilty marriage will not trouble me.
What you intend, Lucile, is odious;
I can't believe it; I'm incredulous;
You are the enemy of your own good name,
And ought to perish of so great a shame.

LUCILE

Such harsh words would be staggering to hear,
If my avenger were not drawing near.
But here's Ascagne, who'll have the pleasure soon
Of teaching you to sing another tune;
It won't be hard.

SCENE EIGHT

———•—•———

Albert, Polidore, Ascagne, Lucile, Éraste, Valère,
Frosine, Marinette, Gros-René, Mascarille

VALÈRE
He couldn't bully me
If he had a hundred arms. Too bad that he
Must risk his life for a guilty sister's sake,
But since he's made so foolish a mistake,
I'll meet his challenge—and yours, too, valiant friend.

ÉRASTE
A while ago, I was enraged no end,
But since Ascagne challenges you thus,
I'll step aside, and let him fight for us.

VALÈRE
That is, no doubt, a wise and prudent action.
But . . .

ÉRASTE
Rest assured, he'll give you satisfaction.

VALÈRE
He?

POLIDORE
Don't be hasty, now. You don't yet know
What a rare lad Ascagne is.

ALBERT
That's so,
And so Ascagne will show him presently.

VALÈRE
All right then, let him show me, let us see.

MARINETTE

In front of everyone?

GROS-RENÉ

It wouldn't be right.

VALÈRE

Are you making fun of me? By God, I'll smite
Whoever dares to laugh. Now, draw your blade.

ASCAGNE

No, no, I'm not so fierce as I'm portrayed;
In this encounter, which concerns all here,
It is my weakness that you'll meet, I fear.
You'll learn that Heaven did not bestow on me
A heart that could resist you, and you'll see
That destiny has chosen you to deal
A death blow to the brother of Lucile.
Yes, far from fighting what the Fates have planned,
Ascagne now must perish by your hand,
And shall be glad to breathe his last, if through
That sacrifice he can bring joy to you,
And, here and now, afford you as your own
A wife who must by law be yours alone.

VALÈRE

No, I shall never, after such treacheries
And shameless acts . . .

ASCAGNE

Oh! Listen to me, please:
The heart that's pledged to you could not, Valère,
Have done you any wrong; to that I'll swear;
Its love is pure, its constancy entire.
I call, as witness to these things, your sire.

POLIDORE

Yes, Son, we've laughed enough at your vexation,

And now it's time you had an explanation.
The one you're pledged to, and your heart's desire,
Stands now before you, concealed in man's attire.
From childhood on, financial reasons made
Her family clothe her thus in masquerade,
And Love, of late, disguised her otherwise,
To trick you and conjoin our family ties.
Don't look around in shock at everyone;
What I have said is serious, my son.
Behold her who, by night, contrived to steal
Your vows, pretending that she was Lucile,
And who, by that contrivance, made us fall
Into a great confusion, one and all.
But now Ascagne shall change to Dorothée,
Your loves shall come into the light of day
And be confirmed now by a holier bond.

ALBERT

That sort of single combat, warm and fond,
Will satisfy us; and that's as well, because
The other kind's forbidden by our laws.

POLIDORE

I know that your bewilderment is great,
But in this matter you cannot hesitate.

VALÈRE

Ah, no, I wouldn't dream of such a thing;
And if this outcome is astonishing,
I relish the surprise, sir. I am seized
By love and wonder, and immensely pleased:
Can it be that those eyes . . .

ALBERT

                 Her clothes, Valère,
Don't suit the tender thoughts you'll soon declare.
Let's let her go and change, and meanwhile you
May learn your wife's whole story hitherto.

VALÈRE

Lucile, I was mistaken; forgive me, please.

LUCILE

Your angry words I can forget with ease.

ALBERT

Come, children; further friendly words can wait.
Let's all go to my house and celebrate.

ÉRASTE

But, sir, you have forgotten that there's still
A chance to see two warriors hack and kill.
Valère and I have found our mates today,
But what of Mascarille and Gros-René?
Which one of them shall win our Marinette?
That won't be settled till some blood is let.

MASCARILLE

My blood's inside me where it likes to be,
And he can marry her, for all of me.
I know her nature, and I can assert
That marriage vows won't make her cease to flirt.

MARINETTE

You think I'd take you for a lover? No.
A husband needn't be a Romeo;
He can be plain and dull and everyday.
But a lover ought to take one's breath away.

GROS-RENÉ

See here; I want you, once we're made one flesh,
To pay no heed when pretty boys get fresh.

MASCARILLE

You'll have her all to yourself, eh? Are you sure?

GROS-RENÉ

I am; I want a wife who's strict and pure,
Or I'll raise the Devil.

MASCARILLE

        Ah, my boy, you'll soften,
As I've seen other husbands do so often.
Before they marry, they're rigid and severe,
But they get meek and tame within a year.

MARINETTE

Dear spouse, don't question my fidelity!
Sweet talkers won't get anywhere with me:
I'll tell you everything.

MASCARILLE

        How nice, to make
One's spouse a confidant!

MARINETTE

        Be still, you snake!

ALBERT

Once more, friends, let's go home and at our ease
Continue these most pleasant colloquies.

SGANARELLE,
OR THE IMAGINARY CUCKOLD

COMEDY IN TWENTY-FOUR
SCENES, 1660

Introduction

This little comedy was first presented by Molière's troupe on May 28, 1660. It was at once a hit, and during the "dead season" of summer, despite the absence of the court and the hot-weather exodus of the rich and fashionable, it played to full houses. By the end of the year, it had been done a remarkable thirty-four times at the Petit-Bourbon, and privately performed a half-dozen times for Cardinal Mazarin or the delighted King. One enthusiast, a man named Neufvillenaine, saw it often enough to memorize the dialogue and to publish, in Molière's honor, a pirated edition of the play. During Molière's lifetime, *Sganarelle* was offered by his company every year, and in all had more performances than any other of his works, with second honors going to *The School for Husbands*.

Sganarelle, or The Imaginary Cuckold has many qualities that may be seen as deriving from the tradition—then two centuries old—of the one-act French farce. Farce is concerned with standard comic types at the mercy of absurd situations, and surely such figures as the young lovers Célie and Lélie, or the earthy and insolent servant Gros-René, are as simple and generic as possible. The plot is a fast-developing imbroglio that, having built to a peak of confusion, concludes with a brisk and convenient denouement. It is loaded with coincidences and ludicrous misunderstandings. There is a certain amount of vulgar language in *Sganarelle*, and though it is scarcely a knockabout piece, it contains a fair bit of physical comedy: the parallel swoons of Célie and Lélie, Sganarelle's examination of Célie's bosom, his avoidances of Lélie in Scene Nine, his bold advances and craven retreats in Scene Twenty-One.

In all these ways, *Sganarelle* partakes of the flavor, rhythm, and general makeup of farce. Yet, having said that, I must begin at once to qualify. The rudimentary persons of farce are commonly subordinate to a hectic plot, and seem to be manipulated by it; but that is not quite the case here. Lélie, Célie, Sganarelle, and Sganarelle's wife are all in some degree mistrustful of their mates or beloveds before they encounter "proof" of inconstancy; and in Scene Twenty-Two, when all has been explained away, we see Sganarelle and his wife still clinging to their doubts of one another. It is the characters, then, who spin the plot of *Sganarelle* with their want of faith; and though the play is far from philosophical, it rests upon thoughts about suspicion, evidence, and trust, which will surface more importantly in *Tartuffe*.

Above all, it is the title character (originally played by Molière himself) who cannot be seen as a mere cog in the plot-machinery. Rather, it is the business of much of the plot to reveal the comic riches of his nature. In his most appealing aspect, Sganarelle is a Falstaffian figure who loves life and does not think much of death, heroic or otherwise. But he is also a prodigy of self-absorption. As one commentator observes, he is "hard on others, soft on himself," and he continually oscillates between blustering self-assertion and timid recoil. So insulated is he that, in these repeated waverings, he seems like a shadow-boxer afraid of his shadow. The play variously shows us the extent of his egoism: he is blithely callous when Célie is thought to be dying; he often thinks himself alone when he is not; and when Célie berates the absent Lélie, he believes that she is uttering *his* grievance. He expresses his complex nature in three distinct voices. One voice is that of a crudely voluble bourgeois who, when addressing his wife, is consistently brutal. The second voice is clownishly ironic and is especially heard in Scene Six where, unable to make a plain statement of his suspicions, he resorts to a buffoonery that has the effect of simultaneous accusation and retraction. The third voice belongs to Sganarelle the fantasist, who drama-tizes his supposed disgrace (Scene Nine) and his temporary courage (Scene Twenty-One) in stilted soliloquies suggestive of tragic theatre. Sganarelle, in short, is a character diversely revealed, who anticipates all those later Molière heroes (Arnolphe, Alceste) who are self-centered, self-assertive, ill-adjusted, and victimized by their own obsessive notions.

"One would call it a farce," a French critic writes of *Sganarelle*, "if it were not written in verse." Certainly it is true that Molière's third verse-comedy, by wedding broad effects to a now-polished poetic technique, makes it hard to speak confidently of low comedy or high; it is somewhat as if a comic strip had been rendered in oils. Much of what might have been expressed by physical violence—Gorgibus's recurrent urge to thrash his daughter, the Punch-and-Judy relationship of Sganarelle and his wife—is realized instead on the verbal plane, a plane on which Célie's maid has leisure to sketch a delectable self-portrait (Scene Two), and Sganarelle to display his mood swings in a lengthy monologue. The sixty-eight-line speech in which he does so constitutes the whole of Scene Seventeen, which was called "*la belle scène*" in Molière's day. It is not hard to see why mid-eighteenth-century editors of Molière, associating well-turned and sustained alexandrines with high comedy, divided *Sganarelle* into three acts, cutting into the play at the two scene endings (Scenes Six and Seventeen) that leave the stage empty.

It was a mistake, of course, to dignify *Sganarelle* with such stately movement; the piece should be done continuously and at a good clip, as Molière intended and as La Grange's edition (1682) makes plain. And M. Neufvillenaine's descriptions of Molière in the title role, which he played without a mask, make it clear that a certain amount of broad clowning is authorized. "No one," says Neufvillenaine, "was ever better at making and unmaking his face, and it is safe to say that in the course of this play he transforms his features more than twenty times . . . his pantomime gives rise to endless bursts of applause." But if some present-day director of *Sganarelle* honors Molière's precedent as to pace and acting style, let him also honor the artful *spokenness* of this comedy, and make sure that the verse dialogue is nowhere sacrificed to irrelevant horseplay and hubbub. Unless the lines are well said and clearly heard, there will be a loss of wit and timing, of character portrayal, and even of plot. This is particularly true toward the end of the play, where the four principals converge, each speaking out of a different—or differently weighted—misunderstanding of the situation. Sganarelle thinks that he is a cuckold, and that his wife is in love with Lélie; Lélie thinks that Célie, his betrothed, has jilted him and married Sganarelle; Célie thinks that her fiancé, Lélie, has betrayed her with Sganarelle's wife; and Sganarelle's wife thinks that her husband is enamored of Célie. Such an interplay of strong delusions can challenge the imaginative agility of an audience, and so give pleasure; or if badly performed, it can be merely chaotic, which does not amuse for long.

Gorgibus, in the fourth speech of the play, makes mention of a number of books that were very well known in Molière's century. *Clélie* (1654–60) was a wildly popular sentimental novel by Madeleine de Scudéry. The *Quatrains* of the magistrate Guy du Faur de Pibrac (d. 1584) and the *Tablettes de la vie et de la mort* of the historian Pierre Matthieu (d. 1621) were edifying texts deemed essential to the education of the young. The *Guide des pêcheurs* was an ascetic devotional book by a Spanish Dominican, Luis of Granada (d. 1588). I have made a few trivial changes in the text, for ease of speaking or of understanding. For example, Célie's maid says in Scene Two, "God rest my poor Martin," but I thought that "God rest my dear dead Jacques" would be easier for an American actress to say. And in the same character's last speech (Scene Twenty-Two), I have substituted "a little pill / Of common sense" for the original's "*peu d'ellébore*," because folk medicine no longer speaks, as it did in the Middle Ages, of hellebore as a cure for madness.

R. W.
Key West
November, 1992

Characters

GORGIBUS, a middle-class Parisian

CÉLIE, his daughter

LÉLIE, a young man in love with Célie

GROS-RENÉ, Lélie's valet

SGANARELLE, a Parisian bourgeois and an imaginary cuckold

SGANARELLE'S WIFE

VILLEBREQUIN, father of Valère, to whom Célie is promised

CÉLIE'S MAID

A RELATIVE OF SGANARELLE'S WIFE

PLACE
The scene throughout: a residential square in Paris

SCENE ONE

Gorgibus, Célie, Célie's Maid

CÉLIE, *entering in tears, followed by her father*
No, no! My heart will never consent to this.

GORGIBUS
What do I hear you say, my saucy miss?
Dare you oppose my wishes, and dispute
A parent's power, which is absolute?
D'you hope to sway, by foolish arguments,
Your father's judgment and mature good sense?
Which of us, in our household, has dominion?
And is it you or I, in your opinion,
Who knows what's best for you, you silly child?
By Heaven, be careful not to get me riled,
Or you'll have cause to know, this very minute,
Whether my arm still has some muscle in it.
You'd better cease your grumbling, Miss Contrary,
And accept the man I've picked for you to marry.
You tell me that I know too little of him,
And should have asked you first if you could love him:
Well, knowing his fortune, which is large indeed,
What other information do I need?
And as for love, does not a husband who
Has twenty thousand ducats appeal to you?
Whatever he's like, a man as rich as he
Is a perfect gentleman, I'll guarantee.

CÉLIE
Alas!

GORGIBUS
Well, well. "Alas," you tell me, eh?
What a very fine alas this girl can say!

Take care, now; if you make me hit the ceiling,
I'll give you cause to say alas—with feeling!
This is what comes, young lady, of your addiction
To all these volumes of romantic fiction;
Your head is full of amorous rigmarole,
And you care more for *Clélie* than for your soul.
Such trashy books, I tell you, should be flung
In the fire, because they much corrupt the young.
Instead of such insidious poppycock,
Go read Matthieu, or the *Quatrains* of Pibrac—
Instructive literature that's sound and wise
And full of maxims you should memorize.
Read, too, the *Sinner's Guide*; no book can give
A young girl better advice on how to live.
Had such books been your only reading, you'd
Have learned a more obedient attitude.

CÉLIE

But, father! Can you mean for me to be
False to the love I've promised to Lélie?
A girl can't wed, I know, at her own whim;
But you yourself, Sir, pledged my hand to him.

GORGIBUS

What if I did? I now transfer my pledge
To another man, whose wealth gives him the edge.
Lélie's a handsome fellow, but do learn
That a suitor's purse should be your first concern,
That gold can make the ugliest mate seem fair,
And that, without it, life's a sad affair.
You don't much like Valère, I know; but still,
Though the lover may not please you, the husband will.
That sweet word *spouse* can cause the heart to soften,
And love is born of marriage, very often.
But I'm a fool to argue and persuade,
When a father should command, and be obeyed!
Let's have no more, please, of your insolence,
And spare me your alases and laments.

My future son-in-law will call tonight;
Be sure, be very sure, to treat him right:
If you dare to be unwelcoming and cold,
I'll . . . Well, I'll say no more. Do as you're told.

SCENE TWO

— • • —

Célie, Célie's Maid

MAID

Dear mistress, what possesses you to spurn
The thing for which so many women yearn—
To greet a marriage offer with streaming eyes,
And balk at saying yes to such a prize?
If only someone asked my hand, there'd be
No need to press the matter, believe you me,
And I'd not find that "yes" was hard to say:
I'd blurt a dozen yesses, right away.
Your little brother's tutor, who comes around
To hear his daily lessons, was very sound
When, telling us of Nature's great design,
He said that woman is like the ivy-vine,
Which, clinging to its oak, grows lush and tall,
But, lacking that support, can't thrive at all.
No truer words were ever spoken, Ma'am,
As well I know, poor sinner that I am.
God rest my dear dead Jacques! Before he died,
My eye was merry, my heart was satisfied,
My cheeks were rosy and my body plump,
And now I'm nothing but a sad old frump.
Back in those sweet days when I had a man,
I slept all winter without a warming pan;
Small need there was to spread my sheets to dry!
But now I shiver even in July.
Believe me, dearest mistress, there's nothing quite
Like having a husband next to you at night,
If only for the cozy thought that he's
Nearby to say "God bless you" when you sneeze.

CÉLIE

Would you have me jilt my dear Lélie, and wed
This ugly-looking man Valère instead?

MAID

Well, your Lélie's a blockhead, in my view,
To take so long a trip away from you,
And his extended absence makes me start
To wonder if he's had a change of heart.

CÉLIE, *showing her a locket containing*
the portrait of Lélie

No, I'll not entertain that dire conjecture.
Look at the noble features in this picture;
They speak to me of love that shall not die.
I can't believe such lineaments could lie,
And since it's he whose face is imaged here,
I know my love will ever hold me dear.

MAID

He has a faithful lover's face, that's true,
And you're quite right to love him as you do.

CÉLIE

But what if I'm forced . . . Oh, hold me!
(*She drops Lélie's portrait.*)

MAID, *supporting Célie as she swoons*
Madam, pray,
What ails you? . . . Heavens! She's fainted dead away!
Help, someone! Hurry!

SCENE THREE

————•◦•————

Célie, Sganarelle, Maid

SGANARELLE
What's up? Did I hear you call?

MAID
Oh, Sir, my lady's dying.

SGANARELLE
Is that all?
You screamed as though all Hell had reared its head.
Let's have a look at her. Madam, are you dead?
Huh! She says nothing.

MAID
I'll go fetch someone who
Will help to carry her. Hold her, I beg of you.

SCENE FOUR

————— •◦•— —————

Célie, Sganarelle, Sganarelle's Wife

SGANARELLE, *supporting Célie, and passing his hand
over her bosom*
She's cold all over; is that a proof of death?
I'll watch her lips, to see if she takes a breath.
My word! I can't be sure, but it seems to me
That her mouth shows signs of life.

SGANARELLE'S WIFE, *looking down from a window*
              Oh, What do I see?
My husband and some woman . . . I'll slip downstairs
And catch that cheating rascal unawares.

SGANARELLE, *to a man whom the Maid has brought in*
Come, we must get her help without delay;
It would be wrong of her to pass away.
The other world's a stupid place to go
When everything's so pleasant here below.

SCENE FIVE

Sganarelle's Wife

SGANARELLE'S WIFE, *alone*

Well, he has suddenly vanished from this place,
And I can't learn the full facts of the case;
But the little I saw has left no room for doubt:
The man's a traitor, and I have found him out.
I now well understand the chilly fashion
Of his responses to my wifely passion:
He saves his hugs for other women, the swine,
And feeds their appetites while starving mine.
Well, that's how husbands are: for them, the joy
Of lawful wedded love soon starts to cloy.
At first they think it wondrous and sublime,
And fervently adore us, but in time
They weary of our kisses, and start to roam,
Bestowing elsewhere what belongs at home.
O for a law that would allow us women
To change our husbands as we change our linen!
What a boon for wives! And I know many a one
Who'd gladly do it if it could be done.
            (*Picking up the portrait dropped by Célie:*)
But what's this locket, which chance drops at my feet?
The enamel's charming, the engraving neat.
I'll open it.

SCENE SIX

Sganarelle, Sganarelle's Wife

SGANARELLE, *thinking himself alone*
Was she dead? No, not a bit.
She'd only fainted, and soon came out of it.
But I see my wife.

WIFE, *thinking herself alone*
Oh, my! It's a miniature!
What a handsome man! What lifelike portraiture!

SGANARELLE, *aside, as he looks over his wife's shoulder*
What is she so absorbed in looking at?
A portrait, eh? I don't much care for that.
A dark suspicion takes possession of me.

WIFE, *not noticing her husband*
I've never laid eyes upon a thing so lovely.
The workmanship's more precious than the gold.
And it smells so fragrant!

SGANARELLE, *aside*
So, I was right! Behold,
She's kissing it!

WIFE, *still unaware of her husband*
I confess that I would be
Ravished if such a man paid court to me,
And that, if his sweet pleadings should persist,
My virtue might not manage to resist.
Ah, why can't I have a mate thus nobly made,
Instead of the bald clown—

SGANARELLE, *snatching away the portrait*
Hold on, you jade!

I've caught you in the act. You dare defame
Your husband, and asperse his honored name.
So then, Milady, in your considered view,
Milord is not quite good enough for you!
Well, by the Devil (and may the Devil take you),
What better gift than me could Heaven make you?
Can you perceive in me a single flaw?
This figure, which the world regards with awe,
This face, which wakens love in each beholder
And makes a thousand beauties sigh and smolder,
Don't these, and all my other charms, provide
A feast with which you should be satisfied?
Or does a tasty husband not suffice,
So that you need a gallant, for added spice?

WIFE

I see right through your sly buffooneries.
You hope thereby to—

SGANARELLE

No evasions, please.

The case is proved, and here in my possession
Is the clearest evidence of your transgression.

WIFE

See here: my anger is already strong,
Without your doing me a second wrong.
Give back my locket, and keep your tongue in check.
What do you mean—

SGANARELLE

I mean to wring your neck.

Oh, how I wish the rogue who's pictured here
Were in my clutches!

WIFE

What for?

SGANARELLE
                              Why, nothing, dear!
I'm wrong to be resentful, and my brow
Should thank you for the gifts it's wearing now.
                    (*Looking at Lélie's portrait:*)
Yes, there he is, your pretty boy, your pet,
The spark by whom your secret fire was set,
The wretch with whom . . .

WIFE
                    With whom . . . Go on.
What's next?

SGANARELLE
With whom, I say . . . and it makes me deeply vexed.

WIFE
What is this drunken idiot trying to say?

SGANARELLE
You take my meaning, strumpet. It's plain as day.
My name's no longer Sganarelle, and folk
Will dub me Mister Staghorn, for a joke.
You've made me lose my honor; but when I'm through,
I shall have made you lose a tooth or two.

WIFE
How dare you speak to me so threateningly?

SGANARELLE
How dare you play such wicked tricks on me?

WIFE
What wicked tricks? Talk plainly. Spell it out.

SGANARELLE

Ah, no, I've nothing to be sore about!
What does it matter if people laugh and stare
At the buck's antlers you have made me wear?

WIFE

So, having wronged me by a grave offense—
The crime a married woman most resents—
You seek now to forestall my rage by feigning
A righteous wrath, and clownishly complaining!
I've never seen so insolent a ruse:
The one you've sinned against, you dare accuse.

SGANARELLE

My! Judging by the haughty speech you've made me,
One might mistake you for a virtuous lady!

WIFE

Go on, pursue your mistresses, address them
With tender words, and lovingly caress them:
But let me have my locket, you lustful ape.
          (*She snatches the portrait from him and flees.*)

SGANARELLE, *running after her*

I'll get that back, don't worry . . . you shan't escape.

SCENE SEVEN

Lélie, Gros-René

GROS-RENÉ
We're home at last. But now, Sir, if you'll hear me,
I'd like to pose to you a little query.

LÉLIE
Well, ask it.

GROS-RENÉ
Are you possessed, Sir, by some devil,
So that you're not worn out by all this travel?
For eight whole days we've galloped, Sir; from dawn
To dusk we've spurred our spavined horses on,
And been so tossed and jolted by their pace
That all my bones feel bruised and out of place,
Not to forget a blister hot as flame
That pains me in a spot I shall not name:
Yet you, once here, rush out on eager feet
Without a moment's rest, or a bite to eat.

LÉLIE
Our swift return was wholly necessary.
I'd heard dire news that Célie soon might marry;
You know I love her; I now must go in haste
And learn on what that dread report was based.

GROS-RENÉ
Yes, but you need a good square meal, Sir, ere
You sally forth to fathom this affair;
T'will fortify your heart, you may be sure
To bear whatever shocks it must endure.
That's how it is with me; when I haven't eaten,
The smallest setback leaves me crushed and beaten;
But when my belly's full, my soul is strong,

And the worst mischance can't trouble me for long.
Be wise, then: stuff yourself, and that will steel you
Against such bitter blows as fate may deal you;
Moreover, make your heart immune to woe
By downing twenty cups of wine or so.

LÉLIE

No, I can't eat.

GROS-RENÉ, *sotto voce, aside*
If I don't eat soon, I'll die!
(*Aloud:*)
Your dinner could be served in the wink of an eye.

LÉLIE

Be still, I tell you.

GROS-RENÉ
How cruel! How unkind!

LÉLIE

It's worry, and not hunger, that's on my mind.

GROS-RENÉ
I'm hungry, Sir, and it worries me to learn
That a foolish passion is your sole concern.

LÉLIE

Let me seek news of her whom I adore;
Go eat, if you wish, and pester me no more.

GROS-RENÉ
I shall not question such a sound command.

SCENE EIGHT

Lélie

LÉLIE, *alone*

No, no, I've let my fears get out of hand;
Her father's solemn promise, and her demure
Avowals of love should make my hopes secure.

SCENE NINE

———————◆•◆———————

Sganarelle, Lélie

SGANARELLE, *not seeing Lélie, and holding
the portrait in his hands*
I've got it back, and I'll study now the face
Of the scoundrel who's the cause of my disgrace . . .
No, I don't know him.

LÉLIE, *aside*
                    Great Heavens! What have I seen?
Is that my portrait? What can this possibly mean?

SGANARELLE, *not seeing Lélie*
Alas, poor Sganarelle, your once proud name
Is doomed to suffer mockery and shame!
Henceforth . . .
    (*Noticing that Lélie is looking at him, he turns away.*)

LÉLIE, *aside*
                    T'will cause my faith in her to waver,
If she has parted with the gift I gave her.

SGANARELLE, *aside*
Henceforth you shall be scorned by all you meet;
They'll point two fingers at you in the street,
And balladeers will jest about the horrid
Growths that a witch has planted on your forehead!

LÉLIE, *aside*
Could I be wrong?

SGANARELLE, *aside*
                    How could you, vicious wife,
Make me a cuckold in my prime of life?

Why, when your mate's well-favored, spry, and dapper,
Were you attracted to this whippersnapper?

LÉLIE, *aside, as he once more looks at the portrait*
in Sganarelle's hands
No, it's my portrait, just as I surmised.

SGANARELLE, *aside, turning his back to Lélie*
That man is nosy.

LÉLIE, *aside*
I'm utterly surprised.

SGANARELLE, *aside*
What does he want?

LÉLIE, *aside*
I'll speak to him.
(*To Sganarelle:*)
If I may . . .
(*Sganarelle starts moving away.*)
Wait! Just one word.

SGANARELLE, *aside, still moving away*
What is it he wants to say?

LÉLIE
I should be grateful if you told me how
You acquired the portrait that you're holding now.

SGANARELLE, *aside*
Why does he want to know? But let me see . . .
(*He studies Lélie and the portrait which he is holding.*)
Ah! Now his feverish air makes sense to me!
This clarifies his actions very nicely.
I've found my man—or my wife's man, more precisely.

LÉLIE

Relieve my mind, and tell me from whose hand—

SGANARELLE

What makes you ask, I now well understand.
This pretty locket, in which your face is painted,
I got from one with whom you're well acquainted;
And I am well aware, Sir, of your dealings
With her, and of your ardent mutual feelings.
I don't know if I have the honor, Sir,
Of being known to you, by way of her,
But do me the honor to pursue no more
A love which, as her husband, I deplore.
When sacred marriage vows are lightly broken—

LÉLIE

What! She, you say, from whom you got this token—

SGANARELLE

Is my wife, and I'm her husband.

LÉLIE

      Her husband? You?

SGANARELLE

Yes, I'm her husband, and her victim, too.
You know my grievance, which I'm off to share
With all her kinfolk.

SCENE TEN

Lélie

LÉLIE, *alone*
Oh, this is hard to bear!
Those rumors that I heard were truthful, then;
She's married, and to the ugliest of men!
Ah, traitress, even if you hadn't sworn
Eternal love to me, you ought in scorn
To have refused that loutish fellow's suit,
And chosen me instead of such a brute.
Yes, faithless woman . . . But now this bitter wrong,
And the strains of traveling so far and long,
Are all at once too much for me; they make
My heart grow feeble and my body quake.

SCENE ELEVEN

———— ◆●◆ ————

Lélie, Sganarelle's Wife

SGANARELLE'S WIFE, *thinking herself alone at first,*
then perceiving Lélie
That traitor took my . . . Sir, are you ill, perhaps?
You look to me as if you might collapse.

LÉLIE
I've had a sudden dizzy spell, I fear.

SGANARELLE'S WIFE
It wouldn't do for you to faint out here.
Come into my house until it passes, do.

LÉLIE
I'll accept your kindness, for a moment or two.

SCENE TWELVE

Sganarelle, a Relative of Sganarelle's Wife

THE RELATIVE

Husbands do well to guard their honor; but surely
You bring these charges rather prematurely.
You're very far, dear boy, from having built
A solid case which demonstrates her guilt.
One shouldn't accuse a wife of this offense
Without strong proof and clinching evidence.

SGANARELLE

One has to catch her clinching, as it were.

THE RELATIVE

By judging hastily, we often err.
Who knows how she acquired that portrait? Can
You prove that she has ever met that man?
Clear up those questions; then, if you're right, we'll be
The first to punish her iniquity.

SCENE THIRTEEN

Sganarelle

SGANARELLE, *alone*

Well said: one should be cautious in such cases,
And take things slowly. Perhaps there was no basis
For the hornish visions that I had just now,
And all that nervous sweat upon my brow.
That portrait, after all, which so dismayed me.
Gives me no certain proof that she's betrayed me.
I'll be more careful . . .

SCENE FOURTEEN

Sganarelle, Sganarelle's Wife, showing Lélie to her door,
Lélie

SGANARELLE, *aside*
                What's this? My blood runs cold!
It's no mere portrait that I now behold;
Look, there he is—the man himself, in person.

SGANARELLE'S WIFE
Stay, Sir, and rest, lest your condition worsen.
If you leave so soon, that seizure may return.

LÉLIE
No, no, I thank you for your kind concern,
And for your timely help in my distress.

SGANARELLE, *aside*
What help the trollop gave him, I can guess!
                (*Sganarelle's Wife retires into her house.*)

SCENE FIFTEEN

———•———

Sganarelle, Lélie

SGANARELLE, *aside*
He's noticed me; let's see what he dares to say.

LÉLIE, *aside*
Ah, there's that creature, vile in every way . . .
But no, in fairness I must curb my hate,
And blame my woes on nothing but my fate.
I shall but envy him his happy lot.
          (*Approaching Sganarelle:*)
Ah, lucky man! What a splendid wife you've got!

SCENE SIXTEEN

Sganarelle, Célie, at her window, seeing the departing Lélie

SGANARELLE, *alone*
Well, that was unambiguous! Now I know.
His brutal frankness stuns me; it's as though
A pair of horns had started from my head.
　　　(*Looking in the direction in which Lélie has gone:*)
Such conduct, Sir, is not at all well-bred!

CÉLIE, *aside, as she enters*
I can't believe it. Just now I saw Lélie;
But why was his return concealed from me?

SGANARELLE, *not seeing Célie*
"Ah, lucky man! What a splendid wife you've got!"
No, luckless me, to have wed a sly cocotte
Whose guilty passion, now revealed, has led
To my disgrace, and left me cuckolded!
As for her lover—after what he'd done,
Why did I stand there like a simpleton
And let him go? I should have smashed his hat,
Thrown mud upon his cloak, and after that
Roused all the neighborhood against that thief
Of honor, to give my fury some relief.
　　　(*During this speech of Sganarelle's, Célie approaches
　　　　bit by bit and waits for his transport to end,
　　　　so that she may speak to him.*)

CÉLIE, *to Sganarelle*
If I may ask, how is it that you know
The man who spoke to you a moment ago?

SGANARELLE
Alas, I do not know the man, not I;
It's my wife who knows him.

CÉLIE
You seem much troubled. Why?

SGANARELLE
My sorrow, I assure you, is not groundless;
I must lament, because my woe is boundless.

CÉLIE
What can have caused you so extreme a pain?

SGANARELLE
It's of no piddling thing that I complain,
And surely there's no man alive who in
My place would fail to feel a deep chagrin.
I am the model of a luckless spouse.
Poor Sganarelle, the honor of your house
Is lost! But honor's nothing to the shame
Of having been deprived of my good name.

CÉLIE
But how?

SGANARELLE
In plain terms, Madam, that popinjay
Has made a cuckold of me, and today
These eyes of mine have witnessed shocking proof
That he meets my wife beneath my very roof.

CÉLIE
The man who just now—

SGANARELLE
Yes, he's filched my honor.
My wife adores him, and he dotes upon her.

CÉLIE
I thought so! He returned in secrecy
So as to hide a base deceit from me;

So as to hide a base deceit from me;
I trembled when I saw him, for I knew
By instinct what has proven all too true.

SGANARELLE

It's very good of you to take my part:
Not everybody has so kind a heart;
And some will view my martyrdom hereafter
Not with compassion but with mocking laughter.

CÉLIE, *addressing the absent Lélie*

What darker deed than yours could one commit?
What vengeance could suffice to punish it?
After this crime, too dreadful to forgive,
Have you not forfeited the right to live?
Gods! Can such vileness be?

SGANARELLE

           Alas, it can.

CÉLIE

O traitor! Scoundrel! False and faithless man!

SGANARELLE

What a generous soul!

CÉLIE

           No, no, Hell cannot offer
Such agonies as you deserve to suffer!

SGANARELLE

What eloquence!

CÉLIE

           To think that you'd deceive
A heart so pure, devoted, and naïve!

SGANARELLE

Well said!

CÉLIE

A guiltless heart which never earned
The fate of being thus betrayed and spurned!

SGANARELLE

Too true.

CÉLIE

A heart . . . but ah, I'm overcome
By mortal sorrow, and am stricken dumb.

SGANARELLE

It moves me deeply that my plight should touch
You so, dear lady; but do not grieve too much.

CÉLIE

Don't dream, however, that I shall be content
With sad reproaches and with vain lament:
I crave revenge, and I shall quickly take it;
That's my resolve, and nothing now can shake it.

SCENE SEVENTEEN

Sganarelle

SGANARELLE, *alone*
May Heaven keep her safe from harm! I find
Her wish to avenge me very sweet and kind.
Indeed, her generous anger at my plight
Prompts me to rouse myself, and show some fight,
For any man who suffers such affronts
Without a word is but a craven dunce.
Come then! I'll track him down, and with a brave
Resolve avenge myself upon the knave.
I'll teach you, churl, to laugh at folks' expense,
And cuckold people with such insolence!
(*Having taken several steps, he comes back again.*)
But not so fast; let's wait a bit. Good gracious,
That fellow looks hot-blooded and pugnacious,
And he might leave his mark, should I attack,
Not merely on my brow but on my back.
I can't stand folk who have a violent streak,
And those I love are peaceable and meek;
I strike no man, for men can turn and hurt you,
And mild good nature is my greatest virtue.
And yet my honor says to me that I
Must take revenge for this affront, or die:
Well, rave on, dearest Honor, talk your fill;
I won't obey you; damn me if I will!
When I have played the hero, and for reward
Have had my guts impaled upon a sword,
And gossips tell my death on every corner,
Will you be happy then, my dearest Honor?
The grave's a dreary domicile, I'm told,
And just the place to catch one's death of cold,
And as for me, I think, when all is said,
It's better to be cuckolded than dead.
What harm does it do a fellow? Does it bow

His legs, or spoil his figure, I'd like to know?
A curse on the demented person who
First thought of such a stupid bugaboo,
And tied the honor of a man to what
His wife may do, if she's a fickle slut.
The guilty one should pay in such a case;
Why must our honor suffer in her place?
The wrongs that others do are charged to us,
And if our spouses prove adulterous
We husbands are to shoulder all the blame:
They're shameless, and it's we who bear the shame!
This is a rank injustice, and should be
Corrected by some statute or decree.
Aren't there sufficient woes and sufferings
That plague us in the normal course of things—
Don't sickness, lawsuits, hunger, thirst, and strife
Sufficiently beset us in this life—
Without our adding to them by conceiving
Another and quite baseless cause for grieving?
Away with this chimera and its fears;
I'll groan no more, and shed no further tears.
If my wife's done wrong, it's she who should lament;
Why should I weep, when I am innocent?
In any case, it comforts me to be
A member of a wide fraternity,
For many husbands nowadays, I've heard,
When their wives cheat them, never say a word.
I'll pick no quarrel, then, but wisely stifle
My ire at what is, after all, a trifle.
If I don't seek vengeance, people may deride me,
But I'd look sillier with a sword inside me.
             (*Placing his hand on his breast:*)
And yet I feel the stirrings of a passion
Which urges me to act in manly fashion:
Yes, I'm enraged; enough of cowardice;
I'll make that low seducer pay for this:
As my first move, I'll let the whole town know
That he's sleeping with my wife, the so-and-so.

SCENE EIGHTEEN

Gorgibus, Célie, Célie's Maid

CÉLIE
Yes, Father, I bow to your authority:
Do as you wish, Sir, with my hand and me,
And let the marriage contract soon be signed;
I do my duty with a willing mind.
I have renounced my former feelings, and
In all things shall obey your least command.

GORGIBUS
Ah! That's the kind of talk I like to hear.
By Jove, your words delight me so, my dear,
That these old legs might caper and cavort
If folk weren't near to see me and make sport.
Come here, my daughter; come to my embrace.
In such behavior there is no disgrace;
A father's free to give his daughter a kiss
Without the neighbors taking it amiss.
Ha-ha! It makes me ten years younger to
Have heard such sweet, submissive words from you.

SCENE NINETEEN

Célie, Célie's Maid

MAID

Your change of mind astounds me.

CÉLIE

                  When I apprise
You of the facts, you'll say that I've been wise.

MAID

Perhaps I will.

CÉLIE

             The fact is that Lélie
Has played me false; without informing me
Of his return, he—

MAID

Here he comes, however.

SCENE TWENTY

Lélie, Célie, Célie's Maid

LÉLIE

Before I take my leave of you forever,
I wish to tell you how my heart resents—

CÉLIE

How can you face me now? What impudence!

LÉLIE

I see; I'm impudent! And I'd be a beast
To question your decision in the least!
Be happy, then, with this most brilliant man
You've chosen, and forget me if you can.

CÉLIE

I mean to be happy, traitor; and my chief
Desire is that my joy should cause you grief.

LÉLIE

What have I done, pray, to enrage you so?

CÉLIE

Ha! What have you done? As if you didn't know!

SCENE TWENTY-ONE

—•••—

Célie, Lélie, Sganarelle, armed from head to foot,
Célie's Maid

SGANARELLE

War, bloody war! I warn the thief who dared
To steal my honor, that war is now declared!

CÉLIE, *to Lélie, pointing to Sganarelle*

Look, there's my answer; you know the man, of course.

LÉLIE

Ah, yes—

CÉLIE

That sight should cause you deep remorse.

LÉLIE

The sight of him should make your cheeks turn red.

SGANARELLE, *aside*

My anger now has gathered to a head;
My courage is in full arousal, too;
And if I find him, carnage will ensue.
Yes, he must perish; nothing shall prevent it;
I've sworn to slay the villain, and I meant it.
  (*With sword half-drawn, he approaches Lélie.*)
I'll cleave his heart with one stupendous blow—

LÉLIE, *turning around*

What foe are you seeking?

SGANARELLE

None; I have no foe.

LÉLIE

Then why this armor?

SGANARELLE
It's something that I wear
In case of rain.
(*Aside:*)
Oh, it would be a rare
Pleasure to kill him! Come now, my heart, be firm.

LÉLIE, *turning around again*

Eh?

SGANARELLE

I said nothing.
(*Aside, after slapping his face several
times to rouse his initiative:*)
Oh, you spineless worm!
You hateful coward!

CÉLIE
His presence here gives rise
To guilty thoughts, and so he offends your eyes.

LÉLIE

Yes, when I look at him I see your guilt;
How could you so unconscionably jilt
A faithful lover, who earned no such rebuff?

SGANARELLE, *aside*

Oh, for some courage!

CÉLIE
Traitor, I've heard enough!
Such brazen insolence I won't abide.

SGANARELLE, *aside*

Hark, Sganarelle, the lady is on your side!
Take heart, my boy, let's see some fire and vim.
Forward! and make a bold attack on him,
And bravely kill him while his back is turned.

LÉLIE, *taking two or three aimless steps, which cause*
Sganarelle, who was approaching to kill him, to retreat

Since all my honest words are fiercely spurned,
I'll flatter you, and say that you've displayed
Sublime good taste in the choice your heart has made.

CÉLIE

My choice is sound, and the world can but commend it.

LÉLIE

You have no choice, alas, but to defend it.

SGANARELLE

She's right indeed, Sir, to defend my cause.
The thing you've done breaks all the moral laws:
You've wronged me, and were I not so self-controlled,
A scene of butchery might now unfold.

LÉLIE

Why this grim threat? Of what am I accused?

SGANARELLE

Enough; you well know how I've been abused;
Conscience should tell you that by Heaven's decree
My wife is my exclusive property,
And that to act as if you owned her, too,
Is not at all a Christian thing to do.

LÉLIE

It's quite ridiculous, this charge you make;
But put your fears to rest, for Heaven's sake:
Your wife is yours, and I shan't appropriate her.

CÉLIE

How smoothly you dissimulate, you traitor!

LÉLIE

What! You suspect me of some gross intent
Which this poor fellow rightly would resent?
D'you think me capable of such low acts?

CÉLIE

Ask him; he can support his charge with facts.

SGANARELLE, *to Célie*

No, Madam, pray speak on in my defense;
I couldn't match your force and eloquence.

SCENE TWENTY-TWO

————————•—•————————

Célie, Lélie, Sganarelle, Sganarelle's Wife, Célie's Maid

SGANARELLE'S WIFE, *to Célie*
Madam, I shall not make a great to-do
And fly into a jealous rage at you;
But I'm no fool, and I see what's taking place:
Some passions, Madam, are scandalous and base,
And you could have a loftier design
Than to seduce a heart that's rightly mine.

CÉLIE
Well, that confession of love was frank and clear.

SGANARELLE, *to his Wife*
Slut, who invited you to interfere?
She was defending me. You're jealous of her
Because you fear she'll lure away your lover.

CÉLIE, *to Sganarelle's Wife*
Don't worry; he doesn't attract me—not one whit.
          (*Turning toward Lélie:*)
So! All I said was true, you must admit.

LÉLIE
What can you mean?

MAID
                    Lord! When and how this mess
Is going to be untangled, I can't guess.
I've held my peace, and listened as best I could,
But the more I've heard, the less I've understood.
It's time for me to play the referee.
          (*She places herself between Lélie and Célie.*)
Now, I'm going to ask some questions. Listen to me.

(*To Lélie:*)
You, Sir: what is it you hold against this lady?

LÉLIE

That she's thrown me over, despite the vows she made me;
That, when her rumored nuptials brought me flying
Hither on wings of love, my heart denying
That all its trustful hopes could have miscarried,
I found, on reaching home, that she was married.

MAID

Married! To whom?

LÉLIE, *pointing at Sganarelle*
To him.

MAID
To him, you say?

LÉLIE
Yes, him!

MAID
Who said so?

LÉLIE
He did, this very day.

MAID, *to Sganarelle*
Is that the truth?

SGANARELLE
I only said that I
Was married to my wife.

LÉLIE
You don't deny
That you had my portrait in your hands just now?

SGANARELLE

No. Here it is.

LÉLIE

And did you not avow
That you'd received it from a woman who
Was joined by matrimonial bonds to you?

SGANARELLE, *pointing to his Wife*

Quite so. I snatched it from her, and learned thereby
What sins she was committing on the sly.

SGANARELLE'S WIFE

Oh, stop these baseless accusations! I found
That locket, quite by chance, upon the ground;
                    (*Pointing to Lélie:*)
And later, when he had a dizzy fit
And I bade him come inside and rest a bit,
I didn't even connect him with that painting.

CÉLIE

I fear I started all of this, by fainting;
I dropped the portrait when I swooned, and he
                    (*Indicating Sganarelle:*)
Then carried me into the house most gallantly.

MAID

If I hadn't given you folks a little pill
Of common sense, you'd all be raving still.

SGANARELLE, *aside*

Is everything cleared up? It is, I guess.
But my brow felt hot for a while there, nonetheless.

SGANARELLE'S WIFE

Not all my painful doubts have been relieved;
Though I'd like to trust you, I'd hate to be deceived.

SGANARELLE

Come, let's suppose each other to be true;
Since that's a greater risk for me than you,
You ought to find the bargain fair and square.

SGANARELLE'S WIFE

All right. But if I catch you out, beware!

CÉLIE, *to Lélie, they having been conversing
in low voices*

Alas! In that case, what have I done? I dread
The fate to which my vengeful wrath has led.
I thought you faithless, and to give you ill
For ill, I bowed then to my father's will,
And have agreed just now to wed at last
A suitor I've discouraged in the past.
I've promised Father, and I'm afraid that he . . .
But I see him coming.

LÉLIE

He'll keep his word to me.

SCENE TWENTY-THREE

————— ◆ —————

Gorgibus, Célie, Lélie, Sganarelle,
Sganarelle's Wife, Célie's Maid

LÉLIE

Sir, as you see, I'm back in town once more,
Full of a love as ardent as before,
And sure that, as you promised, you'll soon confer
Your daughter's hand on me, who worship her.

GORGIBUS

Sir, as I see, you're back in town once more,
Full of a love as ardent as before,
And sure that, as I promised, I'll soon confer
My daughter's hand on you, who worship her.
I am your lordship's humble servant, Sir.

LÉLIE

Sir! Will you dash my hopes? Must I despair?

GORGIBUS

Sir, I but do my duty to Valère,
As will my daughter.

CÉLIE

My duty bids me, rather,
To keep the promise that you gave him, Father.

GORGIBUS

Is that what an obedient girl should say?
Do you forget that you agreed today
To marry Valère? . . . But I see his father heading
This way, perhaps to talk about the wedding.

SCENE TWENTY-FOUR

———— ✦ ————

*Villebrequin, Gorgibus, Célie, Lélie, Sganarelle,
Sganarelle's Wife, Célie's Maid*

GORGIBUS
Ah, my dear Villebrequin, what brings you here?

VILLEBREQUIN
A just-discovered secret which, I fear
Will force me to go back on what I've said.
My son, whom your good daughter agreed to wed,
Has fooled us all: for four months, if you please,
He's covertly been married to Élise.
Since her family's rich, and she a brilliant catch,
I've no good reason to annul the match,
And so it seems—

GORGIBUS
No matter. For if Valère
Has made a marriage of which you weren't aware,
I must confess that, long ago, Célie
Was promised to this fine young man by me,
And that, since his return today, I've banned
All others from applying for her hand.

VILLEBREQUIN
An excellent choice.

LÉLIE, *to Gorgibus*
You've kept your word by this
Decision, Sir, which fills my heart with bliss.

GORGIBUS
Let's go and plan the wedding.

SGANARELLE, *alone*

It seemed so strong,
The evidence that my wife had done me wrong!
(*To the audience:*)
But as you've seen, in matters of this kind,
Appearances can deceive the keenest mind.
Remember my example, and be wise:
When things look simple, don't believe your eyes.

THE SCHOOL FOR HUSBANDS

COMEDY IN THREE ACTS, 1661

for Brian Bedford

Introduction

Molière was devotedly familiar, all his life, with the *commedia dell'arte*, that form of Italian popular comedy in which stock characters like Pantalone (an amorous old miser) and Arlecchino (a foolish servant) improvised their scenes within skeletal plot outlines or "scenarios." During his thirteen years of touring in the provinces, Molière without question saw and learned from those commedia troupes which, in the seventeenth century, traveled to all of the centers of Europe; and his biographer Grimarest says that the company which he brought to Paris in 1658 was "trained to extemporize short comic pieces in the manner of the Italian actors." When, in that year, he pleased the Court with his farce *Le Docteur amoureux*, and secured the patronage of the King's brother, his Troupe de Monsieur was given the use, for half of each week, of the Salle du Petit-Bourbon, sharing that theatre with a resident Italian company headed by the great commedia actor Tiberio Fiorelli. Contemporary accounts tell us that it was a happy association, and that Molière never missed one of Fiorelli's performances.

An admiring indebtedness to Italian comedy, outweighing all other influences, can be seen throughout Molière's plays and entertainments, but seems to me particularly visible in his early success *The School for Husbands* (1661). The single setting of the play is that public square, with its clustered houses or "mansions," which was the traditional backdrop of commedia performances. The action recalls the commonest of commedia plots, in which the *innamorati* or young lovers, balked by their elders and aided by clever servants, manage to outwit their oppressors and marry. As for the characters, Sganarelle is one of Molière's quirky Pantalones, and Lisette and Ergaste are French cousins of those *zanni* who, in the

Italian comedy, represented impudent servants with a taste for intrigue.

The School for Husbands, however, is a firmly constructed, fully written play in the high mode of verse comedy. Nothing is left to improvisation. Such a farcical bit as Valère's and Ergaste's accosting of the oblivious Sganarelle (Act One, Scene Three), which in commedia would give the actors all sorts of inventive latitude, is here wholly worded and choreographed by the dialogue and stage directions. The chief persons of the play, though behind them loom certain stock figures, are variously individuated by Molière's art and endowed with a measure of complexity. In the first act of *Husbands*, we meet two middle-aged brothers, Sganarelle and Ariste, who have promised a dying friend to rear, and perhaps ultimately to marry, his two orphaned daughters. Ariste, an easygoing man of fifty-nine or so, has treated his spirited ward, Léonor, in a considerate and indulgent fashion, thus gaining her grateful affection. Sganarelle, Ariste's junior by twenty years, is a premature fuddy-duddy who has raised his charge, Isabelle, with a domineering strictness, and it will of course be the business of the play to rescue her from his tyranny and unite her with her romantic young neighbor, Valère. Certain peculiarities of Sganarelle (whose central part was originally played by Molière himself) are conveyed in the play's early scenes: his cranky opposition to fashion and to urban social pleasures, his extolling of ancestral ways and standards, his crusty bad manners, his mistrustfulness, his ill-will toward Ariste. All these things, as the second and third acts proceed, become intelligible aspects of his psychology.

As Albert Bermel has noted, the second act—in which the cause of Isabelle is advanced by a series of clever deceptions and dodges—has a number of surprises for us. Isabelle, who in Act One was a poor victim with but twenty-nine syllables to say, emerges in Act Two as a mettlesome, resourceful young woman who, horrified by the prospect of marriage to a bully, drives all the action by improvising one ruse after another. It is surprising, too, that the enamored Valère and his canny valet, Ergaste, who at the end of the first act retired to ponder stratagems, are in the second reactive at best, their behavior being largely confined to the divining of Isabelle's purposes and the abetting of her initiatives. When the figures of a play behave in unexpected and yet credible ways, it increases their dimensionality, and here it is above all the unanticipated actions of Sganarelle which serve to build complex character. The suspicious man of Act One becomes, in Act Two, utterly gullible; the harsh guardian becomes a doting dispenser of pet names; the possessive husband-to-be develops a maudlin sympathy for his young rival. Out of these apparent contradictions we assemble a portrait of an anxious, alienated man, resentful of his brother's sociable aplomb and out of touch with people in general—a man who, significantly, can be blind to others when they are present (Act One, Scene Three) and can fancy them present when they are not ("Who goes there? Ah, I'm dreaming.") His outlandish views and posturings are intended, we perceive, to confer a style upon his isolation and, as Lionel Gossman says, to impress the world by a claim of superiority to it. In his grandiose insecurity, Sganarelle cannot allow others their freedom and their differences; his relation to the world consists in berating it, and in demanding of others that they regard him as a model and embody his values. It is not, after all, surprising that so shaky and fantastic a man should be disarmed by the feigned docility of Isabelle, and duped by the flatteries of Valère.

But the play, as we experience it, is not always busy with the revelation of personality; it is also, and perhaps more densely, concerned with portraying the intricacies of communication in an atmosphere of intrigue—with suspicion, deception, implication, inference, double entendre, the understanding or misunderstanding of look or word. In the latter part of Act Two, Scene Two, for example, Isabelle has asked Sganarelle to convey an ambiguous message which she intends as a signal to Valère that she is aware of his passion; Sganarelle understands the message as a stern rebuff, and delivers it with an admixture of his own jealous vehemence; Valère does not know what to make of this filtered communication, sent by his beloved but spoken by his rival; Ergaste, however,

hypothesizes a secret and favorable meaning, and the departing Sganarelle, looking back at Ergaste and Valère in collo-
quy, more than once misreads the latter's facial expressions.
Given so rich a fabric of doubtful interactions, a critic might
well classify *School for Husbands* as "comedy of intrigue," and
many have done so. Others have as firmly called it "comedy
of character." Some have treated it as a hybrid transitional
piece—an anticipation of deeper character studies to come,
or a sketch for *The School for Wives* (1662), which would
return to its theme and rework certain of its situations. Yet it
seems to me that we may find this play quite sufficient in its
own right, judging with Jacques Guicharnaud that its balance
of elements is "esthetically satisfying"; with Donald Frame
that it represents Molière's "first demonstration of complete
mastery of his craft"; with Martin Turnell that, whatever its
place in the canon, it is a "constant delight."

The title of *School for Husbands* may seem to imply that
the play is a lecture, in which the author advocates permissive
child-rearing and the laissez-faire treatment of young women
and wives. Certainly the comedy appealed to the ladies of
Molière's day, whose enthusiasm was a great factor in its success; and as surely there will be those who, presenting it in this
translation, will be tempted to give it a strong feminist spin.
They will be the more inclined to do so because Ariste, whom
some have taken to be Molière's spokesman, is rewarded by
the plot with the fond fidelity of Léonor. Still, it is well to
remember that the *raisonneurs* of Molière are never effectual
or wholly admirable in their arguments, and that their major
function is to play straight man to the aberrated central figure, exacerbating him and prompting him to display his
imbalance. It is an impoverishment, furthermore, to treat a
dramatic character as a mere mouthpiece, and readers should
bear in mind that Ariste's views and actions are conditioned
by the desire of an aging man to retain the goodwill of a
lively, beautiful young woman. We should also recognize that
Isabelle, though driven by circumstances to hoodwink her
guardian, is not at all a social rebel. Neither she nor Léonor
shares the servants' relish for amorous trickery; she repeat-

edly asks the audience, in asides or little soliloquies, to excuse her subterfuges; and in her letter to Valère she regrets being forced "to overstep the bounds of decorum prescribed for my sex." There is no question, in *School for Husbands*, as to where our sympathies are to lie, but the play seems less a positive case for specific freedoms than a depiction of oppressive folly. If we look in this work for Molière's "ideas," we can most confidently do so by focusing on Sganarelle: in him, as in the Orgon of *Tartuffe*, we see that it is wrong, and deserving of ridicule, to misuse one's authority as parent or husband, and that—on the comic stage at least, where Nature tends to triumph—such tyranny will bring about its own undoing.

This French play, now 330 years old, is like Molière's work generally in requiring little or no mediation; it comes across to us readily, in spite of time and cultural differences. But the reader may be amused by this footnote, which I take from Von Laun's old prose translation, and which has to do with the royal edict brought on stage by Sganarelle at the beginning of Act Two, Scene Six. "It is remarkable that Louis XIV, who was so extravagant himself in his buildings, dress, and general expenses, published sixteen laws against luxury; the law Sganarelle speaks of was promulgated November 27th, 1660, against the use of *guipures, cannetilles, paillettes*, etc., on men's dresses." Sganarelle's speech, then, is topical; and since it praises the King's decree through the lips of a crank, it may be one of those passages in which Molière felt free to josh his royal or noble patrons with a jester's impunity.

In working on this translation, I have been helped at times by the prose versions of Baker and Miller, of Wall, and of Von Laun. My wife, as always, has been my chief consultant. I must also thank Jean Migrenne, William Jay Smith, Sonja Haussmann Smith, and Albert Bermel for their clarifications of particular passages, and James Merrill for his kindness in reading the whole.

R. W.
Cummington
May, 1991

Characters

SGANARELLE, a man approaching forty; brother to Ariste and guardian to Isabelle

ARISTE, Sganarelle's elder brother by twenty years; guardian to Léonor

ISABELLE, Léonor's sister, Sganarelle's young ward

LÉONOR, Isabelle's sister and Ariste's ward

LISETTE, Léonor's maid

VALÈRE, Isabelle's lover

ERGASTE, valet to Valère

A MAGISTRATE

A NOTARY

PLACE
The scene throughout: a residential square in Paris

First produced by the Old Globe Theatre,
San Diego, California, in January 1992

Act One

SCENE ONE

Sganarelle, Ariste

SGANARELLE

Enough talk, Brother; let's give our tongues a rest,
And let's each live his life as he thinks best.
Although you're my superior in age
And old enough, indeed, to be a sage,
Nevertheless I hereby notify you
That I don't care to be corrected by you,
That my own taste suffices to advise me,
And that my way of life quite satisfies me.

ARISTE

Yet all condemn it.

SGANARELLE

            Yes, idiots of your sort,

Dear Brother.

ARISTE

Thank you; what a sweet retort!

SGANARELLE

Since you won't drop the subject, tell me, do,
What these fine critics take exception to.

ARISTE

They blame that surly humor which makes you flee
From all the pleasures of society,
And lends a sort of grim outlandishness
To all you do, even to the way you dress.

SGANARELLE

I see: I mustn't wear what clothes I please,
But must submit to fashion's wise decrees!
Do you propose, by precepts so bizarre,
Dear elder brother—for that is what you are
By twenty blessed years, I must confess,
Although of course it couldn't matter less—
Do you propose, I say, to force me to
Adorn myself as your young dandies do?
To wear those little hats which leave their brains,
Such as they are, exposed to winds and rains,
And those immense blond wigs which hide their features
And make one doubt that they are human creatures?
Those tiny doublets, cut off at armpit-level,
Those collars hanging almost to the navel,
Those sleeves that drag through soups and gravy boats,
And those huge breeches, loose as petticoats?
Those small, beribboned slippers, too neat for words,
Which make them look like feather-footed birds?
Those rolls of lace they force their legs to wear
Like the leg irons that slaves and captives bear,
So that we see each fop and fashion plate
Walk like a pigeon, with a waddling gait?
You'd have me dress like that? I note with loathing
That you're attired in just such modish clothing.

ARISTE

It's best at all times to observe convention
And not, by being odd, attract attention.
For all extremes offend, and wise men teach
Themselves to deal with fashion as with speech,
Accepting calmly, with no fuss or haste,
Whatever changes usage has embraced.
I'm far from recommending those whose passion
Is always to improve upon the fashion,
And who are filled with envy and dismay
If someone else is more extreme than they:
But it is bad, on any ground, to shun

The norm, and not to do the thing that's done;
Better by far to join the foolish throng
Than stand alone and call the whole world wrong.

SGANARELLE

There speaks a vain old man who slyly wears
A black wig to conceal his few white hairs.

ARISTE

It's strange with what persistence and ill grace
You throw my age forever in my face,
And how incessantly I'm forced to hear
You blame my style of dress and my good cheer;
As if old age should bid all joys good-bye,
Thinking of nothing save that it must die,
And doesn't look grotesque enough unless
It's sour of mood and dismal in its dress.

SGANARELLE

However that may be, my firm intent
Is not to alter my habiliment.
Despite the mode, I'll have a hat that's made
To shield my head and give my eyes some shade,
A fine long doublet which will wrap me 'round
To warm my belly and keep digestion sound,
Breeches which fit me well in thighs and seat,
And sturdy shoes which won't torment my feet.
Thus did our forebears dress, and they were wise;
Those I offend are free to shut their eyes.

SCENE TWO

Léonor, Isabelle, Lisette; Ariste and Sganarelle,
talking unobserved at the front of the stage

LÉONOR, *to Isabelle*
I'll take the blame, if he should make a scene.

LISETTE, *to Isabelle*
Shut in your lonely room all day? How mean!

ISABELLE
He's like that.

LÉONOR
Sister, I'm sorry for your plight.

LISETTE, *to Léonor*
His brother and he are just like day and night.
Madam, the Fates were kind in giving you,
As guardian, the sane one of the two.

ISABELLE
I marvel that for one day he should fail
To drag me with him, or shut me in my jail.

LISETTE
I'd send him and his Spanish ruff to Hades,
If—

SGANARELLE, *Lisette having bumped into him*
Where are you going, may I ask, young ladies?

LÉONOR
We don't yet know, but since the weather's fair
I've asked my sister out to take the air,
And—

SGANARELLE, *to Léonor*
You may go where you like, for all of me.
Just run along. (*Pointing to Lisette:*) She'll keep you
company.
(*To Isabelle:*)
But you, if you please, won't go on this excursion.

ARISTE
Oh, Brother, let them go. They need diversion.

SGANARELLE
Your servant, Brother.

ARISTE
Youth must be permitted—

SGANARELLE
Youth, Sir, is foolish; and age can be half-witted.

ARISTE
With Léonor, could she come to any ill?

SGANARELLE
No; but with me she will be safer still.

ARISTE
But—

SGANARELLE
All that she does I strictly oversee,
Thus honoring my responsibility.

ARISTE
And do I neglect her sister, would you say?

SGANARELLE
Well, each man thinks and acts in his own way.
These girls are orphans. Their father, our dear friend,

Entrusted them to us at his life's end,
Bidding us marry them, if so inclined,
Or find them spouses of a proper kind.
Thus we have ruled them with the double sway
Of father and husband, from their childhood's day.
That one, dear Brother, you undertook to rear,
And I took charge of raising this one, here;
Pray govern yours according to your views,
And let me train the other as I choose.

ARISTE

I think—

SGANARELLE
I think, and firmly will declare,
That that's how we should manage this affair.
You let your charge be dashingly arrayed:
So be it; she has a flunky and a maid:
I'm quite content; she idly gads about,
And our young beaux are free to seek her out:
All that is splendid. But my charge, be it known,
Shall live by my desires, and not her own;
She'll dress in serge, in simple browns and grays,
And not wear black except on holidays;
Like any prudent girl, she'll stay indoors
And occupy herself with household chores;
In leisure time she'll mend my linen, or make
Some knitted stockings for amusement's sake;
She'll close her ears to young men's fancy talk,
And never go unguarded for a walk.
The flesh is weak, as each day's gossip warns.
If I can help it, I shall not wear horns,
And since her destiny's to be my wife,
I mean to guard her as I would my life.

ISABELLE
You have no reason—

SGANARELLE
Be still. You know you're not
To leave the house without me. Had you forgot?

LÉONOR
Oh, come, Sir—

SGANARELLE
Madam, I'd rather not debate
With one whose wit and wisdom are so great.

LÉONOR
Are you vexed to find me here with Isabelle?

SGANARELLE
Why yes—because you spoil her, truth to tell.
Frankly, your visits here disturb my peace,
And you'd oblige me if they were to cease.

LÉONOR
Well, shall I speak with equal frankness, Sir?
I don't know how all this may sit with her,
But such mistrust, I know, would rouse my ire;
And, though we share a mother and a sire,
We're not true sisters if the things you do,
Day after day, can make her fond of you.

LISETTE
Yes, all these stern precautions are inhuman.
Are we in Turkey, where they lock up women?
It's said that females there are slaves or worse,
And that's why Turks are under Heaven's curse.
Our honor, Sir, is truly very frail
If we, to keep it, must be kept in jail.
But do you think that such severities
Bar us, in fact, from doing what we please,
Or that, when we're dead set upon some plan,
We can't run rings around the cleverest man?

All these constraints are vain and ludicrous:
The best course, always, is to trust in us.
It's dangerous, Sir, to underrate our gender.
Our honor likes to be its own defender.
It almost gives us a desire to sin
When men mount guard on us and lock us in,
And if my husband were so prone to doubt me,
I just might justify his fears about me.

SGANARELLE, *to Ariste*

Well, teacher, there's what comes of what you teach.
Do you not shudder, hearing such a speech?

ARISTE

Brother, we should but smile at her discourse.
And yet her notions have a certain force:
All women like a bit of freedom, and
It's wrong to rule them with a heavy hand.
It isn't bolts and bars and strict controls
That give our wives and maidens virtuous souls;
No, honor keeps their feet on duty's path,
And not our harshness or our threatened wrath.
I say, indeed, that there's no woman known
Who's good and faithful through constraint alone.
We can't dictate a woman's every move:
If we're to sway her, it must be by love,
And I, whatever curbs I'd put upon her,
Would not feel safe were I to trust my honor
To one who was deterred from wronging me
Only by lack of opportunity.

SGANARELLE

What drivel!

ARISTE

As you like; but still I say
That we should school the young in a pleasant way,

And chide them very gently when they've erred,
Lest virtue come to seem a hateful word.
I've raised Léonor by maxims such as these;
I've not made crimes of little liberties;
To all her young desires I've given consent—
Of which, thank Heaven, I've no cause to repent.
I've let her see good company, and go
To balls, and plays, and every sort of show,
Such social pleasures being well designed,
I've always held, to form a youthful mind.
The world's a school in which we learn to live
By better lessons than any book could give.
She's fond of buying gowns, and bows, and frills:
Well, what of that? I give her what she wills,
For gay attire's a thing we should permit
Young girls to enjoy, if we can pay for it.
She's pledged to wed me by her father's order,
But I shall not be overbearing toward her:
I well know that, in years, we're far apart,
And so I free her to consult her heart.
If the four thousand crowns I yearly earn,
My deep affection, and my dear concern
Can compensate, in her considered view,
For all the years which separate us two,
Then she shall wed me; if not, she'll choose another.
She might be happier without me, Brother,
And I had rather give her up than see
Her forced, against her will, to marry me.

SGANARELLE

How sweet he is! All sugar and spice! My, my!

ARISTE

Well, that's my nature, thank the Lord, and I
Deplore the too-strict training which has led
So many children to wish their parents dead.

SGANARELLE

The more one lets the young run wild, the greater
A task it is to discipline them later;
You'll view her willful habits with misgiving
When the time comes to change her mode of living.

ARISTE

Why should I change it?

SGANARELLE
Why?

ARISTE
Yes.

SGANARELLE
I don't know.

ARISTE

Is there any disgrace, do you think, in living so?

SGANARELLE

Oh, come! If you marry her, will you still allow
The girlish freedoms you permit her now?

ARISTE

Why not?

SGANARELLE
Then you'll indulge her, I suppose,
In wearing ribbons, beauty spots, and bows?

ARISTE

Of course.

SGANARELLE
And let her madly run about
To every ball, or fashionable rout?

ARISTE

Quite so.

SGANARELLE

You'll receive young gallants in your house?

ARISTE

Why, yes.

SGANARELLE

To make merry, and amuse your spouse?

ARISTE

Indeed.

SGANARELLE

And they'll pay her flowery compliments?

ARISTE

No doubt.

SGANARELLE

And you'll stand by at these events,
Looking entirely unconcerned and cool?

ARISTE

Most certainly.

SGANARELLE

Enough! You're an old fool.
(*To Isabelle:*)
Go in; you mustn't hear such shameful rot.

ARISTE

I'll trust my wife's fidelity, and shall not
Do otherwise, when married, than now I do.

SGANARELLE

How I'll enjoy it when she cuckolds you!

ARISTE

I don't know what the stars intend for me,
But if they should deny you cuckoldry
It won't be your fault, for you've taken great
Pains to deserve that horny-headed state.

SGANARELLE

Laugh on, my jester. It's wondrous to behold
A clown who's almost sixty winters old!

LÉONOR

If he should wed me, I'd never make him bear
The fate of which you speak; to that I'll swear.
But were I forced to wear your wedding ring,
I frankly couldn't promise anything.

LISETTE

We owe fidelity to them that trust us;
But cheating folk like you is simple justice.

SGANARELLE

Just hold your cursèd, ill-bred tongue, d'you hear?

ARISTE

You've brought this mockery on yourself, I fear.
Farewell. Do change your views, and realize
That locking up one's wife can be unwise.
Brother, your servant.

SGANARELLE

    I'm not *your* servant, Brother.
    (*Alone:*)
Oh, but those three are made for one another!
What a fine household! An agèd maniac
With foppish clothing on his creaking back;

A girlish mistress who's a wild coquette;
Impudent servants: Wisdom herself would get
Nothing but headaches by attempting to
Correct the ways of that unbalanced crew.
Lest Isabelle, in their loose company,
Should lose the sound ideas she's learned from me,
I'll send her back where she'll be safe from harm
Among the beans and turkeys of my farm.

SCENE THREE

———— • • ————

Valère, Sganarelle, Ergaste

VALÈRE, *at the rear of the stage*
Ergaste, look: there's that Argus I abhor,
The guardian of the girl whom I adore.

SGANARELLE, *thinking himself alone*
It's altogether shocking, the decay
Of manners and of morals in our day!

VALÈRE
I'm going to accost him, if I can,
And strike up an acquaintance with the man.

SGANARELLE, *thinking himself alone*
Where are those standards, stern and absolute,
Which were the basis, once, of good repute?
Our wild young folk indulge their every whim,
And won't . . .
          (*Valère bows to Sganarelle, from a distance.*)

VALÈRE
He didn't see me bow to him.

ERGASTE
Maybe he's blind on this side; what do you say
We walk around him?

SGANARELLE, *thinking himself alone*
                    I must end my stay.
Life in this city only serves to rouse
My worst . . .

VALÈRE, *approaching bit by bit*
I *must* gain entrance to his house.

SGANARELLE, *hearing a noise*

Did I hear a voice?
(*Thinking himself alone:*) In the country, praise the Lord,
The follies of these times can be ignored.

ERGASTE, *to Valère*

Go up to him.

SGANARELLE, *once more hearing a noise*
Eh?
(*Hearing no further sound:*)
My ears are ringing, I guess.
(*Thinking himself alone:*)
There, girls have simple pleasures, simple dress . . .
(*He sees Valère bowing to him.*)
What's this?

ERGASTE, *to Valère*
Get closer.

SGANARELLE, *still staring at Valère*
There, no fops are seen . . .
(*Valère bows to him again.*)
What the devil—
(*He turns and sees Ergaste bowing on the other side.*)
Another? Such bowing! What does it mean?

VALÈRE

Do I disrupt your thoughts, Sir, by this greeting?

SGANARELLE

Perhaps.

VALÈRE
Forgive me; but this happy meeting
Is such a privilege, such a pleasure too,
I couldn't forgo this chance to speak with you.

SGANARELLE

I see.

VALÈRE

And to assure you that I stand
Entirely at your service, heart and hand.

SGANARELLE

I'm sure of it.

VALÈRE

It's my happiness to be
Your neighbor, for which I thank my destiny.

SGANARELLE

Well put.

VALÈRE

But now, Sir, have you heard the new
Gossip at court? Some think it may be true.

SGANARELLE

Does that concern me?

VALÈRE

No; but in such a matter
Folk sometimes like to hear the latest chatter.
Shall you go see the lavish preparations
For our new Dauphin's natal celebrations?

SGANARELLE

If I like.

VALÈRE

Ah, Paris affords us, you must own,
A hundred pleasures which elsewhere are unknown;
The country offers nothing that compares.
What are your pastimes?

SGANARELLE
    Tending to my affairs.

VALÈRE
Still, one needs relaxation, and the brain,
From too much serious use, can suffer strain.
What do you do 'twixt supper time and bed?

SGANARELLE
Just what I please.

VALÈRE
    Ah, Sir, that's nicely said;
A wise reply; we all should see life thus,
And only do what truly pleases us.
Some evening, if you're free of business, I'll
Drop by, if I may, and chat with you a while.

SGANARELLE
Your servant.

SCENE FOUR

———— •◦• ————

Valère, Ergaste

VALÈRE
That crackpot! What did you make of him?

ERGASTE
He gives gruff answers, and his manner's grim.

VALÈRE
Oh, I can't bear it!

ERGASTE
What?

VALÈRE
It irks my soul
That the one I love is under the control
Of a fierce, sharp-eyed dragon who will never
Allow her any liberty whatever.

ERGASTE
Why, that's to your advantage; the situation
Should fill your heart with hope and expectation.
Cheer up; you have no cause to feel undone.
A woman closely watched is halfway won,
And a harsh husband or a crabbèd sire
Is just what any lover should desire.
I don't chase women; for that I have no talent;
And I do not profess to be a gallant;
But I've served woman-chasers by the score
Who told me often that nothing pleased them more
Than meeting with those fractious husbands who
Come grumbling home and scold all evening through,
Those brutes who groundlessly mistrust their wives,

Checking on every moment of their lives,
And act proprietary and unpleasant
When young admirers of their wives are present.
"All this," they said, "is favorable to us.
The lady's pique at being treated thus,
And the warm sympathy which we then express,
Can pave the way to amorous success."
In short, if you have hopes of Isabelle,
Her guardian's cranky ways may serve you well.

VALÈRE

But for four months I've been her worshipper,
And never had one chance to speak with her!

ERGASTE

Love makes men clever; but it's not done much for you.
In your place, I'd—

VALÈRE

But what was there to do?
She's never seen without that beast nearby;
There are no servants in his house whom I
Could tempt with little gifts, and thus obtain
As helpers in my amorous campaign.

ERGASTE

Then she doesn't know, as yet, of your devotion?

VALÈRE

Well, as to that I have no certain notion.
Whenever that barbarian's taken her out,
She's seen me, for I've shadowed her about
And sought by fervent glances to impart
The raging passion that is in my heart.
My eyes have spoken boldly; but how well
She's understood their language, who can tell?

ERGASTE

Such language can be hard to fathom, when
It's not interpreted by tongue or pen.

VALÈRE

How can I end this anguishing ordeal,
And learn if she's aware of what I feel?
Think of some stratagem.

ERGASTE

That's what we must discover.
Let's go inside a while, and think it over.

Act Two

SCENE ONE

———— •• ————

Isabelle, Sganarelle

SGANARELLE
That's quite enough; I know the house, and can,
From what you tell me, recognize the man.

ISABELLE, *aside*
O Heaven! be gracious now, and lend your aid
To the artful plot my innocent love has laid.

SGANARELLE
You've learned, I gather, that his name's Valère?

ISABELLE
Yes.

SGANARELLE
Go then; don't fret; I'll handle this affair.
I'll speak at once to that young lunatic.

ISABELLE, *as she goes in*
It's bold for a girl to play this sort of trick;
But since I'm harshly and unjustly used,
I hope, by all fair minds, to be excused.

SCENE TWO

————— • —————

Sganarelle, Ergaste, Valère

SGANARELLE, *at Valère's door*
Well, here's the house. I'll act without delay.
Who goes there? Ah, I'm dreaming . . . Hullo, I say!
It doesn't surprise me, knowing what now I know,
That he paid court to me an hour ago;
But I'll soon dash the hopes of this fond lover—
      (*To Ergaste, who has come out in haste:*)
You clumsy oaf! Do you mean to knock me over?
Why stand there like a post and block the door?

VALÈRE
I regret, Sir—

SGANARELLE
      Ah! It's you I'm looking for.

VALÈRE
I, Sir?

SGANARELLE
Yes, you. Your name's Valère, I find.

VALÈRE
It is.

SGANARELLE
A word with you, if you don't mind.

VALÈRE
May I serve you somehow? I should be proud to do—

SGANARELLE

No, but there's something I can do for you,
And that is why I've sought your house, and found you.

VALÈRE

You've come to my house, Sir!

SGANARELLE

      Yes. Need that astound you?

VALÈRE

It does indeed, and I'm in ecstasies
At this great honor—

SGANARELLE

    Forget the honor, please.

VALÈRE

Won't you come in?

SGANARELLE

    I see no need of that.

VALÈRE

I beg you, Sir.

SGANARELLE

    I'll stay where I am; that's flat.

VALÈRE

I'd hear you better if we went within.

SGANARELLE

I shall not budge.

VALÈRE

    Ah well, I must give in.

(*To Ergaste:*)
Our guest won't enter, but he must have a seat.
Quick, bring a chair.

SGANARELLE
I'll talk to you on my feet.

VALÈRE
But how can I let you—

SGANARELLE
What infernal stalling!

VALÈRE
Such incivility would be appalling.

SGANARELLE
What in the world is more uncivil, pray,
Than not to hear what people want to say?

VALÈRE
I'll do as you wish, then.

SGANARELLE
That's a splendid notion.
(*They go to great lengths of ceremony, in putting on their hats.*)
These courtesies are a waste of time and motion.
Now, will you listen?

VALÈRE
I shall, Sir, with delight.

SGANARELLE
Do you know that I'm the guardian of a quite
Young girl, who's rather pretty; that we dwell
Nearby, and that her name is Isabelle?

VALÈRE

Yes.

SGANARELLE

I won't say, then, what you know already.
Do you know, likewise, that her charms have led me
To feelings other than a guardian's pride,
And that her destiny is to be my bride?

VALÈRE

No.

SGANARELLE

Then I tell you so. And I bid you cease
Your warm advances, and leave the girl in peace.

VALÈRE

I, Sir?

SGANARELLE

You. Don't deny that you pursue her.

VALÈRE

Who told you, then, of my devotion to her?

SGANARELLE

People whose testimony one can credit.

VALÈRE

But who?

SGANARELLE

She herself.

VALÈRE

She?

SGANARELLE

She. That's twice I've said it.
That good young woman, who, since she was small,
Has loved me, came just now and told me all,
And charged me, furthermore, to let you know
That when, of late, you've dogged her footsteps so,
Her heart, which your attentions scandalize,
Read all too well the language of your eyes;
That what you feel for her is all too clear,
And that t'will be no use to persevere
In shows of passion which can only be
Offensive to a heart that's pledged to me.

VALÈRE

You say that she, of her own accord, besought you—

SGANARELLE

Yes, to convey the message that I've brought you.
She adds that, having plumbed your heart, she would
Have made herself much sooner understood,
If she'd been able, through some messenger,
To express the feelings which arose in her;
At last, in her extreme frustration, she
Had no recourse but to make use of me,
In order to inform you, as I've said,
That I'm the man she loves and means to wed,
That the sheep's eyes you've made were made in vain,
And that, if you have any sort of brain,
You'll take your passion elsewhere. For now, farewell.
I've told you everything I had to tell.

VALÈRE

Good heavens, Ergaste, what do you make of this?

SGANARELLE, *sotto voce, moving away*

How stunned he looks!

ERGASTE, *sotto voce, to Valère*
It's my analysis
That you need not be troubled for a minute.
This message has a secret meaning in it,
And wasn't sent by someone who desires
To terminate the love which she inspires.

SGANARELLE, *aside*
He takes it well.

VALÈRE, *sotto voce, to Ergaste*
You think her words implied—

ERGASTE, *sotto voce*
Yes . . . But he's watching us; let's go inside.

SGANARELLE, *alone*
My, what confusion's written on his visage!
Clearly, he didn't expect so harsh a message.
Let me call Isabelle. In her we find
The effect of sound instruction on the mind.
So perfect is her virtue that if a man
Dares look at her, she puts him under ban.

SCENE THREE

———— •◦• ————

Isabelle, Sganarelle

ISABELLE, *sotto voce, as she enters*
I fear that, in his passion, my lover may
Not fathom what my message meant to say;
And so I must, since I'm a captive here,
Risk yet another to make my meaning clear.

SGANARELLE
Well, I am back.

ISABELLE
What happened?

SGANARELLE
                        Your words quite dashed
Your lover's spirits; he's utterly abashed.
He sought to deny his passion, but once he knew
That you had sent me, and that I spoke for you,
The fellow stood there speechless and nonplussed.
He won't be troubling us again, I trust.

ISABELLE
Ah, won't he, though! I greatly fear he will,
And that he'll give us much more trouble still.

SGANARELLE
What grounds do you have for such a premonition?

ISABELLE
You'd hardly left the house upon your mission
When I went to the window for a breath of air
And saw a young man on that corner there,
Who, much to my amazement, shortly came
And greeted me in my admirer's name,

And then, with further impudence, tossed into
My room a box which held a billet-doux.
I would have thrown it back to him, but his feet
Had far too quickly borne him up the street,
Leaving me full of outrage and distress.

SGANARELLE

Just think of it! Such guile, such craftiness!

ISABELLE

Duty requires that I send back again
Both box and letter to this cursèd swain,
But who's to run the errand I cannot say.
I dare not ask you—

SGANARELLE

My sweet, of course you may.
You prove your love of me by what you ask,
And I accept with joy this little task:
I can't express my pleasure.

ISABELLE

Then take this, do.

SGANARELLE

Let's see, now, what he's dared to say to you.

ISABELLE

Oh, Heavens! Don't break the seal.

SGANARELLE

Not open it? Why?

ISABELLE

He'd think 'twas I it had been opened by.
A decent girl should never read the tender
Communications which young men may send her:
To show such curiosity betrays

A secret appetite for flattering praise.
I think it right, then, that this missive be
Returned unopened, and most speedily,
So that Valère will learn this very day
How much I scorn him, and will without delay
Discard the hopes which he's invested in me,
And make no more absurd attempts to win me.

SGANARELLE

Her point's well taken; this young girl reasons rightly.
My dear, your virtue and good sense delight me:
My teachings have borne fruit, I see with pride,
And you are worthy indeed to be my bride.

ISABELLE

Still, I won't oppose your wishes; I wouldn't dare to.
You have the letter; open it, if you care to.

SGANARELLE

No, no, your reasons cannot be contested.
I'll go and do this errand you've requested,
Make a brief call nearby—ten minutes at best—
And then return to set your mind at rest.

SCENE FOUR

Sganarelle, Ergaste

SGANARELLE, *alone*

It floods my soul with rapture to have found
This girl so utterly discreet and sound!
I have in my house a pearl of purest honor!
She treats a love glance as a slur upon her!
A billet-doux does nothing but offend her!
By *my* hand, she returns it to the sender!
I wonder if my brother's ward, in such
A situation, would have done as much.
This proves, by heaven, that girls are what we make them.
Ho, there!
        (*He knocks on Valère's door.*)

ERGASTE

Yes?

SGANARELLE

    These are your master's property; take them.
Tell him that no more letters need be sent
In small gold boxes; it's most impertinent,
And he has greatly angered Isabelle.
See, it's not even been opened: he can tell
By that how low is her regard for him,
And that the prospects for his love are dim.

SCENE FIVE

Valère, Ergaste

VALÈRE

What were you given by that surly brute?

ERGASTE

A letter, Sir, and a gold box to boot.
He claims that you sent Isabelle this letter,
Which, he declares, has mightily upset her.
She's sent it back unopened. Come, read it, Sir.
Let's see how accurate my conjectures were.

VALÈRE, *reading*

"This letter will doubtless surprise you, and both in my decision to write it and in the manner of its delivery I must seem very rash indeed; but I find myself in such a situation that I cannot observe the proprieties any longer. My just aversion to a marriage with which I am threatened in six days' time has made me ready to dare anything; and in my determination to escape that bondage by whatever means, I have thought it better to turn to you than to embrace Despair. Still, you must not think that you owe everything to my afflicted state; it is not the predicament in which I find myself that has given rise to my feelings for you; but it hastens my avowal of them, and causes me to overstep the bounds of decorum prescribed for my sex. Whether I am soon to be yours is now entirely up to you; I wait only for a declaration of your heart's intentions before acquainting you with the resolution I have taken; but do be aware that time is pressing, and that two hearts attuned by love should need but few words to come to an understanding."

ERGASTE

Well, Sir! Was this a clever ruse, or not?
For a young girl, she lays a brilliant plot!
Love is a game, it seems, that she can play.

VALÈRE

Oh, she's adorable in every way!
This evidence of her wit and warmth of heart
Doubles my love for her, which had its start
When first her beauty caused my head to swim . . .

ERGASTE

Here comes our dupe; think what you'll say to him.

SCENE SIX

Sganarelle, Valère, Ergaste

SGANARELLE, *thinking himself alone*
Ah, thrice and four times may the heavens bless
This law which bans extravagance in dress!
No more will husbands' troubles be so great,
And women's frivolous cravings will abate.
Oh, how I thank the King for such decrees,
And how I wish that, for men's further ease
Of mind, he'd ban not only lace and frills
But coquetry and its attendant ills!
I've bought this edict so that Isabelle
May read it aloud to me, and learn it well.
Some evening, when her tasks are all complete,
We'll have it for an after-supper treat.
                    (*Perceiving Valère:*)
Well, do you plan now, Mister Goldilocks,
To send more love notes in that gilded box?
You thought you'd found a young coquette who'd be
Fond of intrigue and honeyed flattery,
But what a chill response your offerings got!
Believe me, lad, you waste your powder and shot.
She's a sensible girl; it's me she loves; why aim
At one who scorns you? Go hunt for easier game.

VALÈRE
Indeed, your merits, which all the world admires,
Are a hopeless barrier, Sir, to my desires.
Much as I love her, it's folly on my part
To vie with you for Isabelle's hand and heart.

SGANARELLE
Quite right, it's folly.

VALÈRE

I wouldn't, furthermore,
Have yielded to the charms which I adore,
Had I foreseen that I was doomed to meet,
In you, a rival no man could defeat.

SGANARELLE

I quite believe you.

VALÈRE

I now can hope no longer,
And freely grant, Sir, that your claim's the stronger.

SGANARELLE

Well done.

VALÈRE

In this, I merely do what's right,
For, Sir, your many virtues shine so bright
That I'd do wrong to take a grudging view
Of Isabelle's great tenderness toward you.

SGANARELLE

Of course.

VALÈRE

Your victory, then, I don't contest.
But, Sir, I pray you (it's the sole request
Of a poor lover whom you have overthrown,
And whose great pains are due to you alone),
I pray you, Sir, to say to Isabelle
That in these months I've spent beneath her spell
My love's been pure, and never entertained
A thought by which her honor might be pained.

SGANARELLE

Agreed.

VALÈRE

That the one thing I desired of life
Was that I might obtain her for my wife,
Till fate obstructed my desire, revealing
That she was bound to you by tenderest feeling.

SGANARELLE

Good. Good.

VALÈRE

That, whatever happens, she must not
Think that her charms will ever be forgot;
That, let the Heavens treat me as they may,
My fate's to love her till my dying day;
And that your merits, of which I stand in awe,
Are the sole reason why I now withdraw.

SGANARELLE

Well said; I'll go at once and give her this
Message, which she will scarcely take amiss.
But if I may advise you, do your best
To drive this fruitless passion from your breast.
Farewell.

ERGASTE, *to Valère*

What a perfect dupe!

SGANARELLE, *alone*

It makes me sad
To see the anguish of this lovesick lad;
'Twas his misfortune to suppose that he
Could storm a fortress long since won by me.

SCENE SEVEN

———— •• ————

Sganarelle, Isabelle

SGANARELLE
Never did any swain so hang his head
To see his billet-doux come back unread.
He's lost all hope, and will no longer woo you,
But begs me to convey this message to you:
That in his passion, he never entertained
A thought by which your honor might be pained,
And that the one thing he desired of life
Was that he might obtain you for his wife,
Till fate obstructed his desire, revealing
That you were bound to me by tenderest feeling;
That, whatsoever happens, you must not
Think that your charms will ever be forgot;
That, let the Heavens treat him as they may,
His fate's to love you till his dying day;
And that my merits, of which he stands in awe,
Are the sole cause which leads him to withdraw.
Those are his touching words; I cannot hate him;
He's a decent fellow, and I commiserate him.

ISABELLE, *aside*
Those sweet words but confirm my heart's surmise;
I read his pure intentions in his eyes.

SGANARELLE
Eh? What did you say?

ISABELLE
                          I said that I'm distressed
To hear you pity a man I so detest,
And that, if you truly loved me, you would share
My rage at the affronts he's made me bear.

SGANARELLE

But he didn't know, dear, that your heart was mine;
And his intentions were so pure and fine
That one can hardly—

ISABELLE

Is it well-intended, pray,
To seize a person, and carry her away?
Would a man of honor think it a noble course
To snatch me from you, and marry me by force?
As if I were the kind of girl who could
Survive such insults to her maidenhood!

SGANARELLE

Do you mean to tell me—

ISABELLE

Yes; this brutish lover
Talks of abducting me, I now discover.
I don't know by what secret means he can
Have learned so very quickly of your plan
To marry me within a week or so,
Since only yesterday you let me know;
But he intends to strike at once, I find,
Before our loves and fates can be combined.

SGANARELLE

Well, this is bad indeed.

ISABELLE

Oh, no! I'm sure
He's a decent fellow, whose aims are fine and pure!

SGANARELLE

This is no joke; he's wrong in the extreme.

ISABELLE

Your mildness prompts him to this madcap scheme.
If you'd been harsh with him just now, he would
Have feared your wrath and mine, and stopped for good;
But even after his letter was returned
He hatched the shocking plot of which I've learned,
Convinced in spite of all, it would appear,
That in my heart of hearts I hold him dear,
That I am loath to wed you, and cannot wait
For him to free me from my captive state.

SGANARELLE

He's mad.

ISABELLE

With you, he knows how to disguise
His feelings, and pull the wool over your eyes.
But his fair words make sport of you, believe me.
It does, I'm forced to tell you, deeply grieve me
That after all I've done, for honor's sake,
To balk the vile advances of this rake,
I still must find myself exposed to these
Shameful designs and base conspiracies!

SGANARELLE

There, there; don't worry.

ISABELLE

           I swear, if you do not
Rebuke him fiercely for this impudent plot,
And find a way to put a stop at once
To this bold rogue's continual affronts,
I shall embrace some desperate solution
And, once for all, escape his persecution.

SGANARELLE

Come, come, my little dear, don't fret and frown;
I'll go at once and give him a dressing down.

ISABELLE

Tell him it's useless to play innocent,
That I've been fully informed of his intent,
And that, whatever he may now devise,
I challenge him to take me by surprise;
Tell him he wastes his time, and urge him to
Remember what my feelings are toward you;
And add that, lest he pay a bitter price,
He'd best not wait for me to warn him twice.

SGANARELLE

I'll say what's needful.

ISABELLE

                Show him I mean all this
By speaking it with gravest emphasis.

SGANARELLE

Yes, yes, I'll say it all, and I'll be stern.

ISABELLE

I'll wait impatiently for your return.
Please hasten back to me with all your might;
I'm desolate when you are out of sight.

SGANARELLE

Fear not, I'll soon be back with you, my sweet.
             (*Alone:*)
Was ever a girl more prudent, more discreet?
How happy I am! How fortunate to find
A wife so suited to my heart and mind!
Yes, that is how our women ought to be—
Not like some wives I know, whose coquetry
And bold amours have managed to embarrass
Their wretched mates before the whole of Paris.
         (*Knocking at Valère's door:*)
Ho there, my fine and enterprising swain!

SCENE EIGHT

Valère, Sganarelle, Ergaste

VALÈRE

What brings you back, Sir?

SGANARELLE
        Your follies, once again.

VALÈRE

What?

SGANARELLE
    Come, you understand my reference.
Frankly, I thought that you had better sense.
You've hoaxed me with fine speeches, and continue
To harbor vain and foolish hopes within you.
I've wished to treat you gently, but—see here—
If this goes on, my rage will be severe.
Aren't you ashamed that you, a gentleman,
Should stoop to such skullduggery, should plan
To abduct a decent girl, and cheat her of
A marriage which would bring her joy and love?

VALÈRE

Sir, where did you hear this curious news? Do tell.

SGANARELLE

Let's not dissemble; my source is Isabelle,
Who for the last time tells you, through my voice,
That she's informed you plainly of her choice;
That she's mine, and hates this plot that you've devised;
That she'd rather die than be thus compromised,
And that there will be dire results, unless
You put an end to all this foolishness.

VALÈRE

If that is truly what she said, it seems
That there's no future for my ardent dreams:
Those plain words tell me I must yield at last
And bow before the sentence she has passed.

SGANARELLE

If? Do you doubt, then, that they came from her,
These words I've brought you as her messenger?
Would you care to hear them from her lips? I'm quite
Prepared to allow it, just to set you right.
Follow me, then, and learn from her directly
Whom she prefers, and if I spoke correctly.

SCENE NINE

———— ◆▬◆ ————

Isabelle, Sganarelle, Valère

ISABELLE

You've brought him here—to me? With what design?
Have you taken *his* side, and forsaken mine?
Have his merits charmed you so that I'm to be
Compelled to love him, and bear his company?

SGANARELLE

Ah, no. I'd never give you up, my precious.
But he thinks that my reports were meretricious,
That I falsified your feelings when I stated
That you were fond of me, and he was hated;
Therefore I'd have you speak to him, and dispose
Of this delusion on which his hopes repose.

ISABELLE, *to Valère*

What! When I've bared my whole soul to your eyes,
Can you still doubt where my affection lies?

VALÈRE

Madam, this gentleman's reports were such,
I own, as to surprise me very much:
Frankly, I doubted them; and this last decree,
Which sentences my heart to misery,
So stuns me that I dare request of you
That you repeat those words, if they were true.

ISABELLE

No sentence that I've passed should have surprised you:
Of what I feel, my plain words have advised you,
But since my judgments had both truth and strength
I don't mind stating them at greater length.
Yes, hear me, gentlemen, and believe me, too:
Fate here presents two objects to my view

Who agitate my heart with sentiments
Quite different, though equally intense.
The first, whom honor bids me choose, I deem
Worthy of all my love, all my esteem;
The other one's affection gains from me
All my resentment and antipathy.
The presence of the first is dear and sweet,
And makes my soul's felicity complete;
As for the other, my heart is seized by grim
Hatred and horror at the sight of him.
The first I long to marry, while if I
Were forced to wed the other, I'd wish to die.
But I've now said enough of what I feel,
And borne too long the pains of this ordeal;
It's time for him I love to terminate
Decisively the hopes of him I hate,
And by a happy marriage deliver me
From torments worse than death itself could be.

SGANARELLE
There, there: I'll grant your wishes, little one.

ISABELLE
I'll have no happiness till that is done.

SGANARELLE
You'll soon be happy.

ISABELLE
                    It's scandalous, I know,
For a young girl to declare her passions so.

SGANARELLE
No, no.

ISABELLE
                    Yet in my present state of strain
I take the liberty of being plain,

And cannot blush for the fervent things I've said
Of one to whom I feel already wed.

SGANARELLE

Of course not, sweetest angel, dearest dear.

ISABELLE

Let him now prove his love at last.

SGANARELLE

                Yes—here—
Come kiss my hand.

ISABELLE

          Let him delay no more,
But speed the nuptial day I'm yearning for,
And take my promise now that none but he
Shall ever speak his marriage vows to me.
        (*She pretends to embrace Sganarelle, and
           gives Valère her hand to kiss.*)

SGANARELLE

Haha, my pretty duck, my pussycat!
You shall not pine for long, I promise that:
There, now! (*To Valère:*) You see, she cares for me alone.
I didn't prompt her; those words were all her own.

VALÈRE

Well, Madam, you've made your feelings clear indeed:
I grasp your wishes, and shall pay them heed.
I'll rid you very soon, you may be sure,
Of him whose presence you can not endure.

ISABELLE

Do so, and I'll be infinitely grateful;
For merely to behold him is so hateful,
So insupportable, so odious—

SGANARELLE

Now, now.

ISABELLE

I offend you, then, by speaking thus?

SGANARELLE

Oh, mercy, not in the least. But I confess
I feel some pity for the man's distress;
You put your adverse feelings too severely.

ISABELLE

At a time like this, they can't be put too clearly.

VALÈRE

Well, I'll oblige you. In three days from this date
You'll see no more the object of your hate.

ISABELLE

Thank heaven. Farewell.

SGANARELLE, *to Valère*
          I'm sorry for your pain,
But—

VALÈRE

    No, you'll not hear me whimper or complain:
In judging us, *Madame's* been most judicious,
And I'll now strive to gratify her wishes.
Farewell.

SGANARELLE

    Poor lad, he's utterly undone.
Come, I'm her other self; embrace me, son.
          (*He embraces Valère.*)

SCENE TEN

Isabelle, Sganarelle

SGANARELLE

He's much to be pitied.

ISABELLE
I feel no such emotion.

SGANARELLE

In any case, I'm touched by your devotion,
My sweet, and it deserves some recompense;
A week's too long to keep you in suspense;
Tomorrow, then, shall be our wedding day.

ISABELLE

Tomorrow?

SGANARELLE
From modesty, you feign dismay,
But I well know what joy my words created,
And that you wish we were already mated.

ISABELLE

But—

SGANARELLE
Let's prepare for the wedding; come, be quick.

ISABELLE, *aside*
Inspire me, Heaven! I need another trick.

Act Three
SCENE ONE

———•—•———

Isabelle

ISABELLE, *alone*

Yes, death is far less dire to contemplate
Than a forced marriage to an unloved mate,
And I should not be censured, but forgiven
For any subterfuge to which I'm driven.
Time passes; night has fallen; I now must dare
To trust my fate and fortune to Valère.

SCENE TWO

———— • ————

Sganarelle, Isabelle

SGANARELLE (*Enters, muttering to himself:*)
That's done. Tomorrow, when the magistrate—

ISABELLE

Oh, Heaven!

SGANARELLE
                    Is it you, dear? Where are you going so late?
You told me, when I left, that you desired
To go to your chamber, being a little tired;
You even begged that I, upon returning,
Would not disturb you till tomorrow morning.

ISABELLE

That's true, but—

SGANARELLE
                    Yes?

ISABELLE

You see my hesitation;
I fear that you won't like the explanation.

SGANARELLE

Come, tell me.

ISABELLE
                    You'll be amazed. The reason for
My going out is sister Léonor;
She's borrowed my chamber, which she means to use
As part of a disreputable ruse.

SGANARELLE

What?

ISABELLE

Would you believe it? She loves that rogue whom we
Have just sent packing.

SGANARELLE

Valère?

ISABELLE

Yes, desperately:
I've never seen an ardor so intense;
And you may judge her passion's violence
By her coming here, at such an hour, alone,
To make the anguish of her spirit known.
She told me that she surely will expire
Unless she can obtain her heart's desire,
That for a year and more, Valère and she
Were fervent lovers, meeting secretly,
And that, when first they loved, they traded vows,
Each promising to become the other's spouse.

SGANARELLE

The wretched girl!

ISABELLE

That, knowing how I'd sent
The man she worships into banishment,
She begged me to allow her, since her heart
Would break if he were ever to depart,
To bid him in my name to come tonight
And stand beneath my window, so that she might
Impersonate my voice, and in a vein
Of sweet indulgence move him to remain—
Thus using for her own ends, as you see,
The warm regard she knows he feels for me.

SGANARELLE

And do you condone—

ISABELLE

        I? No, I'm much put out.
"Sister," I said, "you're mad beyond a doubt.
Do you not blush to throw your heart away
On a fickle sort who changes every day,
And shame your sex by choosing him instead
Of the trusting man whom Heaven would have you wed?"

SGANARELLE

Just what the fool deserves; I'm most content.

ISABELLE

In short, with many a furious argument
I chided her behavior, and said I quite
Refused to let her use my room, tonight;
But she poured such entreaties in my ears,
And heaved such sighs, and wept so many tears,
And said so often that she would despair
Unless I granted her impassioned prayer,
That love for her compelled me to accede.
Then, to secure the witness I might need
To clear my name, I thought to ask my friend
Lucrèce, whose many virtues you commend,
To spend the night with me. But ere I could go,
Your quick return surprised me, as you know.

SGANARELLE

No! All this jugglery I won't permit.
To spite my brother, I might agree to it;
But from the street they might be seen and heard;
And she on whom my hand's to be conferred
Must be not only chaste by disposition,
And gently bred, but quite above suspicion.
Let's send this wanton girl away, and teach her—

ISABELLE

Oh, no; you'd be too harsh with the poor creature;
And she might very justly take offense
At my betrayal of her confidence.
Since you require me to refuse my sister,
Stay here, at least, until I have dismissed her.

SGANARELLE

Well, do so, then.

ISABELLE

        Pray find some place of hiding,
And let her leave without reproach or chiding.

SGANARELLE

For love of you I'll curb my anger, dear;
But just as soon as she is out of here
I'll run and find my brother; 'twill be a rare
Pleasure to let him know of this affair.

ISABELLE

In your account, please leave my name unsaid.
Good night: when she has left, I'll go to bed.

SGANARELLE

Until tomorrow, my pet. I cannot wait
To see my brother, and tell him of his fate!
He's proven a fool, for all his glib conceit:
Not for a million would I miss this treat.

ISABELLE (*Inside the house:*)

Yes, sister, I'm sorry that you're so distressed,
But I can't grant the favor you request.
The danger to my honor would be too great.
Farewell. Best hurry home; it's growing late.

SGANARELLE

She'll leave, I wager, feeling cross and sore.
For fear she may come back, I'll lock the door.

ISABELLE, *aside, as she emerges in disguise*
Help my cause, Heaven; don't abandon me.

SGANARELLE, *aside*
Where is she going? I'll follow a bit, and see.

ISABELLE, *aside*
At any rate, this dark night serves my end.

SGANARELLE, *aside*
She's gone to Valère's house! What can she intend?

SCENE THREE

Valère, Isabelle, Sganarelle

VALÈRE, *coming out in haste*
Yes, yes; tonight, if some way can be found
To tell her . . . Who's there?

ISABELLE
                Valère, don't make a sound.
You needn't go out; I'm here; it's Isabelle.

SGANARELLE, *aside*
No, you're not she; what a brazen lie you tell!
She lives by honor, whereas you flirt with shame,
And falsely have assumed her voice and name.

ISABELLE, *to Valère*
However, unless your goal is matrimony—

VALÈRE
My heart is moved by that sweet purpose only.
Tomorrow, I assure you, I shall seize
The chance to wed you in any church you please.

SGANARELLE, *aside*
Poor hoodwinked fool!

VALÈRE
                Come in, and have no fear;
That dupe, your guardian, cannot touch you here,
And ere I let him sunder me from you
This arm of mine will run him through and through.

SGANARELLE, *alone*
Oh, rest assured that I won't deprive you of
This shameless girl, who's so enslaved by love;

That what you've promised her does not aggrieve me,
And that I'll *make* you marry her, believe me!
Yes, he must be surprised with that young doxy:
Both as her well-respected father's proxy
And for her sister's name, I must see to it
That she avoids disgrace, if I can do it.
Ho, there!

(*He knocks at the door of a magistrate.*)

SCENE FOUR

*Sganarelle, a Magistrate, a Notary,
an Attendant with a Lantern*

MAGISTRATE

Yes?

SGANARELLE

Magistrate, I'm glad you're here.
You're needed, Sir, in your official gear.
Please follow me, and bring that lantern, too.

MAGISTRATE

We were going—

SGANARELLE

But this is urgent.

MAGISTRATE

What must I do?

SGANARELLE

Go in there, and take two culprits by surprise
Who should be joined by lawful marriage ties.
I know the girl: she, trusting in the vows
Of one Valère, was lured into his house.
She comes of good and noble family, yet—

MAGISTRATE

If that's your purpose, we're indeed well-met,
For we have a notary with us.

SGANARELLE

That would be you, Sir?

NOTARY

Yes, a King's notary.

MAGISTRATE

A man of honor too, Sir.

SGANARELLE

Of course. Well, use that door—tread softly, eh?—
And don't let anybody get away.
You shall be well-rewarded for this endeavor;
Don't let them try to grease your palm, however.

MAGISTRATE

What! Do you think that a jurist of my station—

SGANARELLE

I meant no slur upon your occupation.
I'll go at once and fetch my brother. Kindly
Allow your lantern bearer to walk behind me.
                    (*Aside:*)
Now, gentle brother, I'll pay you a cheery visit.
Hello!
              (*He knocks at Ariste's door.*)

SCENE FIVE

———— • • ————

Ariste, Sganarelle

ARISTE
Who's knocking? Ah there, Brother! What is it?

SGANARELLE
Come, my wise pedagogue, my agèd beau,
There are pretty doings of which you ought to know.

ARISTE
How's that?

SGANARELLE
I bring you pleasant tidings.

ARISTE
                                        Well?

SGANARELLE
Where is your Léonor tonight, pray tell?

ARISTE
Why do you ask? As I recall, she's gone
To a friend's house, for a ball.

SGANARELLE
                              Ha! Well, come on
And see what sort of ball such girls prefer.

ARISTE
What are you saying?

SGANARELLE
                        How well you've tutored her!
"It does no good to censure and upbraid;

No, it's by kindness that young minds are swayed;
It isn't bolts and bars and strict controls
That give our wives and maidens virtuous souls;
Too much constraint can make them misbehave,
And a bit of freedom's what all women crave."
Well, she's been free in the extreme, I'd say,
And her virtue grows more easy every day.

ARISTE

What are you getting at? I cannot quite—

SGANARELLE

Ah, dearest elder brother, this serves you right!
I wouldn't miss it; you shall now find out
What your crazed theories have brought about.
See how these girls reflect what they've been taught;
Mine flees from gallants, yours chooses to be caught.

ARISTE

If you won't stop riddling—

SGANARELLE

                The riddle of this affair
Is that her ball's at the house of young Valère;
That I saw her steal by night into his place,
And that she's, even now, in his embrace.

ARISTE

Who?

SGANARELLE

    Léonor.

ARISTE

    Please, please, let's have no jokes.

SGANARELLE

He dares dismiss my story as a hoax!

Poor fellow, I've told you—and I say once more—
That at Valère's you'll find your Léonor.
Know, too, that they were pledged to marry, well
Before he dreamt of courting Isabelle.

ARISTE

This tale's preposterous. You cannot mean it.

SGANARELLE

He won't believe it, even when he's seen it!
This drives me mad. Old age without a brain
                (*Tapping his forehead:*)
Is not worth much.

ARISTE

          Come, Brother, do you maintain—

SGANARELLE

Lord, no! I maintain nothing. Just follow me,
And you'll be freed from all uncertainty.
You'll see if I lie, and if it isn't so
That their troths were plighted more than a year ago.

ARISTE

Does it seem likely that she would embark
On such a course, and leave *me* in the dark,
When, all her life, I've looked with an entire
Indulgence on her every young desire,
And promised always that I'd not prevent
Her heart from freely following its bent?

SGANARELLE

Come, let your own eyes judge how matters stand.
A magistrate and notary are on hand:
The promised marriage should at once take place,
I think, to rescue her from more disgrace.
You, I assume, care something for your honor,
And would not wed her with this stain upon her—

Unless you fancy that your liberal vision
And fine ideas could save you from derision.

ARISTE

To claim another's heart against her will
Is something I would scorn to do. But still
I'm not convinced that—

SGANARELLE

How you do run on!
Let's go, or we'll be chattering here till dawn.

SCENE SIX

Sganarelle, Ariste, the Magistrate, the Notary

MAGISTRATE

There's no need for compulsion, gentlemen;
If all you want is to see them married, then
I here and now can give you peace of mind.
Both parties, I am told, are so inclined,
And here is a signed statement from Valère
That he means to wed the girl now in his care.

ARISTE

And the girl's—?

MAGISTRATE

      Locked in, and won't come out unless
You grant their wish for wedded happiness.

SCENE SEVEN

———————•—————

Valère, the Magistrate, the Notary, Sganarelle, Ariste

VALÈRE, *at the window of his house*
No, gentlemen; none shall enter here till you've
Assured me formally that you approve.
You know me, Sirs; I've done what I must do
And signed the instrument they'll show to you.
If you are willing, then, for us to marry,
Your signatures are all that's necessary;
If not, you'll have to take my life before
You rob me of the one whom I adore.

SGANARELLE
No, we'll not rob you; set your mind at rest.
            (*Sotto voce, aside:*)
He still believes that Isabelle is his guest:
Well, let him think it.

ARISTE, *to Valère*
            But is it Léonor—?

SGANARELLE, *to Ariste*
Be quiet.

ARISTE
    But—

SGANARELLE
    Hush.

ARISTE
    I want to know—

SGANARELLE

Once more,
Will you be quiet?

VALÈRE

In any case, good Sirs,
Isabelle has my pledge, as I have hers.
Do think it over: I'm not so poor a catch
That you should make objection to the match.

ARISTE, *to Sganarelle*

The name he said was—

SGANARELLE

Quiet! When this is through,
You shall know everything. (*To Valère:*) Yes, without more ado,
We both agree that you shall be the spouse
Of her who is at present in your house.

MAGISTRATE

Just how this contract puts it, to the letter.
The name's left blank, because we've not yet met her.
Sign here. The girl can do so by and by.

VALÈRE

I agree to that.

SGANARELLE

With my whole heart, so do I.
(*Aside:*)
What a laugh I soon shall have! (*To Ariste:*) Sign, Brother dear;
You should go first.

ARISTE

All this is so unclear—

SGANARELLE

Sign, sign, you idiot! What are you waiting for?

ARISTE

He speaks of Isabelle, you of Léonor.

SGANARELLE

What if it's she? Are you not willing, Brother,
To let these two keep faith with one another?

ARISTE

Surely.

SGANARELLE

Then sign, and I shall do the same.

ARISTE

Very well; but I'm baffled.

SGANARELLE

I'll soon explain the game.

MAGISTRATE

We shall return, Sirs.
(*Exeunt Magistrate and Notary into Valère's house.*)

SGANARELLE

Now then, I'll reveal
Some secrets to you.
(*They retire to the back of the stage.*)

SCENE EIGHT

Léonor, Sganarelle, Ariste, Lisette

LÉONOR

Oh, what a grim ordeal!
I find those young men tiresome, one and all.
On their account, I slipped away from the ball.

LISETTE

They all try hard to please you, and be engaging.

LÉONOR

Nevertheless, I find their talk enraging.
I'd rather hear the simplest common sense
Than all that empty prattle they dispense.
They think their blond wigs dazzle every eye,
And that they're fearfully witty when they try
To tease one, in a bright, malicious fashion,
About the limits of an old man's passion.
But I prefer an old man's kindly zeal
To the giddy transports young men claim to feel.
Ah! Don't I see—?

SGANARELLE, *to Ariste*

Well, Brother, now you know.
(*Perceiving Léonor:*)
But look! She's coming, with her maid in tow.

ARISTE

Léonor, I am not angry, but I'm pained:
You know your freedom's never been constrained,
And that you've long been promised, on my part,
Full liberty in matters of the heart.
Yet, as if doubtful that I would approve,
You've gone behind my back to pledge your love.
I don't regret my leniency, but such

Mistrustful conduct hurts me very much,
And what you've done is not a fair return
For my affection and my warm concern.

ＬＥＯＮＯＲ

I cannot guess to what your words refer;
My feelings, though, are what they always were,
And my regard for you is firm and strong.
I could not love another, and do you wrong,
If you would see my chief wish satisfied,
Say that tomorrow I may be your bride.

ＡＲＩＳＴＥ

Then, Brother, on what foundation did you base—

ＳＧＡＮＡＲＥＬＬＥ

What! Didn't you come, just now, from Valère's place?
Didn't you tell your sister, just today,
That, a year ago, he stole your heart away?

ＬＥＯＮＯＲ

Tell me, who took the trouble to devise
Such tales about me, and spin such pretty lies?

SCENE NINE

---•◦•---

Isabelle, Valère, the Magistrate, the Notary,
Ergaste, Lisette, Léonor, Sganarelle, Ariste

ISABELLE

Sister, I fear I've taken liberties
With your good name; will you forgive me, please?
Under the pressure of a sudden crisis
I've stooped, today, to certain low devices:
By your example I am put to shame;
But fortune did not treat us both the same.
                    (*To Sganarelle:*)
Sir, I shall offer no apologies to you;
It is a service, not a wrong, I do you.
The Heavens did not design us to be wed:
I felt unworthy of you, and instead
Of making you an undeserving wife,
I chose another man to share my life.

VALÈRE, *to Sganarelle*

I count it, Sir, my greatest joy and pride
That from your hands I have received my bride.

ARISTE

Best take this quietly, Brother; your own extreme
Behavior forced these two to plot and scheme,
And it will be your sad lot, I foresee,
To be a dupe who gets no sympathy.

LISETTE

Well, I'm delighted. This clever trick's a just
Reward for his suspicion and mistrust.

LÉONOR

I'm not sure that their trick deserves applause,
But I can't blame them, for they had good cause.

ERGASTE

He's a born cuckold, and lucky to get out
Of marriage before his horns began to sprout.

SGANARELLE, *emerging from his stupefaction*

No, I can't fathom it; I'm overcome;
Such treachery is too deep for me to plumb;
I can't believe that Satan himself could be
As wicked as this jade has been to me.
I would have sworn she could not do amiss;
Let no man trust a woman, after this!
The best of them are guileful and perverse;
Their breed was made to be creation's curse.
The Devil take them all! I hereby sever
Relations with their faithless sex forever.

ERGASTE

Good.

ARISTE

Come to my house, friends. Tomorrow we'll assuage,
As best we can, my brother's pain and rage.

LISETTE, *to the audience*

D'you know any churlish husbands? If you do,
Send them to us: we'll teach them a thing or two.

THE SCHOOL FOR WIVES

COMEDY IN FIVE ACTS, 1662

To the memory of
Louis Jouvet
1887–1951

Introduction

As Dorante says in the *Critique de l'École des femmes*, a comic monster need not lack all attractive qualities. Arnolphe, the hero of Molière's first great verse comedy, is a forty-two-year-old provincial bourgeois whom it is possible to like, up to a point, for his coarse heartiness and his generosity with money. He is, however, a madman, and his alienation is of a harmful and unlovable kind. What ails him is a deep general insecurity, which has somehow been focused into a specific terror of being cuckolded. In fear of that humiliation, he has put off marriage until what, for the seventeenth century, was a very ripe age; meanwhile, he has buttressed his frail vanity by gloating over such of his neighbors as have been deceived by their wives. He has, furthermore, become the guardian of a four-year-old child, Agnès, with a view to shaping her into his idea of a perfect bride, and for thirteen years has had her trained to be docile and ignorant. It is his theory, based upon much anxious observation, that a stupid wife will not shame her husband by infidelity. As the play begins, Arnolphe is about to marry Agnès and achieve a double satisfaction: he will quiet his long trepidation by marrying safely, and he will have the prideful pleasure of showing the world how to rig an infallible alliance. It goes without saying that poor, stultified Agnès is not his object but his victim.

Arnolphe, then, is one of Molière's coercers of life. Like Tartuffe, he proposes to manipulate the world for his own ends, and the play is one long joke about the futility of selfish calculation. Agnès is guileless; her young man, Horace, is a rash bumbler who informs his rival of all that he does and means to do; yet despite Arnolphe's mature canniness, and his twenty years' pondering and plotting, he loses out to a *jeune innocente* and a *jeune écervelé*. Why? There is much high talk in the play, especially from Arnolphe, of cruel destiny, fate, and the stars, and this contributes, as J. D. Hubert has noted, to an effect of "burlesque tragedy"; it is not implacable fate, however, but ridiculous chance which repeatedly spoils Arnolphe's designs. And indeed, the plans of other characters, even when benign, meet constantly with the fortuitous: if Horace achieves his goal, it is certainly not because his blundering intrigues have mastered circumstance; and though Oronte and Enrique accomplish the premeditated union of their children, *le hasard* has already brought the pair together. The play seems to assert that any effort to impose expectations on life will meet with surprises, and that a narrow, rigid, and inhumane demand will not be honored by Nature.

The plot of *L'École des femmes* has often been criticized for its unlikelihood. Doubtless Molière was careless of the fact, since, as W. G. Moore has written, "The plot is not the main thing at all. . . . The high points of the play are not the turning points of the action; they are moments when the clash of youth and age, of spontaneity and automatism, takes shape in speech and scene." And yet it may not be too much to say that the absurdity of the plot is expressive, that it presents us with the world as Arnolphe is bound to experience it. To an obsessed man, the world will be full of exasperating irrelevancies: in this case, a dead kitten, a ribbon, the inopportune chatter of a notary. Similarly, a man who has for years left nothing to chance in the prosecution of a maniacal plan, and who encounters difficulties on the very eve of success, will experience the world as a chaos of disruptive accidents, a storm of casualty: in this case, an old friend's son will by chance gain the affections of Arnolphe's intended; in repeated chance meetings he will subject Arnolphe, whose new title he chances not to know, to tormenting confidences; Oronte and Enrique will chance to arrive in town on what was to have been Arnolphe's wedding day, and will reveal the true identity of the young woman whom Arnolphe once chanced to adopt. It is all too much, for Arnolphe and for us, and in the last-minute breathless summary of Enrique's story, delivered by Chrysalde and Oronte in alternating couplets,

Molière both burlesques a species of comic dénouement and acknowledges the outrageousness of his own. At the same time, for this reader, the gay arbitrariness of the close celebrates a truth which is central to the comic vision—that life will not be controlled, but makes a fluent resistance to all crabbèd constraint. The most triumphant demonstration of life's (or Nature's) irrepressibility occurs within Arnolphe himself, when, after so many years of coldly exploiting Agnès for his pride's sake, he becomes vulnerably human by falling in love with her.

Spontaneity versus automatism, life's happy refusal to conform to cranky plans and theories: such terms describe the play for me. Some, however, may wish to be less general, and to discern here a thesis play about, say, education. This comedy is, indeed, permeated with the themes of instruction and learning. Arnolphe has Agnès minimally educated, so that she will have no attractive accomplishments; the nuns teach her to pray, spin, and sew (and somehow, though it is against her guardian's orders, she also learns to read). In Act Three, Arnolphe himself becomes her teacher, or, rather, her priest, and with repeated threats of hell-fire informs her that the function of a wife is to live wholly for her husband, in absolute subjection. *The Maxims of Marriage*, which Agnès is then given to study, are likened by Arnolphe to the rules which a novice must learn on entering a convent; and very like they are, counseling as they do a cloistered and sacrificial life devoted to the worship of one's husband. Arnolphe's whole teaching is that the purpose of marriage is to preserve the husband's honor, which is like saying that the purpose of dancing is not to break a leg; and his whole education of Agnès is intended to incapacitate her for adultery by rendering her spiritless and uninteresting. There are moments, I think, when other characters burlesque Arnolphe as educator: the manservant Alain, informing Georgette in Act Two, Scene Two that "womankind is . . . the soup of man," caricatures his master's attitude toward women, as well as his patronizing pedagogical style; and the notary, torrentially instructing Arnolphe in contract law, resembles in his pedantic formulae the Arnolphe of the smug thesis, the airtight plan, and the *Maxims*. Much else in the play might be seen as extending the motif of instruction: Arnolphe rehearsing or drilling his servants; Chrysalde lecturing Arnolphe on the temperate view of cuckoldry; Arnolphe schooling himself in the causes of marital disaster, being guided by a Greek who counseled Augustus, or advising Oronte on the use of paternal power. But what is more surely pertinent, and stands in opposition to Arnolphe's kind of schooling, is the transformation of Horace and Agnès by that *grand maître*, Love. When we first meet him, Horace is a pretty-boy very full of himself and quite capable of seducing Agnès, but by the fifth act he has come to esteem and cherish her, and had "rather die than do her any wrong." Agnès, awakened by love to her own childish ignorance and dependence, proceeds like Juliet to develop gumption and resourcefulness, and discovers a wit which is the more devastating because of her continuing simplicity.

The play is full of "education"; granted. But it cannot convincingly be interpreted as a thesis play *about* education. What can Molière be said to advocate? Latin for women? The inclusion of love in the curriculum? Clearly Molière had a low opinion of Agnès' convent schooling, which was rather standard for the age; what really interests him, however, is not the deficiencies of such schooling but Arnolphe's ill-intended use of them. Similarly, Molière is concerned not with religion but with Arnolphe's selfish and Orgon-like abuse of it, his turning it into a bludgeon. Nor does he comment on parental authority in itself, but, rather, on Arnolphe's attempt to exploit it for his own ends. It will not do, in short, for the contemporary reader or director to inject this play with Student Unrest or Women's Liberation, or to descry in it a Generation Gap. That way lies melodrama.

Any director of this English version will have to solve for himself certain problems of interpretation and staging, but I shall say what I think. It is my own decided opinion that Chrysalde is *not* a cuckold, and that Arnolphe's second speech in Act One, Scene One is a bit of crude and objectionable ribbing. Chrysalde's discourses about cuckoldry should be regarded, I think, both as frequently dubious "reasoning" and as bear-baiting; a good actor would know where to modulate between them. Arnolphe's distaste for fuss and sophistication is likely to impress some as an endearing quality, but I do not see it so; rather, it is of a piece with the man's anxiety to prove himself superior to a society whose ridicule he fears, and like the "honesty" of the *Misanthrope*'s Alceste, it entails posturing and bad faith. Finally, there is the fact that much of the slapstick in the plot—the throwing of the brick, Horace's tumble from the ladder—occurs off stage, and that the on-stage proceedings consist in fair part of long speeches. I should be sorry to see any director right this apparent imbalance by introducing too much pie-throwing and bottom-pinching of his own invention. Once again, Dorante gives Molière's point of view: the long speeches, he says, "are themselves actions," involving incessant ironic *interplay* between speakers and hearers. To take the most obvious example, Horace's addresses to Arnolphe are rendered wonderfully "busy" by the fact that he does not know he is addressing M. de la Souche, that Arnolphe cannot enlighten him, and that Arnolphe must continually struggle to conceal his glee or anguish. To add any great amount of farcical "business" to such complex comedy would be to divert in an unfortunate sense.

This translation has aimed at a thought-for-thought fidelity, and has sought in its verse to avoid the metronomic, which is particularly fatal on the stage: I have sometimes been very limber indeed, as in the line "He's the most hideous Christian I ever did see." For a few words or phrases I am indebted to earlier English versions in blank verse or prose. I must also thank Jan Miel for helping me to improve these remarks; Robert Hollander, Stephen Porter, and William Jay Smith for reading and criticizing the translation; and John Berryman for encouraging me to undertake it.

R.W.

Characters

ARNOLPHE, also known as MONSIEUR DE LA SOUCHE
AGNÈS, an innocent young girl, Arnolphe's ward
HORACE, Agnès' lover, Oronte's son
ALAIN, a peasant, Arnolphe's manservant
GEORGETTE, a peasant woman, servant to Arnolphe
CHRYSALDE, a friend of Arnolphe's
ENRIQUE, Chrysalde's brother-in-law, Agnès' father
ORONTE, Horace's father and Arnolphe's old friend
A NOTARY

PLACE
The scene is a square in a provincial city.

First produced by the Phoenix Theatre,
New York, on February 16, 1971

Act One

SCENE ONE

———◆◆◆———

Chrysalde, Arnolphe

CHRYSALDE
So, you're resolved to give this girl your hand?

ARNOLPHE
Tomorrow I shall marry her, as planned.

CHRYSALDE
We're quite alone here, and we can discuss
Your case with no one overhearing us:
Shall I speak openly, and as your friend?
This plan—for your sake—troubles me no end.
I must say that, from every point of view,
Taking a wife is a rash step for you.

ARNOLPHE
You think so? Might it be, friend, that you base
Your fears for me upon your own sad case?
Cuckolds would have us think that all who marry
Acquire a set of horns as corollary.

CHRYSALDE
Fate gives men horns, and fate can't be withstood;
To fret about such matters does no good.
What makes me fear for you is the way you sneer
At every luckless husband of whom you hear.
You know that no poor cuckold, great or small,
Escapes your wit; you mock them one and all,
And take delight in making boisterous mention
Of all intrigues which come to your attention.

ARNOLPHE

Why not? What other town on earth is known
For husbands so long-suffering as our own?
Can we not all too readily bring to mind
Ill-treated dupes of every shape and kind?
One husband's rich; his helpmeet shares the wealth
With paramours who cuckold him by stealth;
Another, with a scarcely kinder fate,
Sees other men heap gifts upon his mate—
Who frees his mind of jealous insecurity
By saying that they're tributes to her purity.
One cuckold impotently storms and rants;
Another mildly bows to circumstance,
And when some gallant calls to see his spouse,
Discreetly takes his hat and leaves the house.
One wife, confiding in her husband, mentions
A swain who bores her with his warm attentions;
The husband smugly pities the poor swain
For all his efforts—which are *not* in vain.
Another wife explains her wealthy state
By saying that she's held good cards of late;
Her husband thanks the Lord and gives Him praise,
Not guessing what bad game she truly plays.
Thus, all about us, there are themes for wit;
May I not, as an observer, jest a bit?
May I not laugh at—

CHRYSALDE

          Yes; but remember, do,
That those you mock may someday mock at you.
Now, I hear gossip, I hear what people say
About the latest scandals of the day,
But whatsoever I'm told, I never hear it
With wicked glee and in a gloating spirit.
I keep my counsel; and though I may condemn
Loose wives, and husbands who put up with them,
And though I don't propose, you may be sure,
To endure the wrongs which some weak men endure,

Still, I am never heard to carp and crow,
For tables have been known to turn, you know,
And there's no man who can predict, in fact,
How in such circumstances he would act.
In consequence, should fate bestow on me
What all must fear, the horns of cuckoldry,
The world would treat me gently, I believe,
And be content with laughing up its sleeve.
There are, in fact, some kindly souls who might
Commiserate me in my sorry plight.
But you, dear fellow, with you it's not the same.
I say once more, you play a dangerous game.
Since with your jeering tongue you plague the lives
Of men who are unlucky in their wives,
And persecute them like a fiend from Hell,
Take care lest someday you be jeered as well.
If the least whisper about your wife were heard,
They'd mock you from the housetops, mark my word.
What's more—

ARNOLPHE

   Don't worry, friend; I'm not a fool.
I shan't expose myself to ridicule.
I know the tricks and ruses, shrewd and sly,
Which wives employ, and cheat their husbands by;
I know that women can be deep and clever;
But I've arranged to be secure forever:
So simple is the girl I'm going to wed
That I've no fear of horns upon my head.

CHRYSALDE

Simple! You mean to bind yourself for life—

ARNOLPHE

A man's not simple to take a simple wife.
Your wife, no doubt, is a wise, virtuous woman,
But brightness, as a rule, is a bad omen,
And I know men who've undergone much pain

Because they married girls with too much brain.
I want no intellectual, if you please,
Who'll talk of nothing but her Tuesday teas,
Who'll frame lush sentiments in prose and verse
And fill the house with wits, and fops, and worse,
While I, as her dull husband, stand about
Like a poor saint whose candles have gone out.
No, keep your smart ones; I've no taste for such.
Women who versify know far too much.
I want a wife whose thought is not sublime,
Who has no notion what it is to rhyme,
And who, indeed, if she were asked in some
Insipid parlor game, "What rhymes with drum?"
Would answer in all innocence, "A fife."
In short, I want an unaccomplished wife,
And there are four things only she must know:
To say her prayers, love me, spin, and sew.

CHRYSALDE

Stupidity's your cup of tea, I gather.

ARNOLPHE

I'd choose an ugly, stupid woman rather
Than a great beauty who was over-wise.

CHRYSALDE

But wit and beauty—

ARNOLPHE

        Virtue is what I prize.

CHRYSALDE

But how can you expect an idiot
To know what's virtuous and what is not?
Not only would it be a lifelong bore
To have a senseless wife, but what is more,
I hardly think you could depend upon her

To guard her husband's forehead from dishonor.
If a bright woman breaks her wedding vow,
She knows what she is doing, anyhow;
A simpleton, however, can commit
Adultery without suspecting it.

ARNOLPHE

To that fine argument I can but say
What Pantagruel says in Rabelais:
Preach and harangue from now till Whitsuntide
Against my preference for a stupid bride;
You'll be amazed to find, when you have ceased,
That I've not been persuaded in the least.

CHRYSALDE

So be it.

ARNOLPHE

Each man has his own design
For wedded bliss, and I shall follow mine.
I'm rich, and so can take a wife who'll be
Dependent, in the least respect, on me—
A sweet, submissive girl who cannot claim
To have brought me riches or an ancient name.
The gentle, meek expression which she wore
Endeared Agnès to me when she was four;
Her mother being poor, I felt an urge
To make the little thing my ward and charge,
And the good peasant woman was most pleased
To grant my wish, and have her burden eased.
In a small convent, far from the haunts of man,
The girl was reared according to my plan:
I told the nuns what means must be employed
To keep her growing mind a perfect void,
And, God be praised, they had entire success.
As a grown girl, her simple-mindedness
Is such that I thank Heaven for granting me

A bride who suits my wishes to a T.
She's out of the convent now, and since my gate
Stands open to society, early and late,
I keep her here, in another house I own,
Where no one calls, and she can be alone:
And, to protect her artless purity,
I've hired two servants as naïve as she.
I've told you all this so that you'll understand
With what great care my marriage has been planned;
And now, to clinch my story, I invite
You, my dear friend, to dine with her tonight;
I want you to examine her, and decide
Whether or not my choice is justified.

CHRYSALDE

Delighted.

ARNOLPHE

You'll gain, I think, a lively sense
Of her sweet person and her innocence.

CHRYSALDE

As to her innocence, what you've related
Leaves little doubt—

ARNOLPHE

My friend, 't was understated.
Her utter naïveté keeps me in stitches.
I laugh so that I almost burst my breeches.
You won't believe this, but the other day
She came and asked me in a puzzled way,
And with a manner touchingly sincere,
If children are begotten through the ear.

CHRYSALDE

I'm happy indeed, Monsieur Arnolphe—

ARNOLPHE

For shame!
Why must you always use my former name?

CHRYSALDE

I'm used to it, I suppose. What's more, I find
That *de la Souche* forever slips my mind.
What in the devil has persuaded you
To debaptize yourself at forty-two
And take a lordly title which you base
On an old tree stump at your country place?

ARNOLPHE

The name La Souche goes with the property
And sounds much better than Arnolphe to me.

CHRYSALDE

But why forsake the name your fathers bore
For one that's fantasy and nothing more?
Yet lately that's become the thing to do.
I am reminded—no offense to you—
Of a peasant named Gros-Pierre, who owned a small
Parcel of land, an acre or so in all;
He dug a muddy ditch around the same
And took Monsieur de l'Isle for his new name.

ARNOLPHE

I can dispense with stories of that kind.
My name is de la Souche, if you don't mind.
I like that title, and it's mine by right;
To address me otherwise is impolite.

CHRYSALDE

Your new name is employed by few, at best;
Much of your mail, I've noticed, comes addressed—

ARNOLPHE

I don't mind that, from such as haven't been told;
But you—

CHRYSALDE

Enough. Enough. No need to scold.
I hereby promise that, at our next meeting,
"Good day, Monsieur de la Souche" shall be my greeting.

ARNOLPHE

Farewell. I'm going to knock now on my door
And let them know that I'm in town once more.

CHRYSALDE, *aside, as he moves off*

The man's quite mad. A lunatic, in fact.

ARNOLPHE, *alone*

On certain subjects he's a trifle cracked.
It's curious to see with what devotion
A man will cling to some quite pointless notion.
Ho, there!

SCENE TWO

———————•❦•———————

Alain, Georgette, Arnolphe

ALAIN, *within*

Who's knocking?

ARNOLPHE

Ho! (*Aside:*) They'll greet me, after
My ten days' trip, with smiles and happy laughter.

ALAIN

Who's there?

ARNOLPHE

It's I.

ALAIN

Georgette!

GEORGETTE

What?

ALAIN

Open below!

GEORGETTE

Do it yourself!

ALAIN

You do it!

GEORGETTE

I won't go!

ALAIN

I won't go either!

ARNOLPHE
Gracious servants, these,
To leave me standing here. Ho! If you please!

GEORGETTE
Who's there?

ARNOLPHE
Your master.

GEORGETTE
Alain!

ALAIN
What?

GEORGETTE
Go lift the latch!
It's him.

ALAIN
You do it.

GEORGETTE
I'm getting the fire to catch.

ALAIN
I'm keeping the cat from eating the canary.

ARNOLPHE
Whoever doesn't admit me, and in a hurry,
Will get no food for four long days, and more.
Aha!

GEORGETTE
I'll get it; what are you coming for?

ALAIN

Why you, not me? That's a sneaky trick to play!

GEORGETTE

Get out of the way.

ALAIN

No, *you* get out of the way.

GEORGETTE

I want to open that door.

ALAIN

I want to, too.

GEORGETTE

You won't.

ALAIN

And you won't either.

GEORGETTE

Neither will you.

ARNOLPHE, *to himself*

My patience with these two amazes me.

ALAIN

I've opened the door, Sir.

GEORGETTE

No, I did it! See?
'T was I.

ALAIN

If only the master, here, weren't present,
I'd—

ARNOLPHE, *receiving a blow from Alain,*
meant for Georgette

Blast you!

ALAIN

Sorry, Sir.

ARNOLPHE

You clumsy peasant!

ALAIN

It's her fault too, Sir.

ARNOLPHE

Both of you, stop this row.
I want to question you; no nonsense, now.
Alain, is everything going smoothly here?

ALAIN

Well, Sir, we're—
    (*Arnolphe removes Alain's hat; Alain*
    obliviously puts it back on.)
            Well, Sir—
                (*Hat business again*)
                    Well, thank God, Sir, we're—
    (*Arnolphe removes Alain's hat a third time,*
    and throws it to the ground.)

ARNOLPHE

Where did you learn, you lout, to wear a hat
While talking to your master? Answer me that.

ALAIN

You're right, I'm wrong.

ARNOLPHE
Now, have Agnès come down.
(*To Georgette:*)
Was she unhappy while I was out of town?

GEORGETTE
Unhappy? No.

ARNOLPHE
No?

GEORGETTE
Yes.

ARNOLPHE
For what reason, then?

GEORGETTE
Well, she kept thinking you'd be back again,
So that whatever passed on the avenue—
Horse, mule, or ass—she thought it must be you.

SCENE THREE

—————•••—————

Agnès, Alain, Georgette, Arnolphe

ARNOLPHE

Her needlework in hand! That's a good sign.
Well, well, Agnès, I'm back and feeling fine.
Are you glad to see me?

AGNÈS

Oh, yes, Sir; thank the Lord.

ARNOLPHE

I'm glad to see you too, my little ward.
I take it everything has been all right?

AGNÈS

Except for the fleas, which bothered me last night.

ARNOLPHE

Well, there'll be someone soon to drive them away.

AGNÈS

I shall be glad of that.

ARNOLPHE

Yes, I dare say.
What are you making?

AGNÈS

A headpiece, Sir, for me;
Your nightshirts are all finished, as you'll see.

ARNOLPHE

Excellent. Well, upstairs with you, my dear:
I'll soon come back and see you, never fear;
There's serious talk in which we must engage.

(*Exeunt all but Arnolphe.*)
O learned ladies, heroines of the age,
Gushers of sentiment, I say that you,
For all your verse, and prose, and billets-doux,
Your novels, and your bright accomplishments,
Can't match this good and modest ignorance.

SCENE FOUR

Horace, Arnolphe

ARNOLPHE

What does her lack of money matter to me?
What matters— Oh! What's this? No! Can it be?
I'm dreaming. Yes, it's he, my dear friend's boy.
Well!

HORACE

Sir!

ARNOLPHE

Horace!

HORACE

Arnolphe!

ARNOLPHE

Ah, what a joy!
How long have you been in town?

HORACE

Nine days.

ARNOLPHE

Ah, so.

HORACE

I called at your house, in vain, a week ago.

ARNOLPHE

I'd left for the country.

HORACE
Yes, you were three days gone.

ARNOLPHE
How quickly children grow! How time rolls on!
I am amazed that you're so big and tall.
I can remember when you were—
(*He makes a gesture of measuring from the floor.*)
that small.

HORACE
Yes, time goes by.

ARNOLPHE
But come now, tell me of
Oronte, your father, whom I esteem and love:
How's my old friend? Still spry and full of zest?
In all that's his, I take an interest.
Alas, it's four years since I talked with him,
And we've not written in the interim.

HORACE
Seigneur Arnolphe, he's spry enough for two;
He gave me this little note to give to you,
But now he writes me that he's coming here
Himself, for reasons not entirely clear.
Some fellow-townsman of yours, whom you may know,
Went to America fourteen years ago;
He's come back rich. Do you know of whom I speak?

ARNOLPHE
No. Did the letter give his name?

HORACE
Enrique.

ARNOLPHE
No . . . no . . .

HORACE

My father writes as if I ought
To recognize that name, but I do not.
He adds that he and Enrique will soon set out
On some great errand that he's vague about.

ARNOLPHE

I long to see your father, that sterling man.
I'll welcome him as royally as I can.
(*He reads the note from Oronte.*)
A friendly letter needn't flatter and fuss.
All this politeness is superfluous,
And even without his asking, I'd have desired
To lend you any money you required.

HORACE

I'll take you at your word, Sir. Can you advance
Fifty *pistoles* or so, by any chance?

ARNOLPHE

I'm grateful that you let me be of use,
And what you ask, I happily can produce.
Just keep the purse.

HORACE

Here—

ARNOLPHE

Forget the I.O.U.
Now, how does our town impress you? Tell me, do.

HORACE

It's rich in people, sublime in architecture,
And full of fine amusements, I conjecture.

ARNOLPHE

There's pleasure here for every taste; and those
The world calls gallants, ladies' men, or beaux

Find here the sport on which their hearts are set,
Since every woman in town's a born coquette.
Our ladies, dark or fair, are pliant creatures;
Their husbands, likewise, have permissive natures;
Oh, it's a capital game; it's often made
Me double up with mirth to see it played.
But you've already broken some hearts, I'd guess;
Have you no gallant conquest to confess?
Cuckolds are made by such as you, young man,
And looks like yours buy more than money can.

HORACE

Well, since you ask, I'll lay my secrets bare.
I *have* been having a covert love affair—
Which, out of friendship, I shall now unveil.

ARNOLPHE

Good, good; 't will be another rakish tale
Which I can put into my repertory.

HORACE

Sir, I must beg you: don't divulge my story.

ARNOLPHE

Of course not.

HORACE

        As you know, Sir, in these matters,
One word let slip can leave one's hopes in tatters.
To put the business plainly, then, my heart's
Been lost to a lady dwelling in these parts.
My overtures, I'm very pleased to state,
Have found her ready to reciprocate,
And not to boast, or slur her reputation,
I think I'm in a hopeful situation.

ARNOLPHE, *laughing*

Who is she?

HORACE

A girl whose beauty is past telling,
And yonder red-walled mansion is her dwelling.
She's utterly naïve, because a blind
Fool has sequestered her from humankind,
And yet, despite the ignorance in which
He keeps her, she has charms that can bewitch;
She's most engaging, and conveys a sense
Of sweetness against which there's no defense.
But you, perhaps, have seen this star of love
Whose many graces I'm enamoured of.
Her name's Agnès.

ARNOLPHE, *aside*
Oh, death!

HORACE
The man, I hear,
Is called La Zousse, La Source, or something queer;
I didn't pay much attention to the name.
He's rich, I gather, but his wits are lame,
And he's accounted a ridiculous fellow.
D'you know him?

ARNOLPHE, *aside*
Ugh, what a bitter pill to swallow!

HORACE
I said, do you know him?

ARNOLPHE
Yes, I do, in a way.

HORACE
He's a dolt, isn't he?

ARNOLPHE
Oh!

HORACE
What? What did you say?
He is, I take it. And a jealous idiot, too?
An ass? I see that all they said was true.
Well, to repeat, I love Agnès, a girl
Who is, to say the least, an orient pearl,
And it would be a sin for such a treasure
To be subjected to that old fool's pleasure.
Henceforth, my thoughts and efforts shall combine
To break his jealous hold and make her mine;
This purse, which I made bold to borrow, will lend
Me great assistance toward that worthy end.
As you well know, whatever means one tries,
Money's the key to every enterprise,
And this sweet metal, which all men hanker for,
Promotes our conquests, whether in love or war.
You look disturbed, Sir; can it be that you
Do not approve of what I mean to do?

ARNOLPHE
No; I was thinking—

HORACE
I'm boring you. Farewell, then.
I'll soon drop by, to express my thanks again.

ARNOLPHE, *to himself*
How could this happen—

HORACE, *returning*
Again, Sir, I entreat
You not to tell my secret; be discreet.
(*He leaves.*)

ARNOLPHE, *to himself*
I'm thunderstruck.

HORACE, *returning*
Above all, don't inform
My father; he might raise a dreadful storm.
(*He leaves.*)

ARNOLPHE (*He expects Horace to return again;*
that not occurring, he talks to himself.)
Oh! . . . What I've suffered during this conversation!
No soul has ever endured such agitation.
With what imprudence, and how hastily
He came and told the whole affair . . . to me!
He didn't know I'd taken a new title;
Still, what a rash and blundering recital!
I should, however, have kept myself in hand,
So as to learn what strategy he's planned,
And prompt his indiscretion, and discover
To what extent he has become her lover.
Come, I'll catch up with him; he can't be far;
I'll learn from him precisely how things are.
Alas, I'm trembling; I fear some further blow;
One can discover more than one wants to know.

Act Two

SCENE ONE

———•—•———

Arnolphe

ARNOLPHE
It's just as well, no doubt, that I should fail
To catch him—that I somehow lost his trail:
For I could not have managed to dissemble
The turbulence of soul which makes me tremble;
He'd have perceived my present near-despair,
Of which it's best that he be unaware.
But I'm not one to be resigned and meek
And turn this little fop the other cheek.
I'll stop him; and the first thing I must do
Is find out just how far they've gone, those two.
This matter involves my honor, which I prize;
The girl's my wife already, in my eyes;
If she's been tarnished, I am covered with shame,
And all she's done reflects on my good name.
Oh, why did I take that trip? Oh, dear, oh, dear.
    (*He knocks at his door.*)

SCENE TWO

———◆•◆———

Alain, Georgette, Arnolphe

ALAIN

Ah! *This* time, Sir—

ARNOLPHE

Hush! Both of you come here:
This way, this way. Come, hurry! Do as you're told!

GEORGETTE

You frighten me; you make my blood run cold.

ARNOLPHE

So! In my absence, you have disobeyed me!
The two of you, in concert, have betrayed me!

GEORGETTE, *falling on her knees*

Don't eat me, Sir; don't eat me alive, I beg.

ALAIN, *aside*

I'd swear some mad dog's nipped him in the leg.

ARNOLPHE, *aside*

Oof! I'm too tense to speak. I'd like to shed
These blasted clothes. I'm burning up with dread.
          (*To Alain and Georgette:*)
You cursèd scoundrels, while I was gone you let
A man into this house—
          (*To Alain, who has made a move to flee:*)
                    No, not just yet!
Tell me at once— (*To Georgette:*) Don't move! I want you
two
To tell me— Whff! I mean to learn from you—
          (*Alain and Georgette rise and try to escape.*)
If anyone moves, I'll squash him like a louse.

Now tell me, how did that man get into my house?
Well, speak! Come, hurry. Quickly! Time is fleeting!
Let's hear it! Speak!

ALAIN *and* GEORGETTE, *falling on their knees*
Oh! Oh!

GEORGETTE
My heart's stopped beating.

ALAIN
I'm dying.

ARNOLPHE, *aside*
I'm sweating, and I need some air.
I must calm down: I'll walk around the square.
When I saw him in his cradle, I didn't know
What he'd grow up and do to me. O woe!
Perhaps—yes, I'd do better to receive
The truth from her own lips, I now believe.
I'll mute my rage as well as I know how;
Patience, my wounded heart! Beat softly, now!
(*To Alain and Georgette:*)
Get up, and go inside, and call Agnès.
Wait. (*Aside:*) That way her surprise would be the less.
They'd warn her of my anger, I don't doubt.
I'd best go in myself and bring her out.
(*To Alain and Georgette:*)
Wait here.

SCENE THREE

———— • ————

Alain, Georgette

GEORGETTE
God help us, but his rage is terrible!
The way he glared at me—it was unbearable.
He's the most hideous Christian I ever did see.

ALAIN
He's vexed about that man, as I said he'd be.

GEORGETTE
But why does he order us, with barks and roars,
Never to let the mistress go outdoors?
Why does he want us to conceal her here
From all the world, and let no man come near?

ALAIN
It's jealousy that makes him treat her so.

GEORGETTE
But how did he get like that, I'd like to know?

ALAIN
It comes of being jealous, I assume.

GEORGETTE
But why is he jealous? Why must he rage and fume?

ALAIN
Well, jealousy—listen carefully, Georgette—
Is a thing—a thing—which makes a man upset,
And makes him close his doors to everyone.
I'm going to give you a comparison,
So that you'll clearly understand the word.
Suppose you were eating soup, and it occurred

That someone tried to take what you were eating:
Wouldn't you feel like giving him a beating?

GEORGETTE

Yes, I see that.

ALAIN

Then grasp this, if you can.
Womankind is, in fact, the soup of man,
And when a man perceives that others wish
To dip their dirty fingers into his dish,
His temper flares, and bursts into a flame.

GEORGETTE

Yes. But not everybody feels the same.
Some husbands seem to be delighted when
Their wives consort with fancy gentlemen.

ALAIN

Not every husband is the greedy kind
That wants to have it all.

GEORGETTE

If I'm not blind,
He's coming back.

ALAIN

It's he; your eyes are keen.

GEORGETTE

He's scowling.

ALAIN

That's because he's feeling mean.

SCENE FOUR

Arnolphe, Alain, Georgette

ARNOLPHE, *aside*

A certain Greek presumed once to advise
The great Augustus, and his words were wise:
When you are vexed, he said, do not forget,
Before you act, to say the alphabet,
So as to cool your temper, and prevent
Rash moves which later on you might repent.
In dealing with Agnès, I have applied
That counsel, and I've bidden her come outside,
Under the pretext of a morning stroll,
So that I can relieve my jangled soul
By seeking dulcetly to draw her out
And learn the truth, and put an end to doubt.
(*Calling:*) Come out, Agnès. (*To Alain and Georgette:*) Go in.

SCENE FIVE

Arnolphe, Agnès

ARNOLPHE
The weather's mild.

AGNÈS
Oh, yes.

ARNOLPHE
Most pleasant.

AGNÈS
Indeed!

ARNOLPHE
What news, my child?

AGNÈS
The kitten died.

ARNOLPHE
Too bad, but what of that?
All men are mortal, my dear, and so's a cat.
While I was gone, no doubt it rained and poured?

AGNÈS
No.

ARNOLPHE
You were bored, perhaps?

AGNÈS
I'm never bored.

ARNOLPHE

During my ten days' absence, what did you do?

AGNÈS

Six nightshirts, I believe; six nightcaps, too.

ARNOLPHE, *after a pause*

My dear Agnès, this world's a curious thing.
What wicked talk one hears, what gossiping!
While I was gone, or so the neighbors claim,
There was a certain strange young man who came
To call upon you here, and was received.
But such a slander's not to be believed,
And I would wager that their so-called news—

AGNÈS

Heavens! Don't wager; you'd be sure to lose.

ARNOLPHE

What! Is it true, then, that a man—

AGNÈS

                     Oh, yes.
In fact, he all but lived at this address.

ARNOLPHE, *aside*

That frank reply would seem to demonstrate
That she's still free of guile, at any rate.
    (*Aloud:*)
But I gave orders, Agnès, as I recall,
That you were to see no one, no one at all.

AGNÈS

I disobeyed you, but when I tell you why,
You'll say that you'd have done the same as I.

ARNOLPHE

Perhaps; well, tell me how this thing occurred.

AGNÈS

It's the most amazing story you ever heard.
I was sewing, out on the balcony, in the breeze,
When I noticed someone strolling under the trees.
It was a fine young man, who caught my eye
And made me a deep bow as he went by.
I, not to be convicted of a lack
Of manners, very quickly nodded back.
At once, the young man bowed to me again.
I bowed to him a second time, and then
It wasn't very long until he made
A third deep bow, which I of course repaid.
He left, but kept returning, and as he passed,
He'd bow, each time, more gracefully than the last,
While I, observing as he came and went,
Gave each new bow a fresh acknowledgment.
Indeed, had night not fallen, I declare
I think that I might still be sitting there,
And bowing back each time he bowed to me,
For fear he'd think me less polite than he.

ARNOLPHE

Go on.

AGNÈS

Then an old woman came, next day,
And found me standing in the entryway.
She said to me, "May Heaven bless you, dear,
And keep you beautiful for many a year.
God, who bestowed on you such grace and charm,
Did not intend those gifts to do men harm,
And you should know that there's a heart which bears
A wound which you've inflicted unawares."

ARNOLPHE, *aside*

Old witch! Old tool of Satan! Damn her hide!

AGNÈS

"You say I've wounded somebody?" I cried.
"Indeed you have," she said. "The victim's he
Whom yesterday you saw from the balcony."
"But how could such a thing occur?" I said;
"Can I have dropped some object on his head?"
"No," she replied, "your bright eyes dealt the blow;
Their glances are the cause of all his woe."
"Good heavens, Madam," said I in great surprise,
"Is there some dread contagion in my eyes?"
"Ah, yes, my child," said she. "Your eyes dispense,
Unwittingly, a fatal influence:
The poor young man has dwindled to a shade;
And if you cruelly deny him aid,
I greatly fear," the kind old woman went on,
"That two days more will see him dead and gone."
"Heavens," I answered, "that would be sad indeed.
But what can I do for him? What help does he need?"
"My child," said she, "he only asks of you
The privilege of a little interview;
It is your eyes alone which now can save him,
And cure him of the malady they gave him."
"If that's the case," I said, "I can't refuse;
I'll gladly see him, whenever he may choose."

ARNOLPHE, *aside*

O "kind old woman"! O vicious sorceress!
May Hell reward you for your cleverness!

AGNÈS

And so I saw him, which brought about his cure.
You'll grant I did the proper thing, I'm sure.
How could I have the conscience to deny
The succor he required, and let him die—
I, who so pity anyone in pain,
And cannot bear to see a chicken slain?

ARNOLPHE, *aside*

It's clear that she has meant no wrong, and I
Must blame that foolish trip I took, whereby
I left her unprotected from the lies
That rascally seducers can devise.
Oh, what if that young wretch, with one bold stroke,
Has compromised her? That would be no joke.

AGNÈS

What's wrong? You seem a trifle irritated.
Was there some harm in what I just related?

ARNOLPHE

No, but go on. I want to hear it all.
What happened when the young man came to call?

AGNÈS

Oh, if you'd seen how happy he was, how gay,
And how his sickness vanished right away,
And the jewel-case he gave me—not to forget
The coins he gave to Alain and to Georgette,
You would have loved him also, and you too—

ARNOLPHE

And when you were alone, what did he do?

AGNÈS

He swore he loved me with a matchless passion,
And said to me, in the most charming fashion,
Things which I found incomparably sweet,
And never tire of hearing him repeat,
So much do they delight my ear, and start
I know not what commotion in my heart.

ARNOLPHE, *aside*

O strange interrogation, where each reply
Makes the interrogator wish to die!

(*To Agnès:*)
Besides these compliments, these sweet addresses,
Were there not also kisses, and caresses?

AGNÈS

Oh, yes! He took my hands, and kissed and kissed
Them both, as if he never would desist.

ARNOLPHE

And did he not take—something else as well?
(*He notes that she is taken aback.*)
Agh!

AGNÈS

Well, he—

ARNOLPHE

Yes?

AGNÈS

Took—

ARNOLPHE

What?

AGNÈS

I dare not tell.
I fear that you'll be furious with me.

ARNOLPHE

No.

AGNÈS

Yes.

ARNOLPHE

No, no.

AGNÈS
Then promise not to be.

ARNOLPHE
I promise.

AGNÈS
He took my—oh, you'll have a fit.

ARNOLPHE
No.

AGNÈS
Yes.

ARNOLPHE
No, no. The devil! Out with it!
What did he take from you?

AGNÈS
He took—

ARNOLPHE, *aside*
God save me!

AGNÈS
He took the pretty ribbon that you gave me.
Indeed, he begged so that I couldn't resist.

ARNOLPHE, *taking a deep breath*
Forget the ribbon. Tell me: once he'd kissed
Your hands, what else did he do, as you recall?

AGNÈS
Does one do other things?

ARNOLPHE

No, not at all;
But didn't he ask some further medicine
For the sad state of health that he was in?

AGNÈS

Why, no. But had he asked, you may be sure
I'd have done anything to speed his cure.

ARNOLPHE, *aside*

I've got off cheap this once, thanks be to God;
If I slip again, let all men call me clod.
    (*To Agnès:*)
Agnès, my dear, your innocence is vast;
I shan't reproach you; what is past is past.
But all that trifler wants to do—don't doubt it—
Is to deceive you, and then boast about it.

AGNÈS

Oh, no. He's often assured me otherwise.

ARNOLPHE

Ah, you don't know how that sort cheats and lies.
But do grasp this: to accept a jewel-case,
And let some coxcomb praise your pretty face,
And be complaisant when he takes a notion
To kiss your hands and fill you with "commotion"
Is a great sin, for which your soul could die.

AGNÈS

A sin, you say! But please, Sir, tell me why.

ARNOLPHE

Why? Why? Because, as all authority states,
It's just such deeds that Heaven abominates.

AGNÈS

Abominates! But why should Heaven feel so?

It's all so charming and so sweet, you know!
I never knew about this sort of thing
Till now, or guessed what raptures it could bring.

ARNOLPHE

Yes, all these promises of love undying,
These sighs, these kisses, are most gratifying,
But they must be enjoyed in the proper way;
One must be married first, that is to say.

AGNÈS

And once you're married, there's no evil in it?

ARNOLPHE

That's right.

AGNÈS

Oh, let me marry, then, this minute!

ARNOLPHE

If that's what you desire, I feel the same;
It was to plan your marriage that I came.

AGNÈS

What! Truly?

ARNOLPHE

Yes.

AGNÈS

How happy I shall be!

ARNOLPHE

Yes, wedded life will please you, I foresee.

AGNÈS

You really intend that we two—

ARNOLPHE
Yes, I do.

AGNÈS
Oh, how I'll kiss you if that dream comes true!

ARNOLPHE
And I'll return your kisses, every one.

AGNÈS
I'm never sure when people are making fun.
Are you quite serious?

ARNOLPHE
Yes, I'm serious. Quite.

AGNÈS
We're to be married?

ARNOLPHE
Yes.

AGNÈS
But when?

ARNOLPHE
Tonight.

AGNÈS, *laughing*
Tonight?

ARNOLPHE
Tonight. It seems you're moved to laughter.

AGNÈS
Yes.

ARNOLPHE

Well, to see you happy is what I'm after.

AGNÈS

Oh, Sir, I owe you more than I can express!
With him, my life will be pure happiness!

ARNOLPHE

With whom?

AGNÈS

With . . . him.

ARNOLPHE

With *him*! Well, think again.
You're rather hasty in your choice of men.
It's quite another husband I have in mind;
And as for "him," as you call him, be so kind,
Regardless of his pitiable disease,
As never again to see him, if you please.
When next he calls, girl, put him in his place
By slamming the door directly in his face;
Then, if he knocks, go up and drop a brick
From the second-floor window. That should do the trick.
Do you understand, Agnès? I shall be hidden
Nearby, to see that you do as you are bidden.

AGNÈS

Oh, dear, he's so good-looking, so—

ARNOLPHE

Be still!

AGNÈS

I just won't have the heart—

ARNOLPHE

Enough; you will.

Now go upstairs.

AGNÈS

How can you—

ARNOLPHE

Do as I say.

I'm master here; I've spoken; go, obey.

Act Three
SCENE ONE

———— •••• ————

Arnolphe, Agnès, Alain, Georgette

ARNOLPHE

Yes, I'm most pleased; it couldn't have gone better.
By following my instructions to the letter,
You've put that young philanderer to flight:
See how wise generalship can set things right.
Your innocence had been abused, Agnès;
Unwittingly, you'd got into a mess,
And, lacking my good counsel, you were well
Embarked upon a course which leads to Hell.
Those beaux are all alike, believe you me:
They've ribbons, plumes, and ruffles at the knee,
Fine wigs, and polished talk, and brilliant teeth,
But they're all scales and talons underneath—
Indeed, they're devils of the vilest sort,
Who prey on women's honor for their sport.
However, owing to my watchful care,
You have emerged intact from this affair.
The firm and righteous way in which you threw
That brick at him, and dashed his hopes of you,
Persuades me that there's no cause to delay
The wedding which I promised you today.
But first, it would be well for me to make
A few remarks for your improvement's sake.
    (*To Alain, who brings a chair:*)
I'll sit here, where it's cool.
    (*To Georgette:*) Remember, now—

GEORGETTE

Oh, Sir, we won't forget again, I vow.
That young man won't get round us any more.

ALAIN

I'll give up drink if he gets through that door.
Anyway, he's an idiot; we bit
Two coins he gave us, and they were counterfeit.

ARNOLPHE

Well, go and buy the food for supper, and then
One of you, as you're coming home again,
Can fetch the local notary from the square.
Tell him that there's a contract to prepare.

SCENE TWO

Arnolphe, Agnès

ARNOLPHE, *seated*

Agnès, stop knitting and hear what I have to say.
Lift up your head a bit, and turn this way.
        (*Putting his finger to his forehead:*)
Look at me *there* while I talk to you, right *there*,
And listen to my every word with care.
My dear, I'm going to wed you, and you should bless
Your vast good fortune and your happiness.
Reflect upon your former low estate,
And judge, then, if my goodness is not great
In raising you, a humble peasant lass,
To be a matron of the middle class,
To share the bed and the connubial bliss
Of one who's shunned the married state till this,
Withholding from a charming score or two
The honor which he now bestows on you.
Be ever mindful, Agnès, that you would be,
Without this union, a nonentity;
And let that thought incline your heart to merit
The name which I shall lend you, and to bear it
With such propriety that I shall never
Regret my choice for any cause whatever.
Marriage, Agnès, is no light matter; the role
Of wife requires austerity of soul,
And I do not exalt you to that station
To lead a life of heedless dissipation.
Yours is the weaker sex, please realize;
It is the beard in which all power lies,
And though there are two portions of mankind,
Those portions are not equal, you will find:
One half commands, the other must obey;
The second serves the first in every way;
And that obedience which the soldier owes

His general, or the loyal servant shows
His master, or the good child pays his sire,
Or the stern abbot looks for in the friar,
Is nothing to the pure docility,
The deep submission and humility
Which a good wife must ever exhibit toward
The man who is her master, chief, and lord.
Should he regard her with a serious air,
She must avert her eyes, and never dare
To lift them to his face again, unless
His look should change to one of tenderness.
Such things aren't understood by women today,
But don't let bad example lead you astray.
Don't emulate those flirts whose indiscretions
Are told all over town at gossip-sessions,
Or yield to Satan's trickery by allowing
Young fops to please you with their smiles and bowing.
Remember that, in marrying, I confide
To you, Agnès, my honor and my pride;
That honor is a tender, fragile thing
With which there can be no light dallying;
And that all misbehaving wives shall dwell
In ever-boiling cauldrons down in Hell.
These are no idle lessons which I impart,
And you'll do well to get them all by heart.
Your soul, if you observe them, and abjure
Flirtation, will be lily-white and pure;
But deviate from honor, and your soul
Will forthwith grow as vile and black as coal;
All will abhor you as a thing of evil,
Till one day you'll be taken by the Devil,
And Hell's eternal fire is where he'll send you—
From which sad fate may Heaven's grace defend you.
Make me a curtsey. Now then, just as a novice,
Entering the convent, learns by heart her office,
So, entering wedlock, you should do the same.
                    (*He rises.*)
I have, in my pocket, a book of no small fame

From which you'll learn the office of a wife.
'T was written by some man of pious life.
Study his teaching faithfully, and heed it.
Here, take the book; let's hear how well you read it.

AGNÈS, *reading*

The Maxims of Marriage
or
The Duties of a Married Woman,
Together with Her Daily Exercises.

First Maxim:
A woman who in church has said
She'll love and honor and obey
Should get it firmly in her head,
Despite the fashions of the day,
That he who took her for his own
Has taken her for his bed alone.

ARNOLPHE
I shall explain that; doubtless you're perplexed.
But, for the present, let us hear what's next.

AGNÈS, *continuing*
Second Maxim:
She needs no fine attire
More than he may desire
Who is her lord and master.
To dress for any taste but his is vain;
If others find her plain,
'T is no disaster.

Third Maxim:
Let her not daub her face
With paint and patch and powder-base
And creams which promise beauty on the label.
It is not for their husbands' sake

But vanity's, that women undertake
The labors of the dressing table.

Fourth Maxim:

Let her be veiled whenever she leaves the house,
So that her features are obscure and dim.
If she desires to please her spouse,
She must please no one else but him.

Fifth Maxim:

Except for friends who call
To see her husband, let her not admit
      Anyone at all.
      A visitor whose end
Is to amuse the wife with gallant wit
      Is *not* the husband's friend.

Sixth Maxim:

To men who would confer kind gifts upon her,
She must reply with self-respecting nays.
Not to refuse would be to court dishonor.
Nothing is given for nothing nowadays.

Seventh Maxim:

She has no need, whatever she may think,
Of writing table, paper, pen, or ink.
In a proper house, the husband is the one
To do whatever writing's to be done.

Eighth Maxim:

At those licentious things
Called social gatherings,
Wives are corrupted by the worldly crowd.
Since, at such functions, amorous plots are laid
      And married men betrayed,
      They should not be allowed.

Ninth Maxim:

Let the wise wife, who cares for her good name,
Decline to play at any gambling game.
In such seductive pastimes wives can lose
Far more than coins, or bills, or I.O.U.'s.

Tenth Maxim:

It is not good for wives
To go on gay excursions,
Picnics, or country drives.
In all such light diversions,
No matter who's the host,
The husbands pay the most

Eleventh Maxim—

ARNOLPHE

Good. Read the rest to yourself. I'll clarify
Whatever may confuse you, by and by.
I've just recalled some business I'd forgot;
'T will only take a moment, like as not.
Go in, and treat that precious book with care.
If the notary comes, tell him to have a chair.

SCENE THREE

———•◦•———

Arnolphe

ARNOLPHE

What could be safer than to marry her?
She'll do and be whatever I prefer.
She's like a lump of wax, and I can mold her
Into what shape I like, as she grows older.
True, she was almost lured away from me,
Whilst I was gone, through her simplicity;
But if one's wife must have some imperfection,
It's best that she should err in that direction.
Such faults as hers are easy to remove:
A simple wife is eager to improve,
And if she has been led astray, a slight
Admonitory talk will set her right.
But a clever wife's another kettle of fish:
One's at the mercy of her every wish;
What she desires, she'll have at any cost,
And reasoning with her is labor lost.
Her wicked wit makes virtues of her crimes,
Makes mock of principle, and oftentimes
Contrives, in furtherance of some wicked plan,
Intrigues which can defeat the shrewdest man.
Against her there is no defense, for she's
Unbeatable at plots and strategies,
And once she has resolved to amputate
Her husband's honor, he must bow to fate.
There's many a decent man could tell that story.
But that young fool will have no chance to glory
In my disgrace: he has too loose a tongue,
And that's a fault of Frenchmen, old or young.
When they are lucky in a love affair,
To keep the secret's more than they can bear;
A foolish vanity torments them, till
They'd rather hang, by Heaven, than be still.

What but the spells of Satan could incline
Women to favor men so asinine?
But here he comes; my feelings must not show
As I extract from him his tale of woe.

SCENE FOUR

———— •◆• ————

Horace, Arnolphe

HORACE
I've just been at your house, and I begin
To fear I'm fated never to find you in.
But I'll persist, and one day have the joy—

ARNOLPHE
Ah, come, no idle compliments, my boy.
All this fine talk, so flowery and so polished,
Is something I'd be glad to see abolished.
It's a vile custom: most men waste two-thirds
Of every day exchanging empty words.
Let's put our hats on, now, and be at ease.
Well, how's your love life going? Do tell me, please.
I was a bit distrait when last we met,
But what you told me I did not forget:
Your bold beginnings left me much impressed,
And now I'm all agog to hear the rest.

HORACE
Since I unlocked my heart to you, alas,
My hopes have come to an unhappy pass.

ARNOLPHE
Oh, dear! How so?

HORACE
                    Just now—alas—I learned
That my beloved's guardian has returned.

ARNOLPHE
That's bad.

HORACE

What's more, he's well aware that we've
Been meeting secretly, without his leave.

ARNOLPHE

But how could he so quickly find that out?

HORACE

I don't know, but he has, beyond a doubt.
I went at my usual hour, more or less,
To pay my homage to her loveliness,
And found the servants changed in attitude.
They barred my way; their words and looks were rude.
"Be off!" they told me, and with no good grace
They slammed the door directly in my face.

ARNOLPHE

Right in your face!

HORACE

Yes.

ARNOLPHE

Dreadful. Tell me more.

HORACE

I tried to reason with them through the door,
But whatsoever I said to them, they cried,
"The master says you're not to come inside."

ARNOLPHE

They wouldn't open it?

HORACE

No. And then Agnès,
On orders from her guardian, as one could guess,
Came to her window, said that she was sick
Of my attentions, and threw down a brick.

ARNOLPHE

A brick, you say!

HORACE

A brick; and it wasn't small.
Not what one hopes for when one pays a call.

ARNOLPHE

Confound it! That's no mild rebuff, my lad.
I fear your situation's pretty bad.

HORACE

Yes, that old fool's return has spoiled my game.

ARNOLPHE

You have my deepest sympathy; it's a shame.

HORACE

He's wrecked my plans.

ARNOLPHE

Oh, come; you've lost some ground,
But some means of recouping will be found.

HORACE

With a little inside help, I might by chance
Outwit this jealous fellow's vigilance.

ARNOLPHE

That should be easy. The lady, as you say,
Loves you.

HORACE

Indeed, yes.

ARNOLPHE

Then you'll find a way.

HORACE

I hope so.

ARNOLPHE

You must not be put to flight
By that ungracious brick.

HORACE

Of course you're right.
I knew at once that that old fool was back
And secretly directing the attack.
But what amazed me (you'll be amazed as well)
Was something else she did, of which I'll tell—
A daring trick one wouldn't expect to see
Played by a girl of such simplicity.
Love is indeed a wondrous master, Sir,
Whose teaching makes us what we never were,
And under whose miraculous tuition
One suddenly can change one's disposition.
It overturns our settled inclinations,
Causing the most astounding transformations:
The miser's made a spendthrift overnight,
The coward valiant, and the boor polite;
Love spurs the sluggard on to high endeavor,
And moves the artless maiden to be clever.
Well, such a miracle has changed Agnès.
She cried, just now, with seeming bitterness,
"Go! I refuse to see you, and don't ask why;
To all your questions, here is my reply!"—
And having made that statement, down she threw
The brick I've mentioned, and a letter, too.
Note how her words apply to brick *and* letter:
Isn't that fine? Could any ruse be better?
Aren't you amazed? Do you see what great effect
True love can have upon the intellect?
Can you deny its power to inspire
The gentlest heart with fortitude and fire?
How do you like that trick with the letter, eh?

A most astute young woman, wouldn't you say?
As for my jealous rival, isn't the role
He's played in this affair extremely droll?
Well?

ARNOLPHE
   Yes, quite droll.

HORACE
              Well, laugh, if that's the case!
  (*Arnolphe gives a forced laugh.*)
My, what a fool! He fortifies his place
Against me, using bricks for cannon balls,
As if he feared that I might storm the walls;
What's more, in his anxiety he rallies
His two domestics to repulse my sallies;
And then he's hoodwinked by the girl he meant
To keep forever meek and innocent!
I must confess that, though this silly man's
Return to town has balked my amorous plans,
The whole thing's been so comical that I find
That I'm convulsed whenever it comes to mind.
You haven't laughed as much as I thought you would.

ARNOLPHE, *with a forced laugh*
I beg your pardon; I've done the best I could.

HORACE
But let me show you the letter she wrote, my friend.
What her heart feels, her artless hand has penned
In the most touching terms, the sweetest way,
With pure affection, purest naïveté;
Nature herself, I think, would so express
Love's first awakening and its sweet distress.

ARNOLPHE, *aside*
Behold what scribbling leads to! It was quite
Against my wishes that she learned to write.

HORACE, *reading*

I am moved to write to you, but I am much at a loss as to how to begin. I have thoughts which I should like you to know of; but I don't know how to go about telling them to you, and I mistrust my own words. I begin to perceive that I have always been kept in a state of ignorance, and so I am fearful of writing something I shouldn't, or of saying more than I ought. In truth, I don't know what you have done to me, but I know that I am mortally vexed by the harsh things I am made to do to you, that it will be the most painful thing in the world to give you up, and that I would be happy indeed to be yours. Perhaps it is rash of me to say that; but in any case I cannot help saying it, and I wish that I could have my desire without doing anything wrong. I am constantly told that all young men are deceivers, that they mustn't be listened to, and that all you have said to me is mere trickery; I assure you, however, that I have not yet been able to think that of you, and your words so touch me that I cannot believe them false. Please tell me frankly what you intend; for truly, since my own intentions are blameless, it would be very wicked of you to deceive me, and I think that I should die of despair.

ARNOLPHE, *aside*

The bitch!

HORACE

What's wrong?

ARNOLPHE

Oh, nothing: I was sneezing.

HORACE

Was ever a style so amiable, so pleasing?
Despite the tyranny she's had to bear,
Isn't her nature sweet beyond compare?
And is it not a crime of the basest kind
For anyone to stifle such a mind,
To starve so fine a spirit, and to enshroud

In ignorance a soul so well-endowed?
Love has begun to waken her, however,
And if some kind star favors my endeavor
I'll free her from that utter beast, that black
Villain, that wretch, that brute, that maniac—

ARNOLPHE

Good-bye.

HORACE

What, going?

ARNOLPHE

I've just recalled that I'm
Due somewhere else in a few minutes' time.

HORACE

Wait! Can you think of someone who might possess
An entrée to that house, and to Agnès?
I hate to trouble you, but do please lend
Whatever help you can, as friend to friend.
The servants, as I said, both man and maid,
Have turned against my cause, and can't be swayed.
Just now, despite my every blandishment,
They eyed me coldly, and would not relent.
I had, for a time, the aid of an old woman
Whose talent for intrigue was superhuman;
She served me, at the start, with much success,
But died four days ago, to my distress.
Don't you know someone who could help me out?

ARNOLPHE

I don't; but you'll find someone, I don't doubt.

HORACE

Farewell, then, Sir. You'll be discreet, I know.

SCENE FIVE

Arnolphe

ARNOLPHE

In that boy's presence, what hell I undergo,
Trying to hide my anguish from his eye!
To think that an innocent girl should prove so sly!
Either she's fooled me, and never *was* naïve,
Or Satan's just now taught her to deceive.
That cursèd letter! I wish that I were dead.
Plainly that callow wretch has turned her head,
Captured her mind and heart, eclipsed me there,
And doomed me to distraction and despair.
The loss of her entails a double hell:
My honor suffers, and my love as well.
It drives me mad to see myself displaced,
And all my careful planning gone to waste.
To be revenged on her, I need but wait
And let her giddy passion meet its fate;
The upshot can't be anything but bad.
But oh, to lose the thing one loves is sad.
Good Lord! To rear her with such calculation,
And then fall victim to infatuation!
She has no funds, no family, yet she can dare
Abuse my lavish kindness and my care;
And what, for Heaven's sake, is my reaction?
In spite of all, I love her to distraction!
Have you no shame, fool? Don't you resent her crimes?
Oh, I could slap my face a thousand times!
I'll go inside for a bit, but only to see
How she will face me after her treachery.
Kind Heaven, let no dishonor stain my brow;
Or if it is decreed that I must bow
To that misfortune, lend me at least, I pray,
Such patient strength as some poor men display.

Act Four

SCENE ONE

Arnolphe

ARNOLPHE, *entering from the house, alone*
I can't hold still a minute, I declare.
My anxious thoughts keep darting here and there,
Planning defenses, seeking to prevent
That rascal from achieving his intent.
How calm the traitress looked when I went in!
Despite her crimes, she shows no sense of sin,
And though she's all but sent me to my grave,
How like a little saint she dares behave!
The more she sat there, cool and unperturbed,
The less I thought my fury could be curbed;
Yet, strange to say, my heart's increasing ire
Seemed only to redouble my desire.
I was embittered, desperate, irate,
And yet her beauty had never seemed so great.
Never did her bright eyes so penetrate me,
So rouse my spirit, so infatuate me;
Oh, it would break the heart within my breast
Should fate subject me to this cruel jest.
What! Have I supervised her education
With loving care and long consideration,
Sheltered her since she was a tiny creature,
Cherished sweet expectations for her future,
For thirteen years molded her character
And based my hopes of happiness on her,
Only to see some young fool steal the prize
Of her affection, under my very eyes,
And just when she and I were all but wed?
Ah, no, young friend! Ah, no, young chucklehead!

I mean to stop you; I swear that you shall not
Succeed, however well you scheme and plot,
And that you'll have no cause to laugh at me.

SCENE TWO

———— ◆ ————

The Notary, Arnolphe

NOTARY

Ah, here you are, Sir! I am the notary.
So, there's a contract which you'd have me draw?

ARNOLPHE, *unaware of the notary*

How shall I do it?

NOTARY

According to the law.

ARNOLPHE, *still oblivious*

I must be prudent, and think what course is best.

NOTARY

I shall do nothing against your interest.

ARNOLPHE, *oblivious*

One must anticipate the unexpected.

NOTARY

In my hands, you'll be thoroughly protected.
But do remember, lest you be betrayed,
To sign no contract till the dowry's paid.

ARNOLPHE, *oblivious*

I must act covertly; if this thing gets out,
The gossips will have much to blab about.

NOTARY

If you're so anxious not to make a stir,
The contract can be drawn in secret, Sir.

ARNOLPHE, *oblivious*
But how shall she be dealt with? Can I condone—

NOTARY
The dowry is proportional to her own.

ARNOLPHE, *oblivious*
It's hard to be strict with one whom you adore.

NOTARY
In that case, you may wish to give her more.

ARNOLPHE, *oblivious*
How should I treat the girl? I must decide.

NOTARY
As a general rule, the husband gives the bride
A dowry that's one-third the size of hers;
But he may increase the sum, if he prefers.

ARNOLPHE, *oblivious*
If—

NOTARY, *Arnolphe now noticing him*
As for property, and its division
In case of death, the husband makes provision
As he thinks best.

ARNOLPHE
Eh?

NOTARY
He can make certain of
His bride's security, and show his love,
By jointure, or a settlement whereby
The gift is canceled should the lady die,
Reverting to her heirs, if so agreed;
Or go by common law; or have a deed

Of gift appended to the instrument,
Either by his sole wish, or by consent.
Why shrug your shoulders? Am I talking rot?
Do I know contracts, Sir, or do I not?
Who could instruct me? Who would be so bold?
Do I not know that spouses jointly hold
Goods, chattels, lands, and money in their two names,
Unless one party should renounce all claims?
Do I not know that a third of the bride's resources
Enters the joint estate—

ARNOLPHE
                            All that, of course, is
True. But who asked for all this pedantry?

NOTARY
You did! And now you sniff and shrug at me,
And treat my competence with ridicule.

ARNOLPHE
The devil take this ugly-featured fool!
Good day, good day. An end to all this chatter.

NOTARY
Did you not ask my aid in a legal matter?

ARNOLPHE
Yes, yes, but now the matter's been deferred.
When your advice is needed, I'll send word.
Meanwhile, stop blathering, you blatherskite!

NOTARY
He's mad, I judge; and I think my judgment's right.

SCENE THREE

———————•———————

The Notary, Alain, Georgette, Arnolphe

NOTARY, *to Alain and Georgette*
Your master sent you to fetch me, isn't that so?

ALAIN

Yes.

NOTARY
How you feel about him I don't know,
But I regard him as a senseless boor.
Tell him I said so.

GEORGETTE
We will, you may be sure.

SCENE FOUR

———————— • ▬ ————————

Alain, Georgette, Arnolphe

ALAIN

Sir—

ARNOLPHE

    Ah, come here, my good friends, tried and true:
You've amply proved that I may count on you.

ALAIN

The notary—

ARNOLPHE

          Tell me later, will you not?
My honor's threatened by a vicious plot;
Think, children, what distress you'd feel, what shame,
If some dishonor touched your master's name!
You wouldn't dare to leave the house, for fear
That all the town would point at you, and sneer.
Since we're together, then, in this affair,
You must be ever watchful, and take care
That no approach that gallant may adopt—

GEORGETTE

We've learned our lesson, Sir; he shall be stopped.

ARNOLPHE

Beware his fine words and his flatteries.

ALAIN

Of course.

GEORGETTE

    We can resist such talk with ease.

ARNOLPHE, *to Alain*

What if he said, "Alain, for mercy's sake,
Do me a kindness"—what answer would you make?

ALAIN

I'd say, "You fool!"

ARNOLPHE

Good, good. (*To Georgette:*)
"Georgette, my dear,
I'm sure you're just as sweet as you appear."

GEORGETTE

"Fathead!"

ARNOLPHE

Good, good. (*To Alain:*) "Come, let me in.
You know
That my intent is pure as the driven snow."

ALAIN

"Sir, you're a knave!"

ARNOLPHE

Well said. (*To Georgette:*) "Unless you
take
Pity on my poor heart, it's sure to break."

GEORGETTE

"You are an impudent ass!"

ARNOLPHE

Well said, Georgette.
"I'm not the sort of person to forget
A favor, or begrudge the *quid pro quo*,
As these few coins, Alain, will serve to show.
And you, Georgette, take this and buy a dress.
(*Both hold out their hands and take the money.*)

That's but a specimen of my largesse.
And all I ask is that you grant to me
An hour of your young mistress' company."

GEORGETTE, *giving him a shove*
"You're crazy!"

ARNOLPHE
Good!

ALAIN, *shoving Arnolphe*
"Move on!"

ARNOLPHE
Good!

GEORGETTE, *shoving Arnolphe*
"Out of my sight!"

ARNOLPHE
Good, good—but that's enough.

GEORGETTE
Did I do it right?

ALAIN
Is that how we're to treat him?

ARNOLPHE
You were fine;
Except for the money, which you should decline.

GEORGETTE
We didn't think, Sir. That was wrong indeed.

ALAIN
Would you like to do it over again?

ARNOLPHE
No need;
Go back inside.

ALAIN
Sir, if you say the word, we—

ARNOLPHE
No, that will do; go in at once; you heard me.
Just keep the money; I shall be with you shortly.
Be on your guard, and ready to support me.

SCENE FIVE

Arnolphe

ARNOLPHE

The cobbler at the corner is sharp of eye;
I think that I'll enlist him as a spy.
As for Agnès, I'll keep her under guard,
And all dishonest women shall be barred—
Hairdressers, glovers, handkerchief-makers, those
Who come to the door with ribbons, pins, and bows,
And often, as a sideline to such wares,
Are go-betweens in secret love affairs.
I know the world, and the tricks that people use;
That boy will have to invent some brand-new ruse
If he's to get a message in to her.

SCENE SIX

———•◆•———

Horace, Arnolphe

HORACE

What luck to find you in this quarter, Sir!
I've just had a narrow escape, believe you me!
Just after I left you, whom did I chance to see
Upon her shady balcony, but the fair
Agnès, who had come out to take the air!
She managed, having signaled me to wait,
To steal downstairs and open the garden gate.
We went to her room, and were no sooner there
Than we heard her jealous guardian on the stair;
In which great peril I was thrust by her
Into a wardrobe where her dresses were.
He entered. I couldn't see him, but I heard
Him striding back and forth without a word,
Heaving deep sighs of woe again and again,
Pounding upon the tables now and then,
Kicking a little dog, who yipped in fright,
And throwing her possessions left and right.
What's more, to give his fury full release,
He knocked two vases off her mantelpiece.
Clearly the old goat had some vague, dismaying
Sense of the tricks his captive had been playing.
At last, when all his anger had been spent
On objects which were dumb and innocent,
The frantic man, without a word, went striding
Out of the room, and I came out of hiding.
Quite naturally, we didn't dare extend
Our rendezvous, because our jealous friend
Was still about; tonight, however, I
Shall visit her, quite late, and on the sly.
Our plan is this: I'll cough, three times, outside;
At that, the window will be opened wide;
Then, with a ladder and the assistance of

Agnès, I'll climb into our bower of love.
Since you're my only friend, I tell you this—
For telling, as you know, augments one's bliss.
However vast the joy, one must confide
In someone else before one's satisfied.
You share, I know, my happy expectations.
But now, farewell; I must make preparations.

SCENE SEVEN

Arnolphe

ARNOLPHE
The evil star that's hounding me to death
Gives me no time in which to catch my breath!
Must I, again and again, be forced to see
My measures foiled through their complicity?
Shall I, at my ripe age, be duped, forsooth,
By a green girl and by a harebrained youth?
For twenty years I've sagely contemplated
The woeful lives of men unwisely mated,
And analyzed with care the slips whereby
The best-planned marriages have gone awry;
Thus schooled by others' failures, I felt that I'd
Be able, when I chose to take a bride,
To ward off all mischance, and be protected
From griefs to which so many are subjected.
I took, to that end, all the shrewd and wise
Precautions which experience could devise;
Yet, as if fate had made the stern decision
That no man living should escape derision,
I find, for all my pondering of this
Great matter, all my keen analysis,
The twenty years and more which I have spent
In planning to escape the embarrassment
So many husbands suffer from today,
That I'm as badly victimized as they.
But no, damned fate, I challenge your decree!
The lovely prize is in my custody,
And though her heart's been filched by that young pest,
I guarantee that he'll not get the rest,
And that this evening's gallant rendezvous
Won't go as smoothly as they'd like it to.
There's one good thing about my present fix—

That I'm forewarned of all my rival's tricks,
And that this oaf who's aiming to undo me
Confesses all his bad intentions to me.

SCENE EIGHT

Chrysalde, Arnolphe

CHRYSALDE
Well, shall we dine, and then go out for a stroll?

ARNOLPHE
No, no, the dinner's off.

CHRYSALDE
Well, well, how droll!

ARNOLPHE
Forgive me: there's a crisis I must face.

CHRYSALDE
Your wedding plans have changed? Is that the case?

ARNOLPHE
I have no need of your solicitude.

CHRYSALDE
Tell me your troubles, now, and don't be rude.
I'd guess, friend, that your marriage scheme has met
With difficulties, and that you're upset.
To judge by your expression, I'd almost swear it.

ARNOLPHE
Whatever happens, I shall have the merit
Of not resembling some in this community,
Who let young gallants cheat them with impunity.

CHRYSALDE
It's odd that you, with your good intellect,
Are so obsessive in this one respect,
Measure all happiness thereby, and base

On it alone men's honor or disgrace.
Greed, envy, vice, and cowardice are not
Important sins to you; the one grave blot
You find on any scutcheon seems to be
The crime of having suffered cuckoldry.
Now, come: shall a man be robbed of his good name
Through an ill chance for which he's not to blame?
Shall a good husband lacerate his soul
With guilt for matters not in his control?
When a man marries, why must we scorn or praise him
According to whether or not his wife betrays him?
And if she does so, why must her husband see
The fact as an immense catastrophe?
Do realize that, to a man of sense,
There's nothing crushing in such accidents;
That, since no man can dodge the blows of fate,
One's sense of failure should not be too great,
And that there's no harm done, whatever they say,
If one but takes things in the proper way.
In difficulties of this sort, it seems,
As always, wiser to avoid extremes.
One shouldn't ape those husbands who permit
Such scandal, and who take a pride in it,
Dropping the names of their wives' latest gallants,
Praising their persons, bragging of their talents,
Professing warm regard for them, attending
The parties that they give, and so offending
Society, which properly resents
Displays of laxity and impudence.
Needless to say, such conduct will not do;
And yet the other extreme's improper too.
If men do wrong to flatter their wives' gallants,
It's no less bad when, lacking tact and balance,
They vent their grievances with savage fury,
Calling the whole world to be judge and jury,
And won't be satisfied till they acquaint
All ears whatever with their loud complaint.
Between these two extremes, my friend, there lies

A middle way that's favored by the wise,
And which, if followed, will preserve one's face
However much one's wife may court disgrace.
In short, then, cuckoldry need not be dreaded
Like some dire monster, fierce and many-headed;
It can be lived with, if one has the wit
To take it calmly, and make the best of it.

ARNOLPHE

For that fine speech, the great fraternity
Of cuckolds owes you thanks, your Excellency;
And all men, if they heard your wisdom, would
Make joyous haste to join the brotherhood.

CHRYSALDE

No, that I shouldn't approve. But since it's fate
Whereby we're joined to one or another mate,
One should take marriage as one takes picquette,
In which, if one has made a losing bet,
One takes the setback calmly, and takes pains
To do the best one can with what remains.

ARNOLPHE

In other words, eat hearty and sleep tight,
And tell yourself that everything's all right.

CHRYSALDE

Laugh on, my friend; but I can, in all sobriety,
Name fifty things which cause me more anxiety,
And would, if they occurred, appall me more
Than this misfortune which you so abhor.
Had I to choose between adversities,
I'd rather be a cuckold, if you please,
Than marry one of those good wives who find
Continual reason to upbraid mankind,
Those virtuous shrews, those fiendish paragons,
As violently chaste as Amazons,
Who, having had the goodness not to horn us,

Accord themselves the right to nag and scorn us,
And make us pay for their fidelity
By being as vexatious as can be.
Do learn, friend, that when all is said and done,
Cuckoldry's what you make of it; that one
Might welcome it in certain situations,
And that, like all things, it has compensations.

ARNOLPHE

Well, if you want it, may you get your wish;
But, as for me, it's not at all my dish.
Before I'd let my brow be decked with horn—

CHRYSALDE

Tut, tut! Don't swear, or you may be forsworn.
If fate has willed it, your resolves will fail,
And all your oaths will be of no avail.

ARNOLPHE

I! I a cuckold?

CHRYSALDE

                   Don't let it fret you so.
It happens to the best of men, you know.
Cuckolds exist with whom, if I may be frank,
You can't compare for person, wealth, or rank.

ARNOLPHE

I have no wish to be compared with such.
Enough, now, of your mockery; it's too much.
You try my patience.

CHRYSALDE

                   So, you're annoyed with me?
Ah, well. Good-bye. But bear in mind that he
Who thumps his chest and swears upon his soul
That he will never play the cuckold's role
Is studying for the part, and may well get it.

ARNOLPHE
That won't occur, I swear; I shall not let it.
I shall remove that threat this very minute.
                    (*He knocks at his own gate.*)

SCENE NINE

———— • ————

Alain, Georgette, Arnolphe

ARNOLPHE

My friends, the battle's joined, and we must win it.
Your love for me, by which I'm touched and moved,
Must now, in this emergency, be proved,
And if your deeds repay my confidence,
You may expect a handsome recompense.
This very night—don't tell a soul, my friends—
A certain rascal whom you know intends
To scale the wall and see Agnès; but we
Shall lay a little trap for him, we three.
You'll both be armed with clubs, and when the young
Villain has almost reached the topmost rung
(I meanwhile shall have flung the shutters wide),
You shall lean out and so lambaste his hide,
So bruise his ribs by your combined attack,
That he will never dream of coming back.
Don't speak my name while this is happening, mind you,
Or let him know that I am there behind you.
Have you the pluck to serve me in this action?

ALAIN

If blows are called for, we can give satisfaction.
I'll show you that this good right arm's not lame.

GEORGETTE

Mine looks less strong than his, but all the same
Our foe will know that he's been beaten by it.

ARNOLPHE

Go in, then; and, whatever you do, keep quiet.

(*Alone:*)
Tonight, I'll give a lesson to mankind.
If all endangered husbands took a mind
To greet their wives' intrusive gallants thus,
Cuckolds, I think, would be less numerous.

Act Five

SCENE ONE

———— • ————

Alain, Georgette, Arnolphe

ARNOLPHE

You brutes! What made you be so heavy-handed?

ALAIN

But, Sir, we only did as you commanded.

ARNOLPHE

Don't put the blame on me; your guilt is plain.
I wished him beaten; I didn't wish him slain.
And furthermore, if you'll recall, I said
To hit him on the ribs, not on the head.
It's a ghastly situation in which I'm placed;
How is this young man's murder to be faced?
Go in, now, and be silent as the grave
About that innocent command I gave.
                    (*Alone:*)
It's nearly daybreak. I must take thought, and see
How best to cope with this dire tragedy.
God help me! What will the boy's father say
When this appalling story comes his way?

SCENE TWO

Horace, Arnolphe

HORACE

Who's this, I wonder. I'd best approach with care.

ARNOLPHE

How could I have foreseen . . . I say, who's there?

HORACE

Seigneur Arnolphe?

ARNOLPHE

    Yes—

HORACE

        It's Horace, once more.
My, you're up early! I was heading for
Your house, to ask a favor.

ARNOLPHE

        Oh, God, I'm dizzy.
Is he a vision? Is he a ghost? What is he?

HORACE

Sir, I'm in trouble once again, I fear.
It's providential that you should appear
Just at the moment when your help was needed.
My plans, I'm happy to tell you, have succeeded
Beyond all expectations, and despite
An incident which might have spoiled them quite.
I don't know how it happened, but someone knew
About our contemplated rendezvous;
For, just as I'd almost reached her window sill,
I saw some frightful figures, armed to kill,
Lean out above me, waving their clubs around.

I lost my footing, tumbled to the ground,
And thus, though rather scratched and bruised, was spared
The thumping welcome which they had prepared.
Those brutes (of whom Old Jealous, I suppose,
Was one) ascribed my tumble to their blows,
And since I lay there, motionless, in the dirt
For several minutes, being stunned and hurt,
They judged that they had killed me, and they all
Took fright at that, and so began to brawl.
I lay in silence, hearing their angry cries:
They blamed each other for my sad demise,
Then tiptoed out, in darkness and in dread,
To feel my body, and see if I were dead.
As you can well imagine, I played the part
Of a limp, broken corpse with all my heart.
Quite overcome with terror, they withdrew,
And I was thinking of withdrawing, too,
When young Agnès came hurrying, out of breath
And much dismayed by my supposèd death:
She had been able, of course, to overhear
All that my foes had babbled in their fear,
And while they were distracted and unnerved
She'd slipped from the house, entirely unobserved.
Ah, how she wept with happiness when she found
That I was, after all, both safe and sound!
Well, to be brief: electing to be guided
By her own heart, the charming girl decided
Not to return to her guardian, but to flee,
Entrusting her security to me.
What must his tyranny be, if it can force
So shy a girl to take so bold a course!
And think what peril she might thus incur,
If I were capable of wronging her.
Ah, but my love's too pure for that, too strong;
I'd rather die than do her any wrong;
So admirable is she that all I crave
Is to be with her even to the grave.
I know my father: this will much displease him,

But we shall manage somehow to appease him.
In any case, she's won my heart, and I
Could not desert her, even if I chose to try.
The favor I ask of you is rather large:
It's that you take my darling in your charge,
And keep her, if you will, for several days
In your own house, concealed from the world's gaze.
I ask your help in this because I'm bent
On throwing all pursuers off the scent;
Also because, if she were seen with me,
There might be talk of impropriety.
To you, my loyal friend, I've dared to impart,
Without reserve, the secrets of my heart,
And likewise it's to you I now confide
My dearest treasure and my future bride.

ARNOLPHE

I'm at your service; on that you may depend.

HORACE

You'll grant the favor that I ask, dear friend?

ARNOLPHE

Of course; most willingly. I'm glad indeed
That I can help you in your hour of need.
Thank Heaven that you asked me! There's no request
To which I could accede with greater zest.

HORACE

How kind you are! What gratitude I feel!
I feared you might refuse my rash appeal;
But you're a man of the world, urbane and wise,
Who looks upon young love with tolerant eyes.
My man is guarding her, just down the street.

ARNOLPHE

It's almost daylight. Where had we better meet?
Someone might see me, if you brought her here,

And should you bring her to my house, I fear
'T would start the servants talking. We must look
For some more shadowy and secluded nook.
That garden's handy; I shall await her there.

HORACE

You're right, Sir. We must act with the utmost care.
I'll go, and quickly bring Agnès to you,
Then seek my lodgings without more ado.

ARNOLPHE, *alone*

Ah, Fortune! This good turn will compensate
For all the tricks you've played on me of late.
(*He hides his face in his cloak.*)

SCENE THREE

Agnès, Horace, Arnolphe

HORACE
Just come with me; there's no cause for alarm.
I'm taking you where you'll be safe from harm.
To stay together would be suicide:
Go in, and let this gentleman be your guide.
      (*Arnolphe, whom she does not recognize, takes her hand.*)

AGNÈS
Why are you leaving me?

HORACE
                        Dear Agnès, I must.

AGNÈS
You'll very soon be coming back, I trust?

HORACE
I shall; my yearning heart will see to that.

AGNÈS
Without you, life is miserable and flat.

HORACE
When I'm away from you, I pine and grieve.

AGNÈS
Alas! If that were so, you wouldn't leave.

HORACE
You know how strong my love is, and how true.

AGNÈS
Ah, no, you don't love me as I love you.

(*Arnolphe tugs at her hand.*)
Why does he pull my hand?

HORACE

'T would ruin us,
My dear, if we were seen together thus,
And therefore this true friend, who's filled with worry
About our welfare, urges you to hurry.

AGNÈS

But why must I go with him—a perfect stranger?

HORACE

Don't fret. In his hands you'll be out of danger.

AGNÈS

I'd rather be in *your* hands; that was why—
(*To Arnolphe, who tugs her hand again:*)
Wait, wait.

HORACE

It's daybreak. I must go. Good-bye.

AGNÈS

When shall I see you?

HORACE

Very soon, I swear.

AGNÈS

Till that sweet moment, I'll be in despair.

HORACE, *leaving, to himself*

My happiness is assured; my fears may cease;
Praise be to Heaven, I now can sleep in peace.

SCENE FOUR

———•◦•———

Arnolphe, Agnès

ARNOLPHE, *hiding his face in his cloak, and
disguising his voice*
Come, this is not where you're to stay, my child;
It's elsewhere that you shall be domiciled.
You're going to a safe, sequestered place.
    (*Revealing himself, and using his normal voice:*)
Do you know me?

AGNÈS, *recognizing him*
Aagh!

ARNOLPHE
       You wicked girl! My face
Would seem, just now, to give you rather a fright.
Oh, clearly I'm a most unwelcome sight:
I interfere with your romantic plan.
    (*Agnès turns and looks in vain for Horace.*)
No use to look for help from that young man;
He couldn't hear you now; he's gone too far.
Well, well! For one so young, how sly you are!
You ask—most innocently, it would appear—
If children are begotten through the ear,
Yet you know all too well, I now discover,
How to keep trysts—at midnight—with a lover!
What honeyed words you spoke to him just now!
Who taught you such beguilements? Tell me how,
Within so short a time, you've learned so much!
You used to be afraid of ghosts and such:
Has your gallant taught you not to fear the night?
You ingrate! To deceive me so, despite
The loving care with which you have been blessed!
Oh, I have warmed a serpent at my breast

Until, reviving, it unkindly bit
The very hand that was caressing it!

AGNÈS

Why are you cross with me?

ARNOLPHE

Oh! So I'm unfair?

AGNÈS

I've done no wrong of which I am aware.

ARNOLPHE

Was it right, then, to run off with that young beau?

AGNÈS

He wants me for his wife; he's told me so.
I've only done as you advised; you said
That, so as not to sin, one ought to wed.

ARNOLPHE

Yes, but I made it perfectly clear that I'd
Resolved, myself, to take you as my bride.

AGNÈS

Yes; but if I may give my point of view,
He'd suit me, as a husband, better than you.
In all your talk of marriage, you depict
A state that's gloomy, burdensome, and strict;
But, ah! when *he* describes the married state,
It sounds so sweet that I can hardly wait.

ARNOLPHE

Ah! So you love him, faithless girl!

AGNÈS

Why, yes.

ARNOLPHE

Have you the gall to tell me that, Agnès?

AGNÈS

If it's the truth, what's wrong with telling it?

ARNOLPHE

How dared you fall in love with him, you chit?

AGNÈS

It was no fault of mine; he made me do it.
I was in love with him before I knew it.

ARNOLPHE

You should have overcome your amorous feeling.

AGNÈS

It's hard to overcome what's so appealing.

ARNOLPHE

Didn't you know that I would be put out?

AGNÈS

Why, no. What have you to complain about?

ARNOLPHE

Nothing, of course! I'm wild with happiness!
You don't, I take it, love me.

AGNÈS

        Love you?

ARNOLPHE

                    Yes.

AGNÈS

Alas, I don't.

ARNOLPHE

You *don't*?

AGNÈS

Would you have me lie?

ARNOLPHE

Why don't you love me, hussy? Tell me why!

AGNÈS

Good heavens, it's not I whom you should blame.
He made me love him; why didn't you do the same?
I didn't hinder you, as I recall.

ARNOLPHE

I tried to make you love me; I gave my all;
Yet all my pains and strivings were in vain.

AGNÈS

He has more aptitude than you, that's plain;
To win my heart, he scarcely had to try.

ARNOLPHE, *aside*

This peasant girl can frame a neat reply!
What lady wit could answer with more art?
Either she's bright, or in what concerns the heart
A foolish girl can best the wisest man.
    (*To Agnès:*)
Well, then, Miss Back-Talk, answer this if you can:
Did I raise you, all these years, at such expense,
For another's benefit? Does that make sense?

AGNÈS

No. But he'll gladly pay you for your trouble.

ARNOLPHE, *aside*

Such flippancy! It makes my rage redouble.

(*To Agnès:*)
You minx! How could he possibly discharge
Your obligations to me? They're too large.

AGNÈS

Frankly, they don't seem very large to me.

ARNOLPHE

Did I not nurture you from infancy?

AGNÈS

Yes, that you did. I'm deeply obligated.
How wondrously you've had me educated!
Do you fancy that I'm blind to what you've done,
And cannot see that I'm a simpleton?
Oh, it humiliates me; I revolt
Against the shame of being such a dolt.

ARNOLPHE

Do you think you'll gain the knowledge that you need
Through that young dandy's tutelage?

AGNÈS

                           Yes, indeed.
It's thanks to him I know what little I do;
I owe far more to him than I do to you.

ARNOLPHE

What holds me back, I ask myself, from treating
So insolent a girl to a sound beating?
Your coldness irks me to the point of tears,
And it would ease my soul to box your ears.

AGNÈS

Alas, then, beat me, if you so desire.

ARNOLPHE, *aside*

Those words and that sweet look dissolve my ire,
Restoring to my heart such tender feeling
As makes me quite forget her double-dealing.
How strange love is! How strange that men, from such
Perfidious beings, will endure so much!
Women, as all men know, are fraily wrought:
They're foolish and illogical in thought,
Their souls are weak, their characters are bad,
There's nothing quite so silly, quite so mad,
So faithless; yet, despite these sorry features,
What won't we do to please the wretched creatures?
　　(*To Agnès:*)
Come, traitress, let us be at peace once more.
I'll pardon you, and love you as before.
Repay my magnanimity, and learn
From my great love to love me in return.

AGNÈS

Truly, if I were able to, I would.
I'd gladly love you if I only could.

ARNOLPHE

You can, my little beauty, if you'll but try.
　　(*He sighs.*)
Just listen to that deep and yearning sigh!
Look at my haggard face! See how it suffers!
Reject that puppy, and the love he offers:
He must have cast a spell on you; with me,
You'll be far happier, I guarantee.
I know that clothes and jewels are your passion;
Don't worry: you shall always be in fashion.
I'll pet you night and day; you shall be showered
With kisses; you'll be hugged, caressed, devoured.
And you shall have your wish in every way.
I'll say no more; what further could I say?
　　(*Aside:*)
Lord, what extremes desire will drive us to!

(*To Agnès:*)
In short, no love could match my love for you.
Tell me, ungrateful girl, what proof do you need?
Shall I weep? Or beat myself until I bleed?
What if I tore my hair out—would that sway you?
Shall I kill myself? Command, and I'll obey you.
I'm ready, cruel one, for you to prove me.

AGNÈS

Somehow, your lengthy speeches fail to move me.
Horace, in two words, could be more engaging.

ARNOLPHE

Enough of this! Your impudence is enraging.
I have my plans for you, you stubborn dunce,
And I shall pack you out of town at once.
You've spurned my love, and baited me as well—
Which you'll repent of in a convent cell.

SCENE FIVE

Alain, Arnolphe, Agnès

ALAIN

It's very strange, but Agnès has vanished, Sir.
I think that corpse has run away with her.

ARNOLPHE

She's here. Go shut her in my room, securely.
That's not where he'd come looking for her, surely,
And she'll be there but half an hour, at most.
Meanwhile I'll get a carriage, in which we'll post
To a safe retreat. Go now, and lock up tight,
And see that you don't let her out of sight.
          (*Alone:*)
Perhaps a change of scene and circumstance
Will wean her from this infantile romance.

SCENE SIX

Horace, Arnolphe

HORACE

Seigneur Arnolphe, I'm overwhelmed with grief,
And Heaven's cruelty is beyond belief;
It seems now that a brutal stroke of fate
May force my love and me to separate.
My father, just this minute, chanced to appear,
Alighting from his coach not far from here,
And what has brought him into town this morning
Is a dire errand of which I'd had no warning:
He's made a match for me, and, ready or not,
I am to marry someone on the spot.
Imagine my despair! What blacker curse
Could fall on me, what setback could be worse?
I told you, yesterday, of Enrique. It's he
Who's brought about my present misery;
He's come with Father, to lead me to the slaughter,
And I am doomed to wed his only daughter.
When they told me that, it almost made me swoon;
And, since my father spoke of coming soon
To see you, I excused myself, in fright,
And hastened to forewarn you of my plight.
Take care, Sir, I entreat you, not to let him
Know of Agnès and me; 't would much upset him.
And try, since he so trusts your judgment, to
Dissuade him from the match he has in view.

ARNOLPHE

I shall.

HORACE

That failing, you could be of aid
By urging that the wedding be delayed.

ARNOLPHE

Trust me.

HORACE

On you, my dearest hopes repose.

ARNOLPHE

Fine, fine.

HORACE

You're a father to me, Heaven knows.
Tell him that young men— Ah! He's coming! I spy him.
Here are some arguments with which to ply him.
> (*They withdraw to a corner of the stage, and
> confer in whispers.*)

SCENE SEVEN

Enrique, Oronte, Chrysalde, Horace, Arnolphe

ENRIQUE, *to Chrysalde*

No need for introductions, Sir. I knew
Your name as soon as I set eyes on you.
You have the very features of your late
Sister, who was my well-belovèd mate;
Oh, how I wish that cruel Destiny
Had let me bring my helpmeet back with me,
After such years of hardship as we bore,
To see her home and family once more.
But fate has ruled that we shall not again
Enjoy her charming presence; let us, then,
Find solace in what joys we may design
For the sole offspring of her love and mine.
You are concerned in this; let us confer,
And see if you approve my plans for her.
Oronte's young son, I think, is a splendid choice;
But in this matter you've an equal voice.

CHRYSALDE

I've better judgment, Brother, than to question
So eminently worthy a suggestion.

ARNOLPHE, *to Horace*

Yes, yes, don't worry; I'll represent you well.

HORACE

Once more, don't tell him—

ARNOLPHE

I promise not to tell.
(*Arnolphe leaves Horace, and crosses to
embrace Oronte.*)

ORONTE

Ah, my old friend: what a warm, hearty greeting!

ARNOLPHE

Oronte, dear fellow, what a welcome meeting!

ORONTE

I've come to town—

ARNOLPHE

    You needn't say a word;
I know what brings you.

ORONTE

     You've already heard?

ARNOLPHE

Yes.

ORONTE

 Good.

ARNOLPHE

    Your son regards this match with dread;
His heart rebels at being forced to wed,
And I've been asked, in fact, to plead his case.
Well, do you know what I'd do, in your place?
I'd exercise a father's rightful sway
And tie the wedding knot without delay.
What the young need, my friend, is discipline;
We only do them harm by giving in.

HORACE, *aside*

Traitor!

CHRYSALDE

If the prospect fills him with revulsion,
Then surely we should not employ compulsion.
My brother-in-law, I trust, would say the same.

ARNOLPHE

Shall a man be governed by his son? For shame!
Would you have a father be so meek and mild
As not to exact obedience from his child?
At his wise age, 't would be grotesque indeed
To see him led by one whom he should lead.
No, no; my dear old friend is honor-bound;
He's given his word, and he must not give ground.
Let him be firm, as a father should, and force
His son to take the necessary course.

ORONTE

Well said: we shall proceed with this alliance,
And I shall answer for my son's compliance.

CHRYSALDE, *to Arnolphe*

It much surprises me to hear you press
For this betrothal with such eagerness.
What is your motive? I can't make you out.

ARNOLPHE

Don't worry, friend; I know what I'm about.

ORONTE

Indeed, Arnolphe—

CHRYSALDE

He finds that name unpleasant.
Monsieur de la Souche is what he's called at present.

ARNOLPHE

No matter.

HORACE

What do I hear?

ARNOLPHE, *turning toward Horace*
Well, now you know,
And now you see why I have spoken so.

HORACE

Oh, what confusion—

SCENE EIGHT

Georgette, Enrique, Oronte, Chrysalde,
Horace, Arnolphe

GEORGETTE
Sir, please come. Unless
You do, I fear we can't restrain Agnès.
The girl is frantic to escape, I swear,
And might jump out of the window in despair.

ARNOLPHE
Bring her to me: I'll take her away from here
Posthaste, this very minute.
  (*To Horace:*)
       Be of good cheer.
Too much good luck could spoil you; and, as they say
In the proverb, every dog must have his day.

HORACE
What man, O Heaven, was ever betrayed like this,
Or hurled into so hopeless an abyss?

ARNOLPHE, *to Oronte*
Pray don't delay the nuptials—which, dear friend,
I shall be most delighted to attend.

ORONTE
I shan't delay.

SCENE NINE

———— • • ————

Agnès, Alain, Georgette, Oronte, Enrique,
Arnolphe, Horace, Chrysalde

ARNOLPHE
Come, come, my pretty child,
You who are so intractable and wild.
Here is your gallant: perhaps he should receive
A little curtsey from you, as you leave.
(*To Horace:*)
Farewell: your sweet hopes seem to have turned to gall;
But love, my boy, can't always conquer all.

AGNÈS
Horace! Will you let him take me away from you?

HORACE
I'm dazed with grief, and don't know what to do.

ARNOLPHE
Come, chatterbox.

AGNÈS
No. Here I shall remain.

ORONTE
Now, what's the mystery? Will you please explain?
All this is very odd; we're baffled by it.

ARNOLPHE
When I've more time, I'll gladly clarify it.
Till then, good-bye.

ORONTE
Where is it you mean to go?
And why won't you tell us what we ask to know?

ARNOLPHE

I've told you that, despite your stubborn son,
You ought to hold the wedding.

ORONTE

It shall be done.
But weren't you told that his intended spouse
Is the young woman who's living in your house—
The long-lost child of that dear Angélique
Who secretly was married to Enrique?
What, then, did your behavior mean just now?

CHRYSALDE

His words amazed me, too, I must allow.

ARNOLPHE

What? What?

CHRYSALDE

My sister married secretly;
Her daughter's birth was kept from the family.

ORONTE

The child was placed with an old country dame,
Who reared her under a fictitious name.

CHRYSALDE

My sister's husband, beset by circumstance,
Was soon obliged to take his leave of France,

ORONTE

And undergo great trials and miseries
In a strange, savage land beyond the seas,

CHRYSALDE

Where, through his labors, he regained abroad
What here he'd lost through men's deceit and fraud.

ORONTE

Returning home, he sought at once to find
The nurse to whom his child had been consigned,

CHRYSALDE

And the good creature told him, as was true,
That she'd transferred her little charge to you,

ORONTE

Because of your benevolent disposition,
And the dire poverty of her condition.

CHRYSALDE

What's more, Enrique, transported with delight,
Has brought the woman here to set things right.

ORONTE

She'll join us in a moment, and then we'll see
A public end to all this mystery.

CHRYSALDE, *to Arnolphe*

I know that you're in a painful state of mind;
Yet what the Fates have done is not unkind.
Since your chief treasure is a hornless head,
The safest course, for you, is not to wed.

ARNOLPHE, *leaving in a speechless passion*

Oof!

ORONTE

Why is he rushing off without a word?

HORACE

Father, a great coincidence has occurred.
What in your wisdom you projected, chance
Has wondrously accomplished in advance.
The fact is, Sir, that I am bound already,
By the sweet ties of love, to this fair lady;

It's she whom you have come to seek, and she
For whose sake I opposed your plans for me.

ENRIQUE

I recognized her from the very first,
With such deep joy, I thought my heart would burst.
Dear daughter, let me take you in my embrace.
(*He does so.*)

CHRYSALDE

I have the same urge, Brother, but this place
Will hardly do for private joys like these.
Let us go in, resolve all mysteries,
Commend our friend Arnolphe, and for the rest
Thank Heaven, which orders all things for the best.

DON JUAN

COMEDY IN FIVE ACTS, 1665

For my son Nathan

Introduction

Don Juan, Molière's first full-scale comedy in prose, appropriated a tale which, first told by the Spanish dramatist Tirso de Molina in his *El Burlador de Sevilla* (1630), had been reworked at mid-century for the Italian theatre of Cicignini and Giliberto, and adapted to the conventions of French tragicomedy by the playwrights Dorimon and Villiers. From the box-office point of view, any treatment of the familiar plot was likely to succeed, since it offered sensational misbehavior, the supernatural, and a chance for bang-up special effects. It may be, as some have conjectured, that Molière was partially drawn to retell the Don Juan story—the story of an impious man's punishment—in the hope of placating the religious militants who had forced *Tartuffe* off the boards in 1664. If that was any part of his motivation, Molière miscalculated, for when *Don Juan* opened at the Palais-Royal in February of the next year, a storm of pious censure forced the author to make cuts after the first performance and to close the play—despite good business—after the fifteenth. Molière never published or revived the work, and after his death it was effectively replaced by Thomas Corneille's inoffensive verse adaptation, which Molière's widow had commissioned and which played in French theatres for almost two centuries. Not until 1813 was a full and restored text of Molière's *Don Juan* published in France; not until 1847 did the play enter the repertoire of the Comédie Française.

In the twentieth century, however, this long-suppressed play came to enjoy brilliant productions in France, and so much attention from critics and scholars everywhere that Jacques Guicharnaud, in a 1964 essay on Molière, could call *Don Juan* "the center of attention among all the works." There are many cultural factors which might account for the play's changed fortunes, and for our present receptivity to it, but certainly this is true: that the pervasive ambiguity of the work, which offended the devout of Molière's day, is for us a source of richness and nuance.

Don Juan is not a classically constructed comedy but a loose, two-day sequence of episodes which rambles through the vaguest of Sicilies. It is somewhat held together, in the plot sense, by the continuing stories of the Commander and of Elvira and her brothers, as well as by the theme of damnation, which is present from the first scene onward. But its main coherence lies in a many-angled portrayal, in varying circumstances and social milieux, of the title character, who with his servant Sganarelle is centrally present in all but two scenes. That this character will fulfill his legend by ending in hellfire, and that he will deserve that fate, one assumes from the start; yet Molière is at pains to create a complex Don Juan with whom we can to some extent sympathize, and in whom we can see certain attractive qualities. To this end he eliminates the crudely violent deeds—rape, father-beating, and the like—which earlier Don Juans had performed, soft-pedals the Commander's killing by putting it into the past, and permits his hero little in the way of successful onstage wickedness: the Don's amatory initiatives are frustrated by shipwreck or interruption, the Poor Man stands up to him, and only M. Dimanche is fully victimized. On the positive side, Molière's Don Juan is repeatedly shown to be a courageous, witty, eloquent, and handsome young man, whose behavior can appear to embody a brave independence of every code and orthodoxy. That appearance is made the more possible by the fact that all the conventions, as advocated or embodied in the play, give signs of hollowness or fragility.

There being no *raisonneur* on hand, the cause of religion is argued in muddled commonplaces by the foolish Sganarelle, whose want of true piety is proven when he urges the Poor Man to blaspheme. Though Elvira can be moving and genuine in her fervor for the hero, she damages the idea of courtly love when she reproaches the Don for not telling her elegant lies; and the religious exaltation of her second appearance has a theatrical quality which cannot be sustained, as she help-lessly modulates toward a restatement of her passion. The Poor Man, in Act Three, is a fine example of spiritual integ-rity, yet it may be (as some contend) that we would think even better of him if he did not take money for his prayers. Later in the same act, Molière presents the gentleman's code of honor in a dubious light, both because of Don Carlos's humane reservations about it, and because of his brother's feral eagerness to enforce it. Don Luis's reproaches in Act Four, which nobly assert the idea that high rank is nothing without virtue, are somewhat undermined by the reflection that he has long been using his influence to effect a cover-up of his son's criminal career. The shakiness of codes and conventions in *Don Juan*'s world, and a measure of inau-thenticity in all their representatives, enable the Don to hear people with unnerving silence, to dismiss Sganarelle's argu-ments with curt derision, to respond to the tirades of Elvira or Don Luis with deflating mock-politeness, and in every case to direct the play's laughter against the other characters.

Because the laugh is never on Don Juan, some readers of the play have identified with him, seeing him as the free-spirited, self-determining hero of an "anti-Establishment" satire. Doubtless such readers would also distort *The Misanthrope* (which Molière was working on at the time of *Don Juan*'s composition), taking the self-deceived, self-dramatizing, and antisocial Alceste to be a fearless critic of conventional insin-cerities. Such misreadings are not utterly wrong, but they are oversimple, anachronistic, and a little humorless. We find a truer, subtler sense of *Don Juan* in this sentence of Irving Singer's: "The play—which everyone admits to be a difficult one—achieves its unique ambiguity by using Don Juan to reveal the hypocrisy of everyone else at the same time as they show him to be the monster that he is."

Though he kills no one before our eyes, and though we do not witness what Don Luis calls "the multitude of his misdeeds," the young nobleman whom Molière shows us is indeed a monster. He is a serial lover who, by his own account, is repeatedly "ravished" by beauty, and who, having suffered that "sweet violence," rallies his forces and pursues the woman of the moment until she physically surrenders. Thereafter, he is done with her and ready for another "conquest." To the adolescent fantast in us all, such a program is appealing, yet what it argues is a desperate deficiency—a brutish inability to treat people as persons, an incapacity for the creative act of loving. Don Juan can be bitterly aware of what he lacks, and when, toward the end of Act One, Scene Two, he expresses envy of two happy lovers, and proposes to "mar their felicity" by piratical violence, he sounds like Milton's Satan first beholding Adam and Eve "Imparadised in one another's arms." Because he descends from a chivalrous élite, Don Juan seeks to dignify his amours by likening them to military campaigns; and in fact his martial metaphors *are* appropriate to his conduct, in love or out. Whatever pleasure the Don may gain from beauty, or from successive marriage beds, the thing that really matters to him is victory; for him, every human encounter is a battle that he must win. He must intimidate Pierrot, and hoodwink the peasant girls Charlotte and Mathurine, and frustrate M. Dimanche with false courtesies; and when the Poor Man will not be bribed, the Don must hasten to keep the upper hand by giving him the gold piece anyway. The one restraint upon Don Juan, as we learn in the Cornelian situations of Act Three, is the gentleman's code of honor, which he observes not because he believes in it but because to be seen as a gentleman is an essential underpinning for his pride.

What kind of pride is it that one sees in Don Juan? It is an unbounded pride, which longs for "still more worlds" in which to have its way; at the same time, it is an anxious, driven pride which must bolster itself by incessant acts of domination, and in its uneasy self-absorption can spare no sympathy or respect for humankind. It is not the pride of a free man, but of one who is the slave of his fears and compulsions. For Don Juan the *conquistador*, other people are either antagonists or victims; they are also, despite the Don's pretensions to independence, an audience before whom he plays, and on whose witness to his magnetic singularity he depends. His reformation, he says to Don Luis in Act Five, "will astound the world," and it has always been his need to hold the world's attention. This cold, strange young man, who must at every moment dazzle and prevail, can afford only one intimate or confidant in all creation—his valet and jester Sganarelle. Though Sganarelle ultimately resists Don Juan, and at the close of the play mourns not his master but his unpaid wages, it is easy to see how well he answers the Don's need to be safely open with someone. As a servant, Sganarelle is readily dominated; his speeches can be heard with amused contempt, and he can at any moment be bullied into silence. He is also a captive audience of one, before whom the hero struts and defines himself, and despite his timorous moralism he frequently—as in his treatment of M. Dimanche—pays Don Juan the tribute of imitation.

When Don Juan announces to Sganarelle, in Act Five, his intention to become a hypocrite, it would be a mistake to see it as the capitulation of a once-bold social rebel. As W. G. Moore has said, it will not do to view Don Juan as "a prophet of secularism" and the Enlightenment, and if we want to discover his type in history we should think instead of the arrogant and wilful feudal nobility whose power Louis XIV had tamed. Some critics, dissatisfied with the Don's decision, have accused Molière of twisting the plot in order to motivate a long speech unfavorable to that "cabal of the pious" which had been persecuting him. No doubt that is part of the answer; however, it seems to me that the Don's resort to dissimulation is a sufficiently logical development. His affairs have come to a crisis. He needs to appease his irate father, whose help and protection are vital to him, and his pursuit by Elvira's brothers has made him aware that he needs allies against those he has wronged. In resolving to play the part of reformed sinner, he sacrifices one aspect of himself—the image of the swaggering young lord who is a law unto himself. But there is another side of his prideful character—his scorn for the truth and his relish for deception—of which hypocrisy could be the ultimate expression. There are, in Act Five, two kinds of hypocritical utterance by Don

Juan: his words to his father are plain bamboozlement, but what he says to Don Carlos is a teasing, transparent lie (like his "utterly sincere" address to Elvira in Act One) which the hearer is not in a position to dismiss, and which represents falsehood at its most contemptuous.

When I said earlier that the laugh is never on Don Juan, I was thinking of the audible laughter of a theatre audience. This play also provokes a great deal of inward amusement, even in scenes of a poignant or "tragic" character, and that is what makes it possible for so heterogeneous a work to give a final impression of comic unity. Don Juan is extremely attentive in all situations, because of his compulsion to win, but he can at the same time be unshakably resistant and indifferent. That is the case in the play's third scene, when he finds himself overtaken by Elvira, the wife whom he has deserted. His first reaction is not to look at her or acknowledge her presence. His second response is a brief and wonderfully inadequate expression of surprise. When Elvira then passionately denounces his treachery, and challenges him to account for it, he tells her with Brummellian superciliousness that his valet will explain his departure. Finding that explanation unintelligible, Elvira scaldingly reproaches the Don for lacking a courtier's eloquent excuses, and to that he responds with mocking dishonesty and a preemptive piety, claiming to have left her for reasons of conscience. Her parting tirade, in which she proclaims that Heaven will avenge her, is punctuated by impious banter between Don Juan and Sganarelle, and is immediately followed by the Don's saying, "Now then, let's go ahead with our [next] amorous enterprise." Though Elvira's situation deserves our sympathy, and though her stormy speeches are moving and just, the scene is comic or absurd throughout because in the emotional sense Don Juan hears nothing, and replies only with cold parrying, mockery, and obfuscation. H. Gaston Hall finds a similar comedy of noncommunication in the first scene (Act Four, Scene Four) between Don Luis and his son: "The two characters are in a comic situation because they speak and understand in two incompatible planes." When Don Juan, in Act Three, bids

Sganarelle invite the Commander's statue to dinner, the valet replies, "I'd be crazy if I went and talked to a statue." There is a similar craziness or absurdity in any character's trying to have a heart-to-heart talk with Don Juan, who is at least as stony as the Commander.

Is Don Juan himself a comic figure? Yes. It may be that his disbelief in Heaven is a deficiency, like his inability to love a woman, but it comes across as aggressive and cocksure, and that makes him comic in the circumstances of this play—just as it was comic for certain English scientists, presented in 1798 with the skin of a duck-billed platypus, to declare it a hoax because it did not fit into their rigid scheme of Nature. If we are not to be provincially contemporary, we must—as Gaston Hall says—accept the supernatural in *Don Juan* as we accept the ghost in *Hamlet* or the witches in *Macbeth*. If we do, Hall goes on to say, we may then see "that in refusing to heed the warnings of Sganarelle, of Don Luis, and of Doña Elvira, as in refusing to accept the *evidence* of the miracle wrought in the Statue, Don Juan is comic in exactly the same ways as Orgon when he refuses to consider the evidence gathered against Tartuffe." Don Juan is by far the cleverest person in the play which bears his name, and that makes it all the more ridiculous that he should be stupid about the ultimate question of God's existence. To quote Dr. Hall a final time, "Is there not something comic about a man borne off by a force in which he refused to believe?"

Don Juan is not in verse, like the other Molière plays I have translated, but its prose presents some formal challenges which I hope to have met. There are times when Molière's prose dialogue slips into the rhythms of the alexandrine, and the translation should, at such moments, do something similar without overdoing it. There are in the play a great many styles of speaking to be duplicated, from the lofty periods of Don Luis to the mercantile servility of M. Dimanche, and the hero and his valet have several voices each; indeed, in the very first moments of the play we find Sganarelle assuming a pseudosophisticated tone, and seeking to impress a fellow servant with a fatuous digression on snuff. The chief problem of diction for the translator of *Don Juan* is, of course, how to render the speech of Pierrot, Charlotte, and Mathurine in Act Two. Though those characters are supposedly Sicilian peasants, they are altogether French; Molière has given them French names and has had them speak in a patois of the Paris region which, though incidentally amusing, would have been entirely intelligible to his audience. It seemed to me that the peasants should also be easy to understand in English, and so I have avoided the quaint densities of dialect, settling instead for some ordinary bad grammar and for the familiar locutions of rural New England.

When in doubt, I have sometimes consulted earlier translations by Wall, Gravely, Wood, Frame, or Porter, and am grateful for their help. I thank my wife for her patient criticism, and my friends William Jay Smith and Sonja Haussmann Smith for their great kindness in looking over the finished text.

R. W.
Cummington, 1997

Characters

DON JUAN, son of Don Luis

SGANARELLE, Don Juan's valet

ELVIRA, wife of Don Juan

GUSMAN, squire to Elvira

DON CARLOS, Elvira's brother

DON ALONSO, Elvira's brother

DON LUIS, father of Don Juan

A POOR MAN

CHARLOTTE, a peasant girl

MATHURINE, a peasant girl

PIERROT, a peasant

THE STATUE OF THE COMMANDER

LA VIOLETTE, servant to Don Juan

RAGOTIN, servant to Don Juan

MONSIEUR DIMANCHE, a merchant

LA RAMÉE, a roughneck

ATTENDANTS on Don Carlos and Don Alonso

A SPECTRE

PLACE

The action takes place in Sicily.

Act One

SCENE ONE

———— •◦•‒————

Sganarelle, Gusman
A palace or palatial public building.

SGANARELLE (*With a snuff-box in his hand.*)
Whatever Aristotle and the other old philosophers may
say, there's nothing so fine as snuff. All the best people are
devoted to it, and anyone who lives without snuff doesn't
deserve to live. Not only does it purge and stimulate the
brain, it also schools the soul in goodness, and one learns
in using it how to be a true gentleman. You've noticed,
I'm sure, how whenever a man takes a pinch of snuff, he
becomes gracious and benevolent toward everybody, and
delights in offering his snuff-box right and left, wherever he
happens to be. He doesn't wait to be asked, but anticipates
the unspoken desires of others—so great is the generosity
which snuff inspires in all who take it. But enough of that
subject; let's go back a bit to what we were discussing. So
then, my dear Gusman, your mistress Doña Elvira was
surprised by our sudden departure, and has come galloping
after us. Her heart, you say, is so deeply enamored of my
master that she couldn't live unless she followed him here.
Now, just between us, would you like to hear what I think
about these developments? I fear that her love will be ill-
rewarded, that her trip to this city will be fruitless, and that
you'd have done better to stay at home.

GUSMAN
Pray, why do you say that? What leads you, Sganarelle, to
make so grim a prediction? Has your master confided in you
about this business? Has he told you of some displeasure with
us which caused him to leave?

SGANARELLE

Nothing of the sort. But, judging by certain signs, I know pretty well how things are likely to go. Though he hasn't yet told me anything, I'd almost wager that the affair will end as I said. I could be mistaken, of course; but long experience has given me some insight in these matters.

GUSMAN

What! Do you mean to say that Don Juan's unexpected departure was an act of infidelity? Could he so disdain the chaste love of Doña Elvira?

SGANARELLE

No, no, it's just that he's still young, and can't yet bring himself . . .

GUSMAN

Could a man of his rank behave so basely?

SGANARELLE

Ah yes, his rank! What a quaint idea! As if his rank could deter him from doing what he likes!

GUSMAN

But the man is bound by the sacred ties of marriage!

SGANARELLE

Ah, my poor Gusman, you don't begin to know, believe me, what sort of man Don Juan is.

GUSMAN

It's true indeed that I don't know the man, if he can break faith with us in such a way. I don't understand how, after so many professions of love and importunate desire, so many sighs, promises, and tears, so many ardent letters, so many fervent speeches and reiterated vows, so many wild and passionate actions as well, wherein he went so far as to force the gates of a holy convent to gain possession of Doña

Elvira—I don't understand, I repeat, how after all that he could have the gall to go back on his word.

SGANARELLE

As for me, I've no trouble understanding it; and if you knew his shifty character you'd see that such behavior comes natural to him. I'm not saying that his feelings toward Doña Elvira have altered—I can't as yet be sure about that: as you know, he had me leave town ahead of him, and since his arrival here he's told me nothing. But, just to prepare you for the worst, I tell you *inter nos* that the person you've known as Don Juan, my master, is the greatest scoundrel who ever walked the earth, a mad dog, a demon, a Turk, a heretic who doesn't believe in Heaven, or Hell, or werewolves even. He lives like a brute beast, an Epicurean swine, an absolute Sardanapalus, closing his ears to all reproaches and treating all our noblest credences as nonsense. You mention that he has married your mistress; believe you me, he'd have done more than that if necessary. For the sake of his passion, he'd have married you too, and her dog and her cat to boot. Getting married means nothing to him; it's simply his technique for ensnaring beautiful women, and he'll marry anything. A noble lady, a young woman of quality, a merchant's daughter, a peasant wench—there's nothing narrow about his tastes; and if I told you the names of all the women he's married in one place or another, it would take from now until sundown. You stand there pale and astonished at what I've said; but what you've heard was the merest sketch of the subject, and a true portrait would need many more strokes of the brush. Suffice it to say that the wrath of Heaven hangs over him every day, that I'd be safer in the Devil's employ than in his, and that he involves me in so many enormities that I wish he were already in you-know-where. But a great lord who's a wicked man is a frightening thing; I must be loyal to him, whether I like it or not. I serve him not from zeal but from fear, which makes me hide my true feelings and reduces me, very often, to applauding what my soul detests. But here he comes now, strolling through the halls of this palazzo; we must separate. Bear this in mind, however: I've confided in you very frankly, and my words have spilled out in an unguarded fashion; but if anything I've said should come to his ears, I shall swear up and down that you're a liar.

SCENE TWO

Don Juan, Sganarelle

DON JUAN

With whom were you speaking, just now? I'd say that he looks much like the good Gusman, Doña Elvira's servant.

SGANARELLE

The resemblance could not be closer.

DON JUAN

What? Then it's he?

SGANARELLE

The same.

DON JUAN

And since when has he been in this town?

SGANARELLE

Since yesterday evening.

DON JUAN

And what business brings him here?

SGANARELLE

I think you can surmise what's on his mind.

DON JUAN

Our departure, no doubt?

SGANARELLE

The old fellow is greatly grieved by it, and was asking me to explain your motives.

DON JUAN

And what did you tell him?

SGANARELLE

That you hadn't informed me of them.

DON JUAN

But come now, what's your opinion about this turn of events? What do you suppose is going on?

SGANARELLE

What do I think? I think—no offense intended—that you've got some new beloved on the brain.

DON JUAN

That's what you think?

SGANARELLE

Yes.

DON JUAN

My word, you're quite right! I must own that another charmer has banished Elvira from my thoughts.

SGANARELLE

Of course, what else? I know my Don Juan inside and out, and I know that your heart is the most restless thing in the world; it likes to slither from one sacred bond to another, and it can't bear to settle in one place.

DON JUAN

And have I a right, do you think, to behave that way?

SGANARELLE

Well, Sir. . . .

DON JUAN

What? Go on.

SGANARELLE

Certainly it's your right, if you insist; one wouldn't dare contradict you. But if you didn't insist, one might answer otherwise.

DON JUAN

Very well. I give you leave to speak freely, and to tell me what you truly feel.

SGANARELLE

In that case, Sir, I'll tell you frankly that I don't approve your conduct in the least. I think it's shameful to love in all directions as you do.

DON JUAN

What! You'd have a man tie himself down to the first pretty woman who takes his fancy, and forsake the world for her, and never look at another? How absurd to make a specious virtue of fidelity, and bury oneself forever in a single passion, and be dead from youth onward to all the other beauties by whom one might be dazzled! No, no: constancy is for insensitive clods alone. All fair women have the right to enchant us, and the fact that we've met one of them first shouldn't deprive all the rest of their just claim on our hearts. For myself, I'm ravished by beauty wherever I find it, and I yield at once to the sweet violence with which it takes us captive. It's useless for me to pledge my heart and hand; the love I feel for one charming creature can't pledge me to be unjust to the others; I still have eyes for the merits of them all, and I render to each one the tribute that Nature exacts of us. I can't, in short, deny my heart to anything that strikes me as lovable, and the sight of a beautiful face so masters me that, if I had a thousand hearts, I'd give them all.

There is, besides, an inexpressible charm in the first stirrings of a new passion, and the whole pleasure of love lies in change. It's a delicious thing to subdue the heart of some young beauty by a hundred sweet attentions; to see

yourself making some small progress with her every day;
to combat her modest innocence, and her reluctance to
surrender, with tears and sighs and rapturous speeches;
to break through all her little defenses, one by one; to
vanquish her cherished scruples, and gently bring her round
to granting your desires. But once one is the master, there's
nothing more to say or wish for: the joy of passionate
pursuit is over, and all that remains is the boredom of
a placid affection—until some new beauty appears and
revives one's desires, enchanting the heart with the prospect
of a new conquest. To be brief, then, there's nothing sweeter
than overcoming the resistance of an attractive woman,
and I bring to that enterprise the ambition of a conquering
general, who moves on forever from victory to victory, and
will set no limit to his longings. Nothing can withstand
the impetuousness of my desires: I feel my heart capable
of loving all the earth; and, like Alexander, I wish that
there were still more worlds in which to wage my amorous
campaigns.

SGANARELLE

Bless my soul, what a recitation! You seem to have learned
all that by heart, and you talk just like a book.

DON JUAN

Well—what have you to say to it?

SGANARELLE

Heavens! I've a great deal to say, but I don't know how to
say it. You've twisted things in such a way as to make it
seem that you're in the right; and yet the fact is that you're
not. I was ready with the best arguments in the world, and
you've made a muddle of them. Well, let it go; the next
time I discuss anything with you, I'll put my thoughts in
writing before-hand.

DON JUAN

An excellent idea.

SGANARELLE

But Sir, if I still have your leave to speak out, may I say that I'm more than a little scandalized by the life you lead?

DON JUAN

What do you mean? What life do I lead?

SGANARELLE

A very good one. But, for example, your habit of marrying a different person every month or so. . . .

DON JUAN

Could anything be more pleasant?

SGANARELLE

Yes, I can see that it's very pleasant and very amusing, and I could adjust to it, if there were no harm in it; but, Sir, to trifle so with a holy sacrament. . . .

DON JUAN

Enough, enough. That's a matter between myself and Heaven, and Heaven and I will settle it very nicely without your fretting about it.

SGANARELLE

But, Sir, for mercy's sake! I've always heard that it's dangerous to make light of Heaven, and that freethinkers never come to a good end.

DON JUAN

Hold on there, Master Blockhead! Remember what I've told you. I don't like people who preach at me.

SGANARELLE

Oh, I wasn't speaking of you—God forbid! You, Sir, are a man who knows what he's doing, and if you don't believe in anything, you have your reasons. But there are, in this world, some rash little men who are freethinkers without knowing why, and who play at being unbelievers because they think it gives them style. If I had a master like that, I'd say to him flatly, looking him straight in the face, "How dare you scoff at Heaven as you do? How, without trembling, can you make mock of the most sacred things? What right have you—little earthworm, little pigmy that you are (I'm speaking to the master I mentioned), what right have you to make a joke of what all men hold in reverence? Do you think that because you have a title, and a curly blonde wig, and feathers in your hat, and a gold-embroidered coat, and flaming-red ribbons (I'm speaking to that other person, not to you), do you think, I say, that such things make you a great intellect, and that you're free to act with absolute license, and that no one will dare confront you with the truth? Learn then from me, your valet, that, sooner or later, Heaven will punish the impious man, that an evil life leads to an evil death, and that. . . ."

DON JUAN

Quiet!

SGANARELLE

What's the matter?

DON JUAN

What matters at present, I'll have you know, is that a young beauty has stolen my heart, and that, drawn by her many perfections, I've followed her to this town.

SGANARELLE

Have you no fears about returning here? It was here, Sir, that you killed that Commander, six months ago.

DON JUAN

Why should I be afraid? Didn't I kill him properly?

SGANARELLE

Oh, very properly; a thorough job; he'd be wrong to complain.

DON JUAN

I've been given a full pardon for that affair.

SGANARELLE

Yes, but that pardon may not satisfy the vengeful feelings of his family and friends, and. . . .

DON JUAN

Come, now, let's give no thought to the bad things that might happen to us; let's think only of what might bring us pleasure. The young beauty I mentioned, an utterly delectable creature, is engaged to be married, and she's been brought here to this town by her fiancé. Quite by chance I caught sight of these lovers elsewhere, three or four days before their coming here. Never had I seen two people so enchanted by each other, so radiantly in love. Their open tenderness and mutual delight moved me deeply; it pierced me to the heart, and aroused in me a love that was rooted in jealousy. Yes, from the moment I saw them I found their shared happiness intolerable; envy sharpened my desires, and with keenest pleasure I began to consider how I would mar their felicity, and disrupt a union which it pained my heart to behold. But thus far all my efforts have been in vain, and so I must resort to extreme measures. Today, our husband-to-be plans to entertain his lady with a pleasant sail upon the sea. Without telling you, I've made full preparations for achieving my desire; I've engaged a vessel, and hired a crew of men, and with these it should be quite simple for me to abduct my young beauty.

SGANARELLE

But, Sir! . . .

DON JUAN

Eh?

SGANARELLE

That's a capital idea; just what should be done. Nothing matters in this life but getting what one wants.

DON JUAN

Then get ready to accompany me, and make sure that you bring along all of my weapons, so that. . . .
(*He sees Doña Elvira approaching.*)
Oh, what a tiresome interruption! Scoundrel, you didn't tell me that she also was in town.

SGANARELLE

You didn't ask me, Sir.

DON JUAN

Is she demented, not to have changed her dress, and to come to this place in her country clothes?

SCENE THREE

Doña Elvira, Don Juan, Sganarelle

DOÑA ELVIRA

Will you be so kind, Don Juan, as to acknowledge my presence? Will you not deign, at least, to turn your face this way?

DON JUAN

I must say, Madam, that you take me by surprise, and that I hadn't expected to see you here.

DOÑA ELVIRA

Yes, I see very clearly that you weren't expecting me; and you look surprised, indeed, but not in the way I'd hoped for. Your cold reaction, just now, gave me full proof of all that I've been refusing to believe. I wonder at my simple, foolish heart, which despite so much obvious evidence has persisted in doubting your treachery. I confess that I've been so silly, or rather so stupid, as to try to keep myself in the dark—to deny what my eyes and my judgement were telling me. I sought to explain away what it pained me to perceive, the lessening of your love for me; and I invented a hundred excuses for your abrupt departure, seeking to acquit you of the very crime with which my reason charged you. Day after day, I refused to listen to my own just suspicions, since to hear them would have made you guilty in my eyes. My heart harkened instead to a thousand foolish fantasies, all depicting you as innocent. But after this reception I can doubt no longer. The look with which I was greeted tells me more than I ever wished to know. Nevertheless, it would please me to hear from your own lips the reasons for your departure. Do speak, Don Juan, and let's see with what countenance you can justify your behavior.

DON JUAN

Sganarelle, Madam, will tell you my reasons for leaving.

SGANARELLE (*Aside to Don Juan.*)

I, Sir? If you please, Sir, I know nothing about them.

DOÑA ELVIRA

Very well, then: speak, Sganarelle. It doesn't matter from whose lips I hear those reasons.

DON JUAN (*Signaling Sganarelle to approach Doña Elvira.*)

Go on, now. Speak to Madam.

SGANARELLE (*Aside, to Don Juan.*)

What would you have me say?

DOÑA ELVIRA

Come here, since you're to be his spokesman, and give me some explanation of that hasty departure.

DON JUAN

Aren't you going to answer her?

SGANARELLE

I don't have any answers. You're just making a fool of your poor servant.

DON JUAN

Answer the lady, I tell you.

SGANARELLE

Madam. . . .

DOÑA ELVIRA

Yes?

SGANARELLE (*Turning toward his master.*)

Sir. . . .

DON JUAN (*With a threatening gesture.*)
If you don't. . . .

SGANARELLE
Madam, it was because of conquerors, and Alexander, and
the need of more worlds, that we had to leave. There, Sir;
that's all I could think of to say.

DOÑA ELVIRA
Will you be so kind, Don Juan, as to interpret those
mysterious phrases?

DON JUAN
Madam, to tell the truth. . . .

DOÑA ELVIRA
Oh, really! For a courtier, who ought to be used to this sort
of thing, you're very bad at defending yourself. It's pitiable
to see you so tongue-tied and abashed. Why don't you
clothe your brow with a noble effrontery? Why don't you
swear that your feelings for me are unchanged, that you
love me still with a matchless passion, and that nothing but
death could separate you from me? Why don't you tell me
that affairs of the most urgent nature forced you to leave
without bidding me farewell; that, much against your will,
you're obliged to remain here for a time, and that I may
return whence I came in the assurance that you'll follow me
as soon as possible; that you truly burn to be with me again,
and that when you're far from me, you suffer the anguish of
a body that's been divided from its soul? That's the sort of
thing you should say in your defense, rather than standing
there speechless.

DON JUAN
I assure you, Madam, that I have no talent for dissembling,
and that my heart is utterly sincere. I shan't tell you that
my feelings are unchanged, and that I burn to be with you
again, for the plain truth is that, when I took my departure,

I was in flight from you—not at all for the reasons which
you may imagine, but for pure reasons of conscience, and
from a conviction that it would be sinful to live with you
any longer. I'd begun to feel qualms about my conduct,
Madam; I opened the eyes of my soul, and bade them look
upon my actions. I faced the fact that, in order to make
you my bride, I had stolen you from the holy seclusion of a
convent, that you had broken the vows which pledged you
to a purer life, and that Heaven is much incensed by such
behavior. Remorse swept over me, and I feared the wrath
of the Almighty. I now saw how our marriage was nothing
but an adultery in disguise, that it would bring down some
dire punishment on our heads, and that I must therefore try
to forget you, and let you return to your first commitment.
Surely, Madam, you won't find fault with so pious a
decision, or wish me to incur the displeasure of Heaven by
living with you now. . . .

DOÑA ELVIRA

Ah, you scoundrel! I know you now, through and
through—though, unhappily, that knowledge comes too
late, and can serve only to fill me with despair. Be assured,
however, that your crime won't go unpunished, and that the
Heaven which you take so lightly will avenge me for your
faithlessness.

DON JUAN

Heaven, Sganarelle!

SGANARELLE

Yes, we make fun of such things, you and I.

DON JUAN

Madam. . . .

DOÑA ELVIRA

Enough. I'll hear no more of your speeches, and I blame
myself for having listened so long. When one has been

wronged and humiliated, it's base to discuss the matter; in such cases, a noble heart should act at once, without a lot of talk. Don't expect me to shower you now with revilements and reproaches: no, no, my wrath won't spend itself in empty words, and I'll reserve its full fury for the taking of my revenge. I tell you once again, faithless man, that Heaven will punish you for the wrong you've done me; and if you have no fear of Heaven, fear at least the anger of an outraged woman.

(*She exits.*)

SGANARELLE (*Aside.*)
If only he were capable of remorse!

DON JUAN (*After a moment's reflection.*)
Now then, let's go ahead with our amorous enterprise.

SGANARELLE (*Alone.*)
Oh, what a wicked master I'm forced to serve!

Act Two
SCENE ONE

———◆◆———

Charlotte, Pierrot
The countryside, near the seashore and not far from the city.

CHARLOTTE
Good gracious, Pierrot! I guess you got there in the nick of time.

PIERROT
By golly, t'was only by a hair's breadth that them two wasn't drownded.

CHARLOTTE
So, t'was that big wind this morning that turned 'em over in the sea?

PIERROT
Listen, Charlotte, I can tell you the whole thing just like it happened, for I was on the spot, like the fellow says, and I was the one that spotted 'em first. There we was on the seashore, me and fat Lucas, and we was fooling around with some clods of dirt, chucking 'em at each other's heads; I don't have to tell you how fat Lucas likes to fool around, and sometimes I fool around myself. Well, while we was fooling around, and chucking clods like I said, I seen something far away that was wallowing in the water, and that kept coming towards us in lunges, you might say. I kept my eye right on it, and then suddenly I seen that I couldn't see it no more. "Hey, Lucas," I says, "I think some folks is swimming out there." "Come on," he says to me, "you've et some catnip and you're seeing things." "By gum," I told him, "there's nothing wrong with my eyes; there's men out there." "No sir," he says to me, "you've got the day-blindness." "Do you want to bet," I says, "that I ain't

got no day-blindness," I says, "and that there's two men," I says, "swimming right this way?" "By jiminy," he says, "I'll bet you there ain't." "Well," says I, "I got ten sous that says there is." "I'll take that bet," he says, "and to show that I mean it," he says, "here's my money." Well, I was no fool, and no piker neither; I tossed down five sous, by golly, and five more sous in change, just as bold as I'd have tossed off a glass of wine—for I'm a taker of chances, and nothing holds me back. Anyway, I knew what I was doing. What a fool he was to take my bet! We'd hardly put our money down when two men was floating there in plain sight, waving their arms for us to come and get 'em; and so I bent down, first, and scooped up the stakes. "Come on, Lucas," I says to him, "you can see that they're hollering at us; let's go quick and rescue 'em." "No," says he, "they cost me money." Well, to make a long story short, I badgered him until we got ourselves into a rowboat, and then we hauled and heaved out to where we could pull 'em out of the water, and then we took 'em home to warm up by the fire, and they stripped stark naked so as to dry out, and then in come two more of the same crew, which had rescued themselves, and then Mathurine showed up, and one of 'em took to making eyes at her. There you are, Charlotte; that's how it all come to pass.

CHARLOTTE

Didn't you tell me, Pierrot, that one of 'em was a lot better looking than the others?

PIERROT

Yes, that one's the master. I figure he must be a big, big gentleman, because his clothes is all over gold from head to foot; and them that serve him is gentlemen too. Still and all, however big a gentleman he is, he'd 'a been drownded, by George, if I hadn't 'a been there.

CHARLOTTE

Just think of it!

PIERROT

Yes siree, if it hadn't 'a been for us, he'd 'a drunk his fill of
the sea.

CHARLOTTE

Is he still in your house stark naked, Pierrot?

PIERROT

Nope. They put his clothes on again, right in front of us.
Holy Smoke, I'd never seen one of that sort getting dressed
before! What a lot of crazy doodads and contraptions these
court gentlemen do put on! I'd get lost in all that stuff,
myself, and it made me dizzy to look at it. Lord, Charlotte,
they've got hair that comes on and off, and when they get
dressed they put it on, last thing, like a big straw nightcap.
They've got shirts with sleeves so wide that you and me
together could crawl right into 'em. Instead of breeches,
they've got an apron big as from here to Easter. Instead of a
waistcoat, there's a little vest that don't hardly come down
to their belly. And instead of a neckband there's a huge lace
neckerchief, with four big linen tassels hanging down in
front. On top of that, they've got frilly bands around their
wrists, and big funnels of lace on their legs, and everywhere
there's so many ribbons—so terrible many ribbons—that
it's a disgrace. There's even ribbons stuck all over their
shoes, which if I tried to wear 'em I'd fall down and break
my neck.

CHARLOTTE

My goodness, Pierrot, I must go and have a look at some of
that.

PIERROT

No, wait a bit, Charlotte, and listen to me; I got something
else to say to you, I do.

CHARLOTTE

Well, tell me. What is it?

PIERROT

Look here, Charlotte: like the fellow says, I got to get a load off my mind. I love you; you know that; and I want for us to get married. But, doggone it, I ain't satisfied with you.

CHARLOTTE

You ain't? What's the trouble?

PIERROT

The trouble is that you grieve my heart, and that's the truth.

CHARLOTTE

How come? Why do I grieve you?

PIERROT

Because, dad blast it, you don't love me.

CHARLOTTE

Oh! Is that all?

PIERROT

Yes, that's all, and it's plenty.

CHARLOTTE

Land sakes, Pierrot, you're always telling me the same old story.

PIERROT

I always tell you the same old story because it always *is* the same old story; if it *wasn't* always the same old story, I wouldn't always be telling you the same old story.

CHARLOTTE

But what am I supposed to do? What do you want?

PIERROT

Damn it to hell, I want you to love me.

CHARLOTTE

And don't I love you?

PIERROT

No, you don't love me; and in spite of that, I do everything to make you care for me. I buy you ribbons—I ain't complaining, now—I buy you ribbons from every peddler that passes through; I break my neck robbing blackbirds' nests for you; I have the fiddlers play for you when it's your birthday. But in all that, it's as if I was banging my head agin a wall. Doggone it, when a person loves you it ain't fair or decent not to love him back.

CHARLOTTE

Oh, sakes alive, I *do* love you back.

PIERROT

Yes, yes, you love me in a mighty strange way.

CHARLOTTE

What do you want me to do?

PIERROT

I want you to act the way folks act when they love like they ought to.

CHARLOTTE

I don't love you like I ought to?

PIERROT

No. If you did, t'would be plain to see. When folks love a person truly, they play all kinds of monkey tricks on 'em. Think of that fat girl Thomasse, and how crazy she is for young Robin. She's always hanging 'round and pestering him, and she don't give him a moment's peace. She's always pulling some prank, or giving him a thump as she goes by. The other day, when he was setting on a stool, she yanked it

out from under him, so that he fell down flat on his back.
By jiminy, that's how it is when folks are in love. But you,
you never say a word to me, you just stand there like a
fence-post, and I could walk past you twenty times without
you giving me the least little thump, or saying the least little
thing. By gum, that just ain't human; you're too cold to a
person.

CHARLOTTE

What d'you expect me to do? It's my nature, and I can't
make myself over.

PIERROT

Your nature ain't no excuse. When humans feel affection for
somebody, they always let it show a little.

CHARLOTTE

Well, I love you as much as I can, and if that don't satisfy
you, you'd better go and love somebody else.

PIERROT

So, I've got my walking papers, eh? Damnation! If you
loved me, could you say such a thing as that?

CHARLOTTE

Why did you pester me so, and get me all upset?

PIERROT

Hell's bells, what harm have I done you? All I ask from you
is a little affection.

CHARLOTTE

Well, leave me alone, and don't press me too hard. Maybe
t'will come over me all of a sudden, out of the blue.

PIERROT

Let's shake hands and make up, Charlotte.

CHARLOTTE

All right. There.

PIERROT

Promise that you'll try to love me a little more.

CHARLOTTE

I'll do my best, but it'll have to come of itself. Pierrot, is that the gentleman you was telling about?

PIERROT

Yep, that's him.

CHARLOTTE

Heavenly days, how fine-looking he is, and what a shame if he'd been drownded!

PIERROT

I'll be back in a few minutes; after all that hard rowing, I need a glass or two to get my strength back.

SCENE TWO

Don Juan, Sganarelle, Charlotte
Charlotte only is at stage rear.

DON JUAN

Well, Sganarelle, we're failures. That sudden squall upset both our boat and the clever plans we'd made. But to tell you the truth, the peasant girl whom I left just now makes up for our misfortune, and her charms have swept away my chagrin at the sorry outcome of our adventure. I'm resolved that her heart won't escape me; and I've already worked upon her feelings, so that she won't resist my sighs for long.

SGANARELLE

Sir, I confess that you astound me. An hour ago, we barely escaped from death, yet instead of thanking Heaven for the mercy it's shown us, you invite its wrath by resuming your wilful ways and your amorous wick. . . .
(Don Juan gives him a threatening look.)
Hush, you officious knave! You don't know what you're talking about, and your master knows what he's doing. Mind your tongue.

DON JUAN (*Seeing Charlotte.*)

Well, now! Whence comes this other country maid, Sganarelle? Have you ever seen anything prettier? What do you think—is this one the equal of the other?

SGANARELLE

Most certainly.
(Aside.)
One more victim.

DON JUAN (*To Charlotte.*)

What have I done, fair lady, to deserve this delightful

encounter? Can it be that, in this rustic place, among these rocks and trees, there are creatures who look like you?

CHARLOTTE

There are, Sir, like you see.

DON JUAN

Were you born in this village?

CHARLOTTE

Yes, Sir.

DON JUAN

And do you live here?

CHARLOTTE

Yes, Sir.

DON JUAN

And your name is. . . .

CHARLOTTE

Charlotte. Your servant, Sir.

DON JUAN

Oh, what a beauty! And what flashing eyes she has!

CHARLOTTE

Sir, you're making me all embarrassed.

DON JUAN

Oh, you mustn't be embarrassed to hear the truth about yourself. What do you say, Sganarelle? Could anything be lovelier to look at? Turn around a little, if you will. Ah, what a dainty figure! Now lift your chin a little, please. Ah, what a sweet face! Open your eyes wide. Ah, how beautiful they are! Now let me have a look at your teeth, if you please. Ah, how fetching they are—and those lips, how desirable! For my part, I'm ravished; I've never seen anyone so charming.

CHARLOTTE

You're pleased to say so, Sir, but I wonder if you ain't just making fun of me.

DON JUAN

I make fun of you? God forbid! I love you too much for that, and whatever I say to you comes from the bottom of my heart.

CHARLOTTE

In that case, I'm much obliged.

DON JUAN

Not at all; you owe me nothing for the things I've said about you. It's only your beauty that you have to thank.

CHARLOTTE

Sir, your talk's too fancy for me, and I ain't got the wit to answer you back.

DON JUAN

Just look at her hands, Sganarelle.

CHARLOTTE

Oh, heavens, Sir! They're as black as I don't know what.

DON JUAN

Ha! What are you saying? They're the most beautiful hands in the world. Allow me to kiss them, I beg of you.

CHARLOTTE

You pay me a great honor, Sir, and if I'd known about this aforehand, I'd have given 'em a good scrubbing with bran.

DON JUAN

Now, tell me something, my pretty Charlotte: you're not married, I assume?

CHARLOTTE

No, Sir, but I soon will be—to Pierrot, who's the son of our neighbor, Simonette.

DON JUAN

What? Shall a person like you be the wife of a simple peasant? No, no: that would be a profanation of your beauty, and you weren't born to live in some country town. You deserve a better fate than that, and Heaven, which knows your worth, has expressly sent me here to prevent such a marriage, and do justice to your charms. In short, fair Charlotte, I love you with all my heart, and if you'll but say the word I shall snatch you away from this miserable place and raise you to the station where you belong. Doubtless my love seems rather sudden, but why should it not be? So great is your beauty, Charlotte, that you inspire as much love in ten minutes as another could do in half a year.

CHARLOTTE

Honest to goodness, Sir, I don't know what to do when you carry on like that. The things you say are very nice, and I'd give anything if I could believe them; but I've always been told that great gentlemen ain't to be trusted, and that fine talkers like you are deceivers who only want to seduce us girls and ruin us.

DON JUAN

I'm not that sort of man.

SGANARELLE (*Aside.*)

Oh, no! Perish the thought!

CHARLOTTE

Look here, Sir, it's no joke when a girl lets herself be ruined.
I'm a poor country girl, but my honor is precious to me,
and I'd sooner be dead than see myself disgraced.

DON JUAN

Could I be so wicked as to deceive a young woman like
you? Could I be so base as to besmirch your honor? No,
no: I've too much conscience for that. I love you, Charlotte,
and my intentions are wholly honorable; to show you that
I mean what I say, let me inform you that the one thing
I desire is to marry you. What greater proof could there be
of my sincerity? I stand ready to wed you, whenever you
wish; and let this man here be witness to the promise I
make you.

SGANARELLE

Oh, yes, never fear: he'll marry you as much as you like.

DON JUAN

Ah, Charlotte, I can see that you still don't understand me.
You do me a great wrong when you judge me by other men;
if there are knaves among mankind whose only thought is
to seduce young women, you must not think of me as one
of them, or doubt the sincerity of my word. In any case,
you should feel secure in your beauty. When one has a face
like yours, one should be above all common fears. You bear
no resemblance, I assure you, to the sort of girl whom men
deceive and cast aside; and I swear that, if the thought of
betraying you crossed my mind, I'd pierce myself to the
heart a thousand times.

CHARLOTTE

Heavens alive! I don't know whether you're telling the truth
or not, but you make a body believe you.

DON JUAN

Now that you believe me, and give me the trust I deserve,

let me repeat the promise that I made you. Won't you accept my offer, and consent to be my wife?

CHARLOTTE

Yes, so long as my aunt says I can.

DON JUAN

Your hand on it then, Charlotte, since for your part you see no obstacle.

CHARLOTTE

But please, Sir, don't go and deceive me; that would give you a bad conscience, for you see how I'm trusting you.

DON JUAN

What's this? It seems that you still doubt my sincerity! Would you have me swear some terrible oath or other? May Heaven. . . .

CHARLOTTE

Oh, mercy! Don't swear, I'll believe you.

DON JUAN

Then give me a little kiss to seal our engagement.

CHARLOTTE

Oh, Sir! I beg you, wait until we're married and all; after that, I'll kiss you as much as you want.

DON JUAN

Very well, fair Charlotte, your wish shall be my law. But do at least yield me your hand, and let me express my rapture by a thousand kisses. . . .

SCENE THREE

———•———

Don Juan, Sganarelle, Pierrot, Charlotte

PIERROT (*Stepping between the two,
and pushing Don Juan backwards.*)
Hold on there, Sir; go easy, if you please. You're getting
overheated, and you might catch your death of something.

DON JUAN (*Giving Pierrot a hard shove.*)
Why does this low-brow interfere?

PIERROT (*Jumping back between Don Juan and Charlotte.*)
Keep your hands off, I tell you, and don't be kissing our
fiancées.

DON JUAN (*Pushing him again.*)
Oh, how noisy he is!

PIERROT
Hang it! You hadn't ought to push people like that.

CHARLOTTE (*Catching Pierrot by the arm.*)
Leave him alone, now, Pierrot.

PIERROT
What? Leave him alone? I ain't a-going to.

DON JUAN
No?

PIERROT
By gar! Just because you're a fine gentleman, you think you
can come here and kiss our women right under our noses.
Go kiss your own women.

DON JUAN

You mean that?

PIERROT

I mean that.
>   (*Don Juan slaps him in the face.*)
Damnation, don't hit me!
>   (*Another slap.*)
Ouch, doggone it!
>   (*Another slap.*)
Goldarn it!
>   (*Another slap.*)
Drat and thunderation! It ain't right to beat people, and it's a fine reward to give a person who saved you from being drownded.

CHARLOTTE

Now, Pierrot, don't get sore.

PIERROT

I sure as heck *will* get sore; and you're a slut, you are, to let yourself get trifled with.

CHARLOTTE

Oh, Pierrot, it ain't like you think it is. This gentleman wants to marry me, and so you've got nothing to be upset about.

PIERROT

What do you mean? Damn it, you're engaged to me.

CHARLOTTE

That don't matter, Pierrot. If you love me, shouldn't it make you happy that I'm going to be a lady?

PIERROT

By golly, no! I'd sooner see you dead than belonging to somebody else.

CHARLOTTE

Now, now, Pierrot, don't get all worked up: if I get to be a lady, there'll be something in it for you. You can supply our house with butter and cheese.

PIERROT

By gar, I won't supply you with nothing ever, not even if you pay me double. So this is what comes of you listening to that feller's talk! Damme, if I'd known that a while ago, I wouldn't have pulled him out of the water; I'd have knocked him over the head with an oar.

DON JUAN (*Approaching Pierrot,
with a hand raised to strike him.*)

What did you say?

PIERROT (*Backing off, slipping behind Charlotte.*)

By gar, I ain't afeared of nobody.

DON JUAN (*Moving around Charlotte, pursuing Pierrot.*)

Just wait till I catch you.

PIERROT (*Moving around to Charlotte's other side.*)

I ain't scared of nothing, not me.

DON JUAN (*Following after Pierrot.*)

We shall see.

PIERROT (*Once more taking refuge behind Charlotte.*)

I've stood up to many of your sort.

DON JUAN

Hah!

SGANARELLE

Oh, Sir, leave the poor wretch alone. T'would be a sin to beat him.

(*To Pierrot, stepping between him and Don Juan.*)
Listen, my poor boy: be off with you, and say no more to
him.

PIERROT (*Stepping around Sganarelle
and boldly addressing Don Juan.*)
I've got more to say to him, and I'm going to say it!

DON JUAN (*Raising his hand to slap Pierrot,
who ducks his head so that Sganarelle receives the blow.*)
Ha! I'll teach you.

SGANARELLE (*Looking at Pierrot,
who has bent over to avoid the slap.*)
A curse on that yokel!

DON JUAN (*To Sganarelle.*)
There's the reward for your charity.

PIERROT
By jeepers, I'm going to tell her aunt about all this funny-
business.
(*He exits.*)

DON JUAN (*To Charlotte.*)
Now then, Charlotte: I'm soon to be the most fortunate of
men, and I wouldn't exchange my happiness for anything in
creation. How delicious our married life is going to be, and
how. . . .

SCENE FOUR

Don Juan, Sganarelle, Charlotte, Mathurine

SGANARELLE (*Who sees Mathurine approaching.*)
Oh, no!

MATHURINE (*To Don Juan.*)
Why, Sir! What are you doing here with Charlotte? Are you making love to her too?

DON JUAN (*Aside to Mathurine.*)
No, quite the reverse. She expressed, just now, a wish to be my wife, and I was informing her of my engagement to you.

CHARLOTTE (*To Don Juan.*)
What does that Mathurine want of you?

DON JUAN (*Aside to Charlotte.*)
She's jealous because she found me talking to you, and she wants me to marry her; but I've told her that it's you I care for.

MATHURINE
Look here, Charlotte. . . .

DON JUAN (*Aside to Mathurine.*)
Anything you say to her will be a waste of time; she's obsessed with that wild notion.

CHARLOTTE
Listen, Mathurine. . . .

DON JUAN (*Aside to Charlotte.*)
T'will be useless for you to talk with her; she won't give up that fantasy.

MATHURINE
If you don't mind. . . .

DON JUAN (*Aside to Mathurine.*)
There's no way to make her listen to reason.

CHARLOTTE
I'd like to know. . . .

DON JUAN (*Aside to Charlotte.*)
She's as stubborn as the Devil himself.

MATHURINE
Do you honestly. . . .

DON JUAN (*Aside to Mathurine.*)
Don't bother with her; she's mad.

CHARLOTTE
If you ask me. . . .

DON JUAN (*Aside to Charlotte.*)
Let her be; she's quite demented.

MATHURINE
No, no, I've got to talk with her.

CHARLOTTE
I want to know what she thinks she's doing.

MATHURINE
Why? . . .

DON JUAN (*Aside to Mathurine.*)
She'll claim, I wager, that I've promised to marry her.

CHARLOTTE
I. . . .

DON JUAN (*Aside to Charlotte.*)
It's a safe bet that she'll tell you how I've sworn to make her my wife.

MATHURINE
Listen, Charlotte, it ain't fair for you to horn in on my affairs.

CHARLOTTE
You've got no right to get jealous, Mathurine, when this gentleman talks to me.

MATHURINE
The gentleman saw me first.

CHARLOTTE
If he saw you first, he saw me second, and he's promised to marry me.

DON JUAN (*Aside to Mathurine.*)
There! What did I tell you?

MATHURINE (*To Charlotte.*)
Go on with you. It's me, and not you, that he's promised to marry.

DON JUAN (*Aside to Charlotte.*)
Just as I predicted!

CHARLOTTE
Go tell that to the birds; it's me, like I said.

MATHURINE
You're joking. I tell you again, it's me.

CHARLOTTE
This gentleman can say if I'm right or not.

MATHURINE

This gentleman can correct me if I'm wrong.

CHARLOTTE

Sir, is it true that you promised to marry her?

DON JUAN (*Aside to Charlotte.*)

You can't be serious.

MATHURINE

Sir, did you give your word to be her husband?

DON JUAN (*Aside to Mathurine.*)

How can you think such a thing?

CHARLOTTE

You see how she keeps insisting.

DON JUAN (*Aside to Charlotte.*)

Let her insist.

MATHURINE

She won't stop saying it.

DON JUAN (*Aside to Mathurine.*)

Let her talk.

CHARLOTTE

No, no, let's have the truth.

MATHURINE

It's got to be decided.

CHARLOTTE

Yes, Mathurine, I want this gentleman to show you up for a silly goose.

MATHURINE

Yes, Charlotte, I want this gentleman to take you down a peg.

CHARLOTTE

You'll see.

MATHURINE (*To Charlotte.*)

It's you that'll see.

CHARLOTTE (*To Don Juan.*)

Speak, Sir.

MATHURINE (*To Don Juan.*)

Tell us.

DON JUAN (*Flustered, and addressing them both at once.*)

What would you have me say? Both of you contend that I've promised to marry you. Since each of you knows what I really said, why need I explain myself further? Why force me to repeat myself? The one to whom, in fact, I gave my promise should be able to laugh off the pretensions of the other; nothing should trouble her, provided I keep my word. But all this talk accomplishes nothing; it's actions that count, not words, and it's by deeds, not speeches, that matters are decided. It's in that concrete sense that I shall settle this affair, and it will be clear, when I marry, which of you two has won my heart.

(*Aside to Mathurine.*)

Let her believe what she likes.

(*Aside to Charlotte.*)

Let her enjoy her fantasies.

(*Aside to Mathurine.*)

I adore you.

(*Aside to Charlotte.*)

I am your slave.

(*Aside to Mathurine.*)
All faces are ugly, compared to yours.
(*Aside to Charlotte.*)
Once one has seen you, one can't bear the sight of others.
I have one or two little orders to give; I shall be back with
you in a quarter-hour.
(*He exits.*)

CHARLOTTE (*To Mathurine.*)
Well, anyway I'm the one he loves.

MATHURINE (*To Charlotte.*)
It's me he's going to marry.

SGANARELLE
Ah, you poor girls, I pity your innocence, and I can't bear
to see you in such a hurry to be undone. Take my advice,
both of you: don't let yourselves be led astray by all the lies
you've been hearing: stay here in your little village, and be
safe.

DON JUAN (*Speaking to himself, as he reenters.*)
Why didn't Sganarelle follow me, I wonder? What can he
be doing?

SGANARELLE (*To the girls.*)
My master is a trickster. All he wants is to seduce you, as
he has so many others. He's quite ready to marry the whole
human race: he. . . .
(*He notices Don Juan.*)
All that, of course, is false, and if anyone says those things
to you, you must tell him that he is a liar. My master is
not prepared to marry the whole human race, he is not a
trickster, he has no intention of deceiving you, and he has
never seduced anybody. But ah, here he is! If you don't
believe me, ask him.

DON JUAN (*Eyeing Sganarelle,*
and suspicious of what he may have said.)
By all means.

SGANARELLE

Sir, since the world is full of slanders, I've been anticipating
what malicious tongues might say; and I've told these
young ladies that if anyone speaks ill of you, they must
refuse to believe him, and tell him flatly that he's a liar.

DON JUAN

Sganarelle!

SGANARELLE (*To Charlotte and Mathurine.*)
Yes, my master is a man of honor, I can vouch for that.

DON JUAN

Ahem!

SGANARELLE

His detractors are wicked men.

SCENE FIVE

———•••———

Don Juan, La Ramée, Charlotte, Mathurine, Sganarelle

LA RAMÉE (*Aside to Don Juan.*)
Sir, I've come to warn you that you're not safe in these parts.

DON JUAN
How's that?

LA RAMÉE
Twelve men on horseback are hunting for you, and they could arrive here at any moment. I don't know how they've managed to trace you, but I got this news from a peasant they'd questioned and to whom they'd given your description. There's no time to lose, and the quicker you get out of here, the better.

DON JUAN (*To Charlotte and Mathurine.*)
A pressing matter obliges me to go, now; but remember the promise I gave you, and be assured that you'll hear from me before tomorrow evening.
(*Exeunt Charlotte and Mathurine.*)
Since we're so outnumbered by our foes, I shall have to resort to cunning, and escape this danger by means of some stratagem. Let me see: I'll have Sganarelle put on my clothes, and. . . .

SGANARELLE
Oh, Sir, you're only joking. If I were in your clothes, someone might kill me, and. . . .

DON JUAN
Come now, be quick. I offer you a very great honor; it's a lucky valet who can have the glory of dying for his master.

SGANARELLE

For such an honor, I can't thank you enough.

(*Alone.*)

O Heaven, if there's dying to be done, don't let me die of mistaken identity.

Act Three
SCENE ONE

Don Juan, in country clothing
Sganarelle, in the garb of a doctor
A forest near the sea, and not far from the town.

SGANARELLE
You must admit that I was right, Sir, and that both of us are now admirably disguised. Your first idea wasn't at all practical, and these costumes are far better camouflage than what you had in mind.

DON JUAN
You look quite marvelous, it's true; I can't imagine where you dug up that ridiculous garment.

SGANARELLE
Really? It's the professional gown of an old doctor, which I picked up at a pawnshop, and which cost me a good bit of money. Would you believe, Sir, that this gown has already brought me many signs of respect, that people bow to me as I pass, and that they consult me as if I were a learnèd man?

DON JUAN
They do? On what subjects?

SGANARELLE
Five or six peasants, both men and women, have run up to me when they saw me coming by, and asked my advice about one sickness or another.

DON JUAN
You told them, I suppose, that you knew nothing of medicine?

SGANARELLE

Why, certainly not. I felt I should uphold the honor of my gown, and so I pondered their symptoms and in each case prescribed some treatment.

DON JUAN

And what remedies did you prescribe?

SGANARELLE

Good Lord, Sir, I just said whatever came into my head; I tossed off prescriptions at random. It would be a funny thing, wouldn't it, if the sick actually got well, and came to thank me for healing them?

DON JUAN

Why shouldn't they? Why shouldn't you have the same rewards as all the other doctors? They do no more than you to heal the sick, and their science is purest humbug. The one thing they know how to do is to take credit when patients get better; and you should profit, as they do, from the gratitude of those who ascribe to your remedies what they really owe to Nature and good fortune.

SGANARELLE

What, Sir! Are you irreverent about medicine as well?

DON JUAN

It's one of the worst superstitions of mankind.

SGANARELLE

You don't believe, then, in senna, or cassia, or emetic wine?

DON JUAN

Why would you have me believe in such things?

SGANARELLE

You have a very doubting nature. But surely you know that, for some time, there's been great public excitement about

emetic wine. Its miraculous effects have won over the most
skeptical, and I myself, not three weeks ago, witnessed a
wonderful proof of its virtue.

DON JUAN

How so?

SGANARELLE

There was a man who, for six whole days, had lain at death's
door. All remedies had failed, and no one knew what else to
do for him. At last, they decided to give him some emetic
wine.

DON JUAN

And he recovered, did he?

SGANARELLE

No, he died.

DON JUAN

A wondrous result!

SGANARELLE

It certainly was! For six whole days he'd been unable to die,
and it finished him off in a minute. What could be more
effective?

DON JUAN

What, indeed?

SGANARELLE

But let's drop the subject of medicine, since you don't
believe in it, and talk of other things. This costume has
sharpened my wits, and I feel in the mood to debate. You'll
recall that you allow me to debate with you, and that the
only thing you forbid is preaching.

DON JUAN

Very well, go ahead.

SGANARELLE

I just want to know your thoughts about some fundamental questions. Is it possible that you don't believe in Heaven at all?

DON JUAN

Let's table that question.

SGANARELLE

In other words, you don't. What about Hell?

DON JUAN

Huh!

SGANARELLE

Same answer. And the Devil, do you believe in him?

DON JUAN

Yes, yes.

SGANARELLE

So you doubt him too. Have you no faith whatever in the life to come?

DON JUAN

Come, come.

SGANARELLE (*Aside.*)

I can see that I'm going to have trouble converting this man.

(*To Don Juan.*)

Tell me, now: what are your beliefs regarding the Bogeyman? What about him, eh?

DON JUAN

Don't be an idiot.

SGANARELLE

Now, there you go too far, for there's nothing truer in this world than the Bogeyman; I'll stake my life on that. But one has to believe in something; what is it that you believe?

DON JUAN

What do I believe?

SGANARELLE

Yes.

DON JUAN

I believe that two and two are four, Sganarelle, and that four and four are eight.

SGANARELLE

What a fine creed that is! So far as I can see, your religion consists of arithmetic. Men, I must say, can get some weird notions in their heads, and people who've studied a lot aren't always a lot wiser. As for me, Sir, I've never studied like you, thank God, and no one can boast of having taught me anything; but with my small wits, and my small judgement, I see things more clearly than all those books do, and I know for certain that this world we behold is not a mushroom that shot up overnight of its own doing. I'd like to ask you who made those trees, those rocks, this earth, and the sky we see up there, and if all those things created themselves? Look at yourself, for example; here you are: did you make yourself singlehanded, or wasn't it necessary for your father to beget you on your mother before you could exist? Can you look at all the inventions which compose the human apparatus, without marveling at the way they're designed to work together, one with the other? These nerves, these bones, these veins, these arteries, these . . . this lung, this heart, this liver, and all the other ingredients which are in there, and which. . . . Oh, my God, interrupt me, won't you? I can't argue if I'm not interrupted. You're deliberately keeping quiet, and you're letting me run on out of sheer malice.

DON JUAN

I'm waiting for your argument to be finished.

SGANARELLE

My argument, whatever you may say, is that there's something wonderful in man which all the wise heads can't explain. Isn't it marvelous that I'm here, and that I have something in my head that can think a hundred different things in a second, and can make my body do whatever it likes? I can choose to clap my hands, lift my arms, raise my eyes to Heaven, bow my head, shift my feet, move to the right, to the left, forward, backward, turn around. . . .
(*In turning around, he falls down.*)

DON JUAN

Good! There lies your argument with a broken nose.

SGANARELLE

Curses! I'm a fool to waste my time arguing with you. Believe what you like: a lot I care if you're damned!

DON JUAN

What with all this reasoning, I think we've lost our way. Give a shout to that man over there, and ask him for directions.

SGANARELLE

Ho there, my man! Ho there, fellow! Ho, my friend! A word with you, if you please.

SCENE TWO

———— •—•— ————

Don Juan, Sganarelle, A Poor Man

SGANARELLE

Kindly tell us by what route we may get to the town.

THE POOR MAN

You've only to follow this road, Sirs, and bear to the right when you come out of the woods. I warn you, however, to be on your guard, because for some time there have been robbers hereabouts.

DON JUAN

I'm much obliged to you, my friend, and I thank you with all my heart.

THE POOR MAN

Would you be so good, Sir, as to spare me some alms?

DON JUAN

Aha! You charge for your advice, I see.

THE POOR MAN

I'm a poor man, Sir, who for ten years has lived all alone in these woods. I shall ask Heaven, in my prayers, to give you every good thing.

DON JUAN

Huh! Ask Heaven to give you a warm coat, and don't trouble so about the needs of others.

SGANARELLE (*To the Poor Man.*)

You don't know this gentleman, my good fellow: he believes only in two-and-two-are-four, and in four-and-four-are-eight.

DON JUAN

What's your occupation, here among these trees?

THE POOR MAN

I pray to Heaven, all day long, for the prosperity of the good, charitable people who have helped me.

DON JUAN

I assume, then, that you live very comfortably?

THE POOR MAN

Alas, Sir! I live in the greatest possible privation.

DON JUAN

You can't be serious; a man who prays to Heaven all day is bound to be well taken care of.

THE POOR MAN

I assure you, Sir, that most of the time I haven't a crust of bread to chew on.

DON JUAN

It's strange that you should be so shabbily rewarded for all your trouble. See here, I'll give you a gold Louis right now, if you'll just utter one blasphemous oath.

THE POOR MAN

Take the Lord's name in vain? Sir, would you have me commit such a sin?

DON JUAN

It's up to you. Do you want to earn a gold piece or not? Here's one that I'll give you, if you'll just swear that oath. Come now, let's hear it.

THE POOR MAN

Sir. . . .

DON JUAN

You can't have this unless you do.

SGANARELLE

Go on, blaspheme a little. It'll do no harm.

DON JUAN

Here it is, take it, take it. Take it, I tell you. But first you must blaspheme.

THE POOR MAN

No, Sir, I'd rather starve to death.

DON JUAN

Well then, I'll give it to you for the love of humanity. But what do I see over there? One man set upon by three others? That's not a fair contest, and I mustn't permit such dastardly behavior.

SCENE THREE

———•●———

Don Juan, Don Carlos, Sganarelle

SGANARELLE (*Alone.*)
My master is a real madman, to go looking for danger when it's not looking for him. But, my word! His intervention has tipped the balance, and the two of them have put the three to flight.

DON CARLOS (*With sword in hand.*)
It's plain to see, from the way those robbers fled, what help your strong arm gave me. Allow me, Sir, to thank you for a most courageous action, which. . . .

DON JUAN (*Returning, sword in hand.*)
I did nothing, Sir, that you wouldn't have done in my place. One's own honor is challenged when one sees another in such a plight, and not to oppose the base actions of those rogues would have made me their accomplice. But how did you happen to fall into their hands?

DON CARLOS
I had by chance become separated from my brother, and the rest of our party; and as I was seeking to rejoin them I encountered those brigands, who began by killing my horse and, but for your brave assistance, would have done the same to me.

DON JUAN
Is your party going in the direction of the town?

DON CARLOS
Yes, though we don't intend to enter it; my brother and I must keep to the countryside, because we're involved in one of those vexing affairs wherein a gentleman must sacrifice himself and his family to the tyranny of honor. In such

matters, the most fortunate outcome is still a disaster, for if
one doesn't lose one's life one must lose one's country, and
be thrust into exile. It is, I think, an unfortunate thing to
be a gentleman, who can't rest secure in the wisdom and
prudence of his own conduct, but is bound by the laws of
honor to punish the misconduct of others. Our lives, our
fortunes, and our peace of mind are at the mercy of any
fool who deals us one of those insults which oblige a man
of honor to fight to the death.

DON JUAN

Well, there's this compensation—that those so foolish as
to do us wrong must suffer the same danger and distress of
mind as we. But would it be indiscreet to ask the nature of
this affair you mention?

DON CARLOS

The matter can't be kept secret for much longer; and since
the affront to our family will soon be public knowledge,
honor lies not in concealing our shame but in openly
declaring our intent to be avenged. Therefore, Sir, I don't
hesitate to tell you that the wrong we mean to avenge is the
seduction of our sister and her abduction from a convent,
and the wrongdoer is one Don Juan Tenorio, the son of
Don Luis Tenorio. We've been seeking him for several days
now, and this morning we picked up his trail, informed
by a lackey that he'd ridden out along this coast with a
company of four or five men. But all our searching has been
fruitless, and we've no idea what's become of him.

DON JUAN

This Don Juan of whom you speak—do you know him, Sir?

DON CARLOS

Not personally, no. I've never seen him, and I know him
only through my brother's descriptions of him; but his
reputation is by no means good, and he's a man whose
life. . . .

DON JUAN

If you please, Sir, say no more. He is something of a friend of mine, and it would be cowardly of me to stand by and hear him denigrated.

DON CARLOS

For your sake, Sir, I'll say not a word more about him. The least I can do for you, since you've saved my life, is to hold my peace in your presence about a man whom you know, and of whom I can't speak without speaking ill. But, friend though he may be, I hope that you don't approve his actions, or think it strange that we should seek vengeance on their account.

DON JUAN

On the contrary, I want to be of service in your quest, and spare you some unnecessary trouble. I'm a friend of Don Juan, I can't help that; but he mustn't expect to offend good gentlemen with impunity, and I promise to make him give you satisfaction.

DON CARLOS

For such great wrongs, what satisfaction could be given?

DON JUAN

Whatever your family honor may require. What's more, to save you the bother of a further search for Don Juan, I take it upon myself to produce him at whatever place you wish, and at whatever time you choose.

DON CARLOS

That promise, Sir, is balm to our offended hearts; but in view of what I owe you, it would much distress me if you yourself took part in the encounter.

DON JUAN

I'm so attached to Don Juan that he could never fight without my fighting also. In any case, I can answer for him

as for myself, and if you'll just name a time and place, he'll
appear and satisfy your honor.

DON CARLOS

Oh, what a cruel twist of fate! Why must I owe my life to
you, when Don Juan is one of your friends?

SCENE FOUR

———————●———————

Don Alonso and three attendants,
Don Carlos, Don Juan, Sganarelle

DON ALONSO (*Speaking to his attendants,*
not seeing Don Carlos or Don Juan.)
Water my horses over there, then bring them along behind;
I want to go on foot awhile.
(*Perceiving the two men.*)
Great God, what do I see? You, Brother, conversing with
our mortal enemy!

DON CARLOS

Our mortal enemy?

DON JUAN (*Backing off several paces,*
and proudly placing a hand on his sword-hilt.)
Yes, I myself am Don Juan. Though you outnumber me, I
shan't deny my name.

DON ALONSO (*Drawing his sword.*)
Ah, treacherous villain, you must die! Prepare. . . .
(*Sganarelle runs away to hide.*)

DON CARLOS

No, Brother, hold! I'm indebted to him for my life; without
the help of his arm, I'd have been killed by some brigands
who fell upon me.

DON ALONSO

And should that fact stand in the way of our revenge?
Whatever services a foe may render, he can't thereby disarm
our enmity. Compare your debt to him with his offenses,
Brother, and any gratitude must seem absurd. Since honor's
infinitely more precious than life, we owe nothing to a man
who has saved your life but robbed us of our honor.

DON CARLOS

As between life and honor, Brother, I well know which a
gentleman must value more, and my debt of gratitude in
no way lessens my wrath at his misdeeds. But permit me
now to return what he has lent me, and pay him back at
once for the life I owe him: let me postpone our vengeance,
and grant him a few days in which to enjoy the fruits of his
good deed.

DON ALONSO

No, no, if we put off our vengeance we shall run the risk
of losing it; there might never be another chance. Heaven
offers us this opportunity, and we must seize it. When one's
honor has been mortally wounded, one should not respond
with timid half-measures; if you have no stomach for
what must be done, then step aside, and leave our glorious
retribution to my sword alone.

DON CARLOS

Brother, I beg you. . . .

DON ALONSO

All this talk is pointless; the man must die.

DON CARLOS

Stop, Brother; stop, I tell you. I shan't allow his blood to
be spilt, and I swear by Heaven to defend him against any
man, shielding him with the very life he saved. If your
sword would reach him, it must first run me through.

DON ALONSO

So, you take our enemy's side against me! And, far from
sharing the rage I feel at the sight of him, you treat him
with a sweet solicitude!

DON CARLOS

Brother, let's achieve our just end in a moderate spirit, and
not avenge our honor with such fury as you now display.

Let's be the masters of our courage, and let our valor have
nothing savage in it; let's be moved to action by the calm
use of our reason, and not by blind passion. I don't wish,
Brother, to be obligated to my enemy, and so I ask that,
first of all, I may discharge my debt to him. Our vengeance
will lose no lustre by having been deferred: on the contrary,
it will gain in glory, and our having passed up this chance
will make it appear more just in the world's eyes.

DON ALONSO

Oh, what utter folly, what delusion, to endanger the cause
of one's honor for the sake of a fancied obligation!

DON CARLOS

Don't worry, Brother. If I'm making a mistake, I shall know
how to rectify it, and I take upon myself a full responsibility
for our cause: I know what our honor asks of us, and this
one-day's delay, which my gratitude requires, will only
increase my determination to meet its demands. Don Juan,
you see that I'm at pains to return the good deed you did
me, and you should judge my character by that, and know
that I discharge all my debts with the same zeal; believe
me, I shall repay the injury as scrupulously as I've repaid
the kindness. I've no wish to force you, here and now, to
declare your intentions, and you are free to consider, at
leisure, the decisions that you must make. You well know
the magnitude of the offense that you've given, and you
may judge for yourself what reparations are called for. There
are peaceful means by which you might satisfy us, and
there are others both violent and bloody. But whatever you
may decide, I have your word that you'll make Don Juan
give me satisfaction; remember to do so, I pray you, and
remember also that, from this moment on, my only debt is
to my honor.

DON JUAN

I didn't plead for this delay, and I shall keep my promise.

DON CARLOS

Let's go, Brother; a moment's clemency won't impair our stern resolve to do our duty.

SCENE FIVE

Don Juan, Sganarelle

DON JUAN

Ho there! I say! Sganarelle!

SGANARELLE (*Coming out of hiding.*)

You called?

DON JUAN

So, you knave! When I'm attacked, you run away, do you?

SGANARELLE

Pardon me, Sir; I had to slip into the bushes. I think that this gown has medicinal virtues, and that to wear it is like taking a laxative.

DON JUAN

A plague on your impudence! Do at least cloak your cowardice in a better lie than that. Do you know who he was, the man whose life I saved just now?

SGANARELLE

Do I know him? No.

DON JUAN

He's one of Elvira's brothers.

SGANARELLE

One of her bro . . . !

DON JUAN

He's a decent man; he behaved rather well, and I'm sorry to be at odds with him.

SGANARELLE

You could easily settle all this in a peaceful way.

DON JUAN

Yes, but my passion for Doña Elvira has expired, and it doesn't suit me to be tied down. I like to be free in love, as you know, and I could never confine my heart within four walls. As I've told you many a time, it's my nature to yield to whatever bewitches my eye. My heart belongs to all beautiful women, and it's their business to claim it, each in her turn, and to keep it as long as they can. But what's the grand edifice that I see between those trees?

SGANARELLE

You don't know?

DON JUAN

No, I don't.

SGANARELLE

Why, Sir! It's the tomb that the Commander was having built, at the time when you killed him.

DON JUAN

Ah, yes; quite so. I didn't know that it was in this location. Everyone's told me of its wondrous architecture, and of the Commander's statue; I'd like to have a look at it.

SGANARELLE

Oh, Sir, don't go in there.

DON JUAN

Why not?

SGANARELLE

It's not seemly to call on a man whom you've killed.

DON JUAN

On the contrary, my visit will do him a courtesy, and if he's
a man of breeding, he'll receive me graciously. Come, let's
go in.

*(The tomb opens, revealing a splendid mausoleum
and the Statue of the Commander.)*

SGANARELLE

Oh, how beautiful it is! What beautiful statues! And the
beautiful marble! The beautiful columns! Oh, how beautiful
it is! What do you think of it, Sir?

DON JUAN

I think that a dead man's vanity could scarcely go farther
than this. Strange that a man who, while he lived, was
content with a modest dwelling, should desire such a
mansion when he needs a house no longer.

SGANARELLE

Here's the statue of the Commander.

DON JUAN

Dear God! How ridiculous he looks, got up like a Roman
emperor!

SGANARELLE

My word, Sir, what a fine likeness it is! It's as if he were
alive, and about to speak. The way he's looking at us would
scare me, if I were alone, and I think he's not pleased to see
us.

DON JUAN

He'd be wrong to glower at us; t'would be a poor way to
acknowledge the honor of my visit. Ask him if he'd care to
come and have dinner with me.

SGANARELLE

Dinner, I think, is something he no longer needs.

DON JUAN

Ask him, I tell you.

SGANARELLE

You're not serious. I'd be crazy if I went and talked to a statue.

DON JUAN

Do as I tell you.

SGANARELLE

What a curious whim! My lord Commander . . .
(*Aside.*)
I can't help laughing at what I'm doing, but my master's making me do it.
(*Aloud.*)
My lord Commander, my master Don Juan asks that you do him the honor of joining him for dinner.
(*The Statue nods its head.*)
Aagh!

DON JUAN

What is it? What's the matter? Speak up, will you?

SGANARELLE (*Nodding his head
as the Statue did.*)

The Statue. . . .

DON JUAN

Come, knave, what are you trying to say?

SGANARELLE

The Statue, I tell you. . . .

DON JUAN

Well, what about the Statue? Out with it, or I'll break your neck.

SGANARELLE

The Statue nodded its head.

DON JUAN

The Devil take this idiot.

SGANARELLE

It nodded at me, I tell you: that's the God's honest truth.
Go on and speak to it yourself, if you doubt me. Maybe
you'll. . . .

DON JUAN

Come here, you wretch, come here. I'll make you ashamed
of your craven fantasies. Now, watch. Will my lord
Commander be so kind as to come and dine with me?
        (*The Statue nods its head once more.*)

SGANARELLE

I wouldn't have missed that for ten pistoles. Well, Sir?

DON JUAN

Come, let's get out of here.

SGANARELLE (*Alone.*)

So much for your free-thinkers, who won't believe in
anything!

Act Four

SCENE ONE

———◆—◆———

Don Juan, Sganarelle, Ragotin
Don Juan's residence.

DON JUAN

Whatever may have happened, let's say no more about that
trivial incident. Most likely we were deceived by the dim
light, or by some momentary dizziness which blurred our
vision.

SGANARELLE

Oh, no, Sir! Don't try to explain away what we both so
clearly saw. Nothing could be more real than that nod of
the head, and I'm convinced that Heaven, shocked by your
behavior, wrought that miracle so as to make you see the
light, and pull you back from the brink of. . . .

DON JUAN

Listen to me. If you pester me any further with your silly
moralizings, if you say one more word on this subject, I'll
send for a bull-whip, and have you held down by three
or four men, and give you a thousand lashes. Do you
understand me?

SGANARELLE

Very well, Sir, very well indeed. You express yourself most
clearly. That's one of the best things about you, that you
don't in the least beat around the bush: you put things with
an admirable directness.

DON JUAN

Now then, let my dinner be served as quickly as possible.
Bring me a chair, boy!
(Ragotin brings a chair.)

SCENE TWO

———◆●◆———

Don Juan, Sganarelle, La Violette, Ragotin

LA VIOLETTE

Sir, your tailor, Monsieur Dimanche, is here, and he asks to speak with you.

SGANARELLE

Splendid; just what we needed, a visit from a creditor. What makes him think that he can come here and dun us for money, and why didn't you tell him that the master wasn't at home?

LA VIOLETTE

I've been telling him that for three quarters of an hour, but he won't believe me, and he's set himself down in there to wait.

SGANARELLE

Let him wait as long as he likes.

DON JUAN

No; on the contrary, have him come in. It's very bad policy not to be at home to one's creditors. It's only fair to give them something or other, and I know the secret of sending them away happy without paying them a penny.

SCENE THREE

*Don Juan, Monsieur Dimanche, Sganarelle,
La Violette, Ragotin*

DON JUAN (*Being effusively polite.*)
Ah, Monsieur Dimanche, do come in. How delighted I am
to see you, and how annoyed I am with my servants for not
showing you in right away! I *had* given orders that no one
should be admitted; but those orders didn't apply to you,
for whom—of course—my door is always open.

M. DIMANCHE
I'm greatly obliged to you, Sir.

DON JUAN (*Speaking to La Violette and Ragotin.*)
Confound it, you rascals, I'll teach you to keep Monsieur
Dimanche waiting in an antechamber! You must learn how
to treat important people.

M. DIMANCHE
It was nothing, Sir.

DON JUAN
What! Nothing? To tell you that I wasn't at home? You,
Monsieur Dimanche, my dearest friend!

M. DIMANCHE
Your servant, Sir. I came here today. . . .

DON JUAN
Quickly now, bring a seat for Monsieur Dimanche.

M. DIMANCHE
I'm quite comfortable as I am, Sir.

DON JUAN

No, no, I insist that we sit down together.

M. DIMANCHE

That's not at all necessary.

DON JUAN

Take that stool away, and bring an armchair.

M. DIMANCHE

Sir, you must be joking. I. . . .

DON JUAN

Not at all; I wish to give you your due, and I won't have any distinctions between us.

M. DIMANCHE

Sir. . . .

DON JUAN

Come, have a seat.

M. DIMANCHE

There's no need of that, Sir; I only want to say one word to you. I came here. . . .

DON JUAN

Do sit down, I beg of you.

M. DIMANCHE

No, Sir, I'm quite all right. I came here to. . . .

DON JUAN

No, I shall not listen unless you sit down.

M. DIMANCHE

Well then, I'll do as you wish, Sir. I. . . .

DON JUAN

By Heaven, Monsieur Dimanche, you're looking well!

M. DIMANCHE

I'm well, Sir, and at your service. What brings me here. . . .

DON JUAN

You have a fine, healthy constitution: red lips, ruddy
cheeks, sparkling eyes.

M. DIMANCHE

My reason for. . . .

DON JUAN

How is Madame Dimanche, your wife?

M. DIMANCHE

Very well, Sir, thank the Lord.

DON JUAN

She's an excellent woman.

M. DIMANCHE

She's your humble servant, Sir. I came. . . .

DON JUAN

And your little daughter Claudine, how is she?

M. DIMANCHE

She couldn't be better.

DON JUAN

What a pretty little girl she is! I love her with all my heart.

M. DIMANCHE

You're too kind, Sir. I'd like. . . .

DON JUAN

And little Colin, does he still make as much noise as ever with that drum of his?

M. DIMANCHE

The same as always, Sir. I. . . .

DON JUAN

And what about your little dog Brusquet? Does he growl as fiercely as ever, and does he still gnaw the legs of all your visitors?

M. DIMANCHE

He gets worse every day, Sir; we just can't break him of the habit.

DON JUAN

Don't be surprised at my asking for news of your family; I take a great interest in them all.

M. DIMANCHE

We're infinitely obliged to you, Sir. But now. . . .

DON JUAN (*Holding out his hand.*)

Give me the hand of friendship, Monsieur Dimanche. You *are* my friend, I hope?

M. DIMANCHE

I'm your servant, Sir.

DON JUAN

By Heaven, I'm yours with all my heart.

M. DIMANCHE

You do me too much honor. I. . . .

DON JUAN

There's nothing I wouldn't do for you.

M. DIMANCHE

Sir, your kindness is overwhelming.

DON JUAN

And there's no self-interest in it, believe me.

M. DIMANCHE

I don't deserve your gracious favor. But, Sir. . . .

DON JUAN

Now then, Monsieur Dimanche, let's forget the formalities; will you dine with me?

M. DIMANCHE

Oh no, Sir, I must go back home at once. I. . . .

DON JUAN (*Rising.*)

Quick, a torch to light the way for Monsieur Dimanche. And have four or five men get their muskets and escort him home.

M. DIMANCHE (*Also rising.*)

There's no need of that, Sir; I can very well get home alone. But. . . .

(*Sganarelle whisks the chairs away.*)

DON JUAN

Certainly not! I insist that you be escorted, for your safety concerns me deeply. I am your servant and, what's more, I am your debtor.

M. DIMANCHE

Yes, Sir! That's. . . .

DON JUAN

I make no secret of it; indeed, I tell everybody.

M. DIMANCHE

If. . . .

DON JUAN

Would you like me to escort you home, myself?

M. DIMANCHE

Oh, Sir, you're not serious. But, Sir. . . .

DON JUAN

Embrace me then, if you please. I beg you once again to believe that I'm wholly at your service, and that there's nothing in the world I wouldn't do for you.

(*He exits.*)

SGANARELLE

You must admit that my master's very devoted to you.

M. DIMANCHE

That's true; he's so gracious to me, and pays me so many compliments, that I never know how to ask him for money.

SGANARELLE

I assure you that his whole household would gladly die for you. I could almost wish that something bad would happen to you—that someone would take a notion to thrash you with a cane or club; then you'd see how zealously we all. . . .

M. DIMANCHE

I'm sure of it; but, Sganarelle, I beg you to give him a little reminder of the money he owes me.

SGANARELLE

Oh, you mustn't worry about that! He'll pay you royally.

M. DIMANCHE

And you too, Sganarelle, you owe me something on your own account.

SGANARELLE

Tut! Don't mention it.

M. DIMANCHE

What do you mean? I. . . .

SGANARELLE

D'you think I'm not aware of what I owe you?

M. DIMANCHE

No, but. . . .

SGANARELLE

Come, Monsieur Dimanche, I'll light your way to the door.

M. DIMANCHE

But my money. . . .

SGANARELLE (*Taking M. Dimanche by the arm.*)
You can't be serious.

M. DIMANCHE

I want. . . .

SGANARELLE (*Pulling him.*)
Come.

M. DIMANCHE

I came here. . . .

SGANARELLE (*Pushing him.*)
Tut! Tut! Don't talk of trifles!

M. DIMANCHE

But. . . .

SGANARELLE (*Pushing him.*)
Tut, Monsieur Dimanche!

M. DIMANCHE

I. . . .

SGANARELLE (*Pushing him offstage.*)

Tut, I tell you!

SCENE FOUR

———— •◦• ————

Don Luis, Don Juan, La Violette, Sganarelle

LA VIOLETTE (*To Don Juan, who has reentered.*)
Sir, your father is here.

DON JUAN

Well, how opportune! It's just what was needed to drive me out of my mind.

DON LUIS

I can see that I discommode you, and that you'd gladly do without a visit from me. Each of us, in fact, is wonderfully vexing to the other, and if you're tired of the sight of me, I in my turn am tired of your low behavior. Alas, how foolish men are when, instead of letting the Lord decide what's good for them, they presume to know better than He, and plague him with their blind desires and thoughtless entreaties! To have a son was the dearest wish of my heart; for that I prayed unceasingly and with a matchless fervor; and the son I got by wearying Heaven with my pleas is the sorrow and torment of my life, rather than its joy and consolation. Can you conceive how pained I am by the multitude of your misdeeds, the endless stream of scandals which I seek in vain to excuse before the world? They have forced me, again and again, to beg the King's indulgence, so straining his patience that the merit of my services, and the influence of my friends, will soon be powerless to sway him. Oh, how low you have sunk! Are you not ashamed, to be so unworthy of your origins? What right have you now to take pride in your birth? And what have you done in the world that would prove you a gentleman? Do you think that it suffices to bear the name and the coat of arms—that we may glory in our noble blood and at the same time wallow in infamy? No, no, birth is nothing if virtue doesn't attend it. We share the glory of our ancestors only in proportion as we strive to resemble them; and their splendid deeds, which shed a lustre upon us, oblige us to honor them in kind—to follow in their footsteps, and not to forsake their fine example if we wish to be their true descendants. It means nothing, therefore, that you're descended from the forebears who begot you: they disown you as not of their blood, and their illustrious acts reflect no credit on you; on the contrary, their radiance but reveals your dark dishonor, and their glory is a torch whereby all eyes can see the squalor of your ways. Know, then, that a gentleman who lives wickedly is a monster, a freak of nature, and that virtue is our best claim to nobility. The name that a man may sign matters less to me than the deeds he does, and I'd think more highly of a porter's son who was a decent man than of a king's son who lived like you.

DON JUAN

Sir, if you'd take a chair, you could talk more comfortably.

DON LUIS

No, insolent wretch, I've no wish to sit down or to speak further, and I can see that nothing I've said has touched your heart or mind. But be aware, my unworthy son, that your actions have strained my paternal feelings to the breaking-point, and that I shall manage, sooner than you think, to put a stop to your depravities, forestall the wrath of Heaven, and by your punishment cleanse myself of the shame of having given you life.

(*He exits.*)

SCENE FIVE

Don Juan, Sganarelle

DON JUAN

Aagh! The best thing you could do is to die as soon as possible. Every man should have his turn, and it's an outrage when fathers threaten to outlive their sons.
(*He sits down in his armchair.*)

SGANARELLE

Oh, Sir, you shouldn't. . . .

DON JUAN

I shouldn't what?

SGANARELLE (*Quaking.*)

Well, Sir. . . .

DON JUAN (*Rising from his chair.*)

I shouldn't what?

SGANARELLE

Sir, you shouldn't have let him say those things to you; indeed, you should have seized him by the shoulders and thrown him out. What could be more impertinent than for a father to reproach his son, and bid him mend his ways, and remember his ancestors, and lead a decent life, and a hundred other stupidities of the kind? Why should a man like you, who knows how to live, put up with that sort of thing? I'm amazed by your patience; had I been in your place, I'd have sent him packing.
(*Aside.*)
O damnable servility! What have you made me say?

DON JUAN

Will my dinner soon be served?

SCENE SIX

———•—•———

Don Juan, Doña Elvira, Ragotin, Sganarelle

RAGOTIN

Sir, there's a lady in a veil who wants to speak with you.

DON JUAN

Who could it be?

SGANARELLE

We'll soon know.

DOÑA ELVIRA (*Veiled, and wearing
a species of cassock.*)

Don't be surprised, Don Juan, to see me at this hour and
in this costume. The most urgent motives compel me to
make this visit, and what I have to say will permit of no
delay. I don't come here full of that wrath which I displayed
before, and you see me much changed from what I was this
morning. No longer am I that Doña Elvira who prayed
for your punishment, whose angry spirit spoke nothing
but threats, breathed nothing but vengeance. Heaven
has purged my soul of all the unworthy passion I felt for
you, all the stormy emotions of a guilty attachment, all
the shameful transports of a gross and earthly love; the
love for you that remains in my heart is a flame cleansed
of everything sensual; a holy tenderness; a detached,
disinterested love which asks nothing for itself and thinks
only of your welfare.

DON JUAN (*Sotto voce to Sganarelle.*)

I do believe you're crying.

SGANARELLE

Forgive me.

DOÑA ELVIRA

It was that pure and perfect love which led me here to help
you, to convey to you a warning from Heaven, and to pull
you back, if possible, from the precipice toward which you
are blindly rushing. Yes, Don Juan, I'm now well aware of
all the excesses of your life, and the same Heaven which
has touched my heart, and made me confront my errors,
has inspired me to come and see you, and to tell you on its
behalf that your offenses have exhausted its mercy, that its
terrible wrath is ready to fall upon you, that it lies within
your power to avert that wrath by a prompt repentance,
and that you have, perhaps, no more than a day in which
to save yourself from the worst of calamities. As for me,
I am no longer tied to you by any earthly bond; I've
recovered, thanks to Heaven, from all my passionate follies;
I'm resolved to retire from the world, and all I ask is time
enough in which to expiate my lapse, and to gain a pardon,
through austere penitence, for the madness that came of
my sinful infatuation. But it would greatly grieve me, in
my peaceful convent, if someone I had tenderly cherished
were made a dread example of the justice of Heaven; and it
will be an infinite joy to me if I can persuade you to ward
off the terrible blow that threatens you. Don Juan, I entreat
you, as a last favor, to grant me that sweet consolation;
don't refuse me your salvation, for which I ask with tears in
my eyes; and if your own self-interest doesn't move you, be
moved at least by my prayers, and spare me the agony of
seeing you condemned to eternal torments.

SGANARELLE (*Aside.*)
Poor woman!

DOÑA ELVIRA
I loved you with the utmost tenderness; nothing in the
world was so dear to me as you; I forgot my vows for you;
for you, there was nothing that I would not do; and all I ask
in return is that you amend your life and avoid your eternal
ruin. Save yourself, I beg you, whether for your sake or for

mine. Once again, Don Juan, I ask it with tears in my eyes; and if the tears of one you have loved are not enough, I beseech you by whatever is most able to touch your heart.

SGANARELLE (*Aside, looking at Don Juan.*)
His *heart*! He has the heart of a tiger.

DOÑA ELVIRA
With those words I shall leave you, having said all that I had to say.

DON JUAN
Madam, it's late. Stay here: we shall make you as comfortable as we can.

DOÑA ELVIRA
No, Don Juan, don't detain me.

DON JUAN
Madam, you will give me pleasure by staying, I assure you.

DOÑA ELVIRA
No, I tell you; let's waste no time in idle talk. Let me go quickly, don't offer to see me out, and think only of profiting by my good counsel.

SCENE SEVEN

Don Juan, Sganarelle, La Violette, Ragotin

DON JUAN

D'you know, I still have some slight feeling for her, and I found a certain charm in that bizarre new style of hers. Her careless dress, her languishing look, her tears stirred up in me a few small embers of a dead fire.

SGANARELLE

In short, her words had no effect on you at all.

DON JUAN

Quick now, my dinner.

SGANARELLE

Very good, Sir.

DON JUAN (*Sitting down at the table.*)

Still, Sganarelle, we must give some thought to reforming.

SGANARELLE

Oh, Sir! Do you mean that?

DON JUAN

Yes, indeed, we must reform; twenty or thirty more years of this sort of life, and then we'll think about it.

SGANARELLE

Oh.

DON JUAN

What do you say to that?

SGANARELLE

Nothing. Here comes your dinner.

(*Sganarelle takes a piece of food from one of the platters which are being carried in, and pops it into his mouth.*)

DON JUAN

You seem to have a swollen cheek; what's the matter? Speak up, now; what's happened to you?

SGANARELLE

Nothing.

DON JUAN

Let me look. Good Lord, his cheek is all distended. Quick, bring me a lancet to pierce it with. The poor fellow's in dreadful shape, and that abscess might choke him. Wait.
. . . My, what a great lump it was. Ah, you thieving rascal!

SGANARELLE

Heavens, Sir, I only wanted to make sure that your cook hadn't used too much salt, or too much pepper.

DON JUAN

Come, sit down there and eat. I'll have a task for you when I've finished with dinner. You're hungry, it seems.

SGANARELLE (*Sitting down at the table.*)

I should say I am! I've had nothing to eat since morning. Do have a taste of that, it couldn't be more delicious.
(*Ragotin repeatedly removes Sganarelle's plate, as soon as the latter has served anything upon it.*)
My plate, my plate! Not so fast, if you please. For goodness' sake, my young friend, you're a bit too quick with the clean dishes! And you, La Violette, you know just when to pour the wine, don't you?
(*While La Violette is pouring wine for Sganarelle, Ragotin snatches his plate away again.*)

DON JUAN

Who could be knocking in that manner?

SGANARELLE

Who in the devil has come disrupting our dinner-hour?

DON JUAN

I intend to dine in peace; let no one be admitted.

SGANARELLE

Leave it to me; I'll go to the door myself.

DON JUAN (*To Sganarelle, who returns looking frightened.*)
Well, what is it? What's the matter?

SGANARELLE (*Nodding his head as the Statue did.*)
The . . . it's there!

DON JUAN

I'll go and see; and I'll show you that nothing can frighten me.

SGANARELLE

Oh, poor Sganarelle, where can you hide?

SCENE EIGHT

———————◆━━

Don Juan, the Statue of the Commander,
Sganarelle, La Violette, Ragotin

DON JUAN (*To La Violette and Ragotin.*)
Quick now, a chair, and set another place.
(*Don Juan and the Statue sit down at the table.*
To Sganarelle.)
Come, come, sit down with us.

SGANARELLE

Sir, I'm not hungry any more.

DON JUAN

You heard me, sit down. Bring the wine! Join me in a toast,
Sganarelle: to the Commander's health! Give him some
wine.

SGANARELLE

Sir, I'm not thirsty.

DON JUAN

Drink your wine, and sing us a song to amuse the
Commander.

SGANARELLE

I have a cold, Sir.

DON JUAN

That doesn't matter. Let's have it. And the rest of you,
gather round and sing the harmony.

THE STATUE

Don Juan, that will do. I invite you to come and dine with
me tomorrow. Have you the courage to accept?

DON JUAN

Yes, I shall come, accompanied only by Sganarelle.

SGANARELLE

Thank you kindly, but tomorrow is a fast day for me.

DON JUAN (*To Sganarelle.*)

Here, take this torch and light the Commander's way.

THE STATUE

There's no need for light when Heaven is our guide.

Act Five

SCENE ONE

— • —

Don Luis, Don Juan, Sganarelle
In the country, near the city gates.

DON LUIS

Ah, my son, can it be that Heaven, in its mercy, has heard my prayers? Is it really true, what you tell me? You wouldn't delude me, I'm sure, with a false hope. . . . Dare I believe this miraculous change of heart?

DON JUAN (*Playing the hypocrite.*)

Yes, I've renounced all my sinful ways, and I'm not the same man whom you saw yesterday evening. Heaven has wrought in me a sudden change—a change that will astound the world: It's awakened my soul and opened my eyes, so that I look back with horror on my long blindness, and the wicked excesses of the life I've led. When I review in my mind all the abominable things I've done, it amazes me that Heaven has suffered them for so long, without sending down its just wrath upon my head. I'm thankful for the mercy it's shown in not punishing my crimes; and I mean to make good use of that forbearance, showing the world a swift amendment of my ways, atoning thereby for my scandalous past, and striving to win a full pardon from Heaven. Those things are what I undertake to do, and I beg you, Sir, to support me in that effort, and to help me select a spiritual advisor who will guide my steps on the path of redemption.

DON LUIS

Ah, my dear son, how readily a father's love can be restored, and how quickly a few words of repentance can make a son's offenses vanish! I've already forgotten the hours of anguish you've cost me; all that is erased from my mind by the words you've just spoken. I'm beside myself with joy; these tears are tears of happiness; all my prayers are answered, and I have nothing more to ask of the Lord. Embrace me, my son, and don't fail, I implore you, to persevere in your laudable intentions. As for me, I'll go at once and bear this glad news to your mother, share my rapturous delight with her, and render thanks to Heaven for the holy decision it's moved you to make.

SCENE TWO

Don Juan, Sganarelle

SGANARELLE

Oh, Sir, how I rejoice in your conversion! I've waited a long time for this, and now, thank Heaven, my dearest wish is granted.

DON JUAN

Don't be an ass!

SGANARELLE

How am I an ass?

DON JUAN

Come, now! Did you take my words for the real thing? Did you think my lips were speaking for my heart?

SGANARELLE

What! Didn't you. . . . You mean. . . . You mean you didn't. . . .

(*Aside.*)

Oh, what a man! What a man!

DON JUAN

No, no, I haven't changed at all, and my views are what they always were.

SGANARELLE

You're not shaken, then, by the awesome mystery of a statue that walks and talks?

DON JUAN

There is, indeed, something there that I don't understand; but whatever it may be, it's not enough to sway my mind and intimidate my soul; and if I've announced an intention

to mend my ways, and embark on an exemplary mode of
life, I've done so from pure calculation and self-interest.
I said what I said as part of a scheme, a tactic, a prudent
strategy of deception which I'm forced to adopt, in order
to humor a father whose help I need, and protect myself
from all sorts of vexations that men might visit upon me. I
take you into my confidence, Sganarelle, because it pleases
me that someone should know my true feelings, and the
reasons which compel me to act as I do.

SGANARELLE

What! You still don't believe in anything at all, and yet you
intend to pose as a pious, right-thinking man?

DON JUAN

Why not? There are plenty of others who play that game,
and who wear the same mask as I to deceive the world.

SGANARELLE

Oh, what a man! What a man!

DON JUAN

It's no longer shameful to be a dissembler; hypocrisy is
now a fashionable vice, and all fashionable vices pass for
virtues. The part of God-fearing man is the best possible
role to play nowadays, and in our present society the
hypocrite's profession has extraordinary advantages. It's
an art whose dishonesty always goes unchallenged; even if
the whole world sees through the imposture, no one dares
denounce it. All the other vices of mankind are subject
to censure, and anyone is free to upbraid them roundly;
but hypocrisy is a privileged vice which knows how to
silence every tongue and enjoy a perfect impunity. The
hypocrite, by means of pious pretenses, attaches himself to
the company of the devout, and anyone who then assails
him is set upon by a great phalanx of the godly—wherein
those who act sincerely, and have a true religious fervor,
are always the dupes of the others. The true believers are

easily hoodwinked by the false, and blindly second those who ape their piety. I can't tell you how many men I know who, by means of a feigned devotion, have glossed over the sins of their youth, wrapped themselves in the cloak of religion, and in that holy disguise are now free to be the worst of scoundrels! It makes no difference if their intrigues are sometimes exposed and their true natures laid bare; they don't cease, on that account, to be respected, since by soulful groans, and bowings of the head, and rollings of the eye toward Heaven, they can readily persuade the world to excuse whatever they do.

I propose to take refuge in this modish style of deception, and thus protect myself and my interests. I shan't give up any of my cherished pursuits, but I'll be careful to pursue them quietly and on the sly. If ever my secret life is discovered, I won't have to lift a finger: the whole cabal of the pious will take my side, and defend me against all comers. In short, I've found the ideal way to do whatever I like and go scot-free. I'll set myself up as censor of the conduct of others, I'll condemn everybody, and I'll approve of no one but myself. If anyone offends me, however slightly, I'll never forgive him, but shall nurse instead a secret and implacable hatred. I'll appoint myself the Avenger of Heaven, and with that convenient pretext I'll harass my enemies, accuse them of impiety, and stir up against them a swarm of ignorant zealots, who'll assail them in public, heap them with defamations, and officiously doom them to Hell. A clever man will thus exploit men's follies, and adapt his style to the vices of the age.

SGANARELLE

Great Heavens! What do I hear you say? All that was needed to perfect your immorality was that you become a hypocrite, and now it's happened—you've embraced the very worst of iniquities. Sir, this crowning horror is too much for me, and I can't keep silent about it. Do whatever you like to me—beat me, bludgeon me, kill me if you want to; I must nevertheless speak my mind and say to you what, as your loyal valet, I feel bound to say. Remember, Sir, that if the pitcher goes to the well too often, it gets broken at last; and as an author whose name I forget has memorably said, man in this world is like a bird upon a bough; the bough is attached to the trunk; whoever's attached to the trunk has upright values; upright values are better than fine words; fine words are what you hear at court; the court is full of courtiers; courtiers follow the fashion; fashion derives from fancy; fancy is a faculty of the soul; the soul is what gives us life; life ends in death; death makes us think of Heaven; Heaven is above the earth; the earth is both land and sea; the sea is subject to storms; storms toss ships; a ship needs a good pilot; a good pilot has prudence; prudence is seldom found in the young; the young should obey the old; the old are fond of comfort and riches; riches make people rich; the rich aren't poor; the poor live in dire necessity; necessity has no law; whoever knows no law lives like a brute beast; and consequently you shall be condemned to dwell below with all the devils.

DON JUAN

What a fine chain of reasoning!

SGANARELLE

If you don't repent after that, so much the worse for you.

SCENE THREE

Don Carlos, Don Juan, Sganarelle

DON CARLOS

This chance encounter, Don Juan, is most opportune;
I'll be glad to discuss matters here, rather than at your
lodgings, and to learn from you what decisions you've
made. You'll remember that I took on, in your presence,
the responsibility for settling our quarrel. As for me,
it's my frank and fervent wish that the affair be settled
without violence; I hope that I may persuade you to take
the peaceable course, and that I may see you publicly
acknowledge my sister as your wife.

DON JUAN (*In a hypocritical tone of voice.*)

Alas! I wish with all my heart that I could give you the
satisfaction that you desire; but Heaven expressly forbids
me to do so. It's inspired in me a determination to lead a
better life, and I now have no other thought than to sever
all worldly attachments, cast aside all hollow vanities, and
seek henceforward, by austere disciplines, to atone for the
transgressions of my heedless youth.

DON CARLOS

Your intentions, Don Juan, don't jar with what I've
proposed; the companionship of a lawful wife could accord
very well with the laudable ideas that Heaven has inspired
in you.

DON JUAN

Alas, it would never do, as your sister has already decided.
She has retired to a convent. We both saw the light at the
same moment.

DON CARLOS

Her retirement is unacceptable to us, because it might well seem the result of your scorn for her and for our family; our honor demands that she live with you.

DON JUAN

That cannot be, I assure you. For my part, I've desired that happiness more than anything in the world, and even today I asked Heaven's aid and advice in the matter; but while I was communing with Heaven, I heard a voice say that I must think no more about your sister, and that I would never find salvation if she and I lived together.

DON CARLOS

Do you expect us, Don Juan, to be impressed by these high-flown excuses?

DON JUAN

I merely obey the voice of Heaven.

DON CARLOS

Am I to settle for such an unlikely story?

DON JUAN

It's Heaven's will.

DON CARLOS

You've taken my sister out of her convent, and now you abandon her?

DON JUAN

So Heaven ordains.

DON CARLOS

And we're to swallow this insult to our honor?

DON JUAN

You must take that up with Heaven.

DON CARLOS

Heaven! Can you think of nothing but Heaven?

DON JUAN

That's what Heaven would have me do.

DON CARLOS

Enough, Don Juan; I understand you. I shan't settle accounts with you here; this is not the place for it. But I shall find you soon again.

DON JUAN

Do as you wish; you know that I don't lack courage, and that I know how to use my sword when I must. In a few minutes I shall be passing along the quiet little side-street that leads toward the great monastery. I declare to you, however, that I have no wish to fight; Heaven forbids me to harbor such a thought. But should you attack me, we'll see what happens.

DON CARLOS

We'll see. Yes, we shall see.

SCENE FOUR

Don Juan, Sganarelle

SGANARELLE

Sir, what's this infernal new manner you've adopted? It's the worst yet by far; and, wicked though you were, I liked you better as you used to be. I always had hopes for your salvation, but now I despair of it, and I think that Heaven, which has put up with you till now, won't tolerate this last enormity.

DON JUAN

Nonsense. Heaven isn't so fussy as you think. Why, if every time a man. . . .
   (*A Spectre enters, in the form of a veiled woman.*)

SGANARELLE (*Seeing the Spectre.*)

Oh, Sir, Heaven has something to say to you! It's giving you a warning.

DON JUAN

If Heaven's giving me a warning, and wants me to understand, it must speak a bit more clearly.

SCENE FIVE

Don Juan
A Spectre, in the form of a veiled woman
Sganarelle

THE SPECTRE

Don Juan has only a moment left in which to avail himself of Heaven's mercy. If he does not repent at once, he is doomed to perdition.

SGANARELLE

Do you hear that, Sir?

DON JUAN

Who dares address me so? I think I recognize that voice.

SGANARELLE

It's a ghost, Sir! I can tell by its way of walking.

DON JUAN

Ghost, or shadow, or devil—whatever it is—I mean to have a look at it.
(*The Spectre changes shape, and now represents
Time with his scythe in hand.*)

SGANARELLE

Oh, Heavens! Do you see, Sir, how it's changed its shape?

DON JUAN

Hah! Nothing on earth can terrify me, and I mean to find out, with my sword, whether this thing is body or spirit.
(*The Spectre vanishes before Don Juan can strike it.*)

SGANARELLE

Oh, Sir! After so many signs and warnings, you must give in and hasten to repent.

DON JUAN

No, no. Whatever may happen, it won't be said of me that I stooped to repentance. Come, follow me.

SCENE SIX

The Statue, Don Juan, Sganarelle

THE STATUE

Stay, Don Juan! You promised yesterday to come and dine
with me.

DON JUAN

Yes. Where are we to go?

THE STATUE

Give me your hand.

DON JUAN

Here it is.

THE STATUE

Obstinacy in sin, Don Juan, leads to a terrible death. Those
who refuse the mercy of Heaven invite its thunderbolts.

DON JUAN

O God, what's this I feel? An invisible fire consumes me;
I can't bear any more of this; my whole body's become a
blazing furnace. Oh . . . !
(*Thunder and lightning descend upon Don Juan,
with great noise and bright flashes. The earth opens
and swallows him up, and great flames rise out
of the pit into which he has fallen.*)

SGANARELLE

Oh! My back wages! What about my wages? My master's
death gives satisfaction to everyone: the Heaven he
offended, the girls he ruined, the families he dishonored,
the laws he broke, the parents he outraged, the wives he led

astray, the husbands he drove to despair—they're all well pleased. I'm the only one who's unhappy. Alas, my wages! My wages! Who'll pay me my wages?

An Interview with the Translator

By Dana Gioia

No major modern American poet had a longer or closer relationship with theater than Richard Wilbur (1921–2017). He was active in the field for six decades—starting with his translation of Molière's *Misanthrope*, which opened in 1955 at the legendary Poets' Theatre in Cambridge, Massachusetts, and continuing until the final decade of his long life. But Wilbur's sustained and prolific involvement in theater was unusual. He did not write plays, not even verse drama. All of Wilbur's theatrical works, with the notable exception of lyrics for one Broadway musical—Leonard Bernstein's *Candide*—are translations of classical French theater, especially the comedies of Molière.

The son of a painter, Wilbur was born in New York City in 1921 but was raised in rural New Jersey. He attended Amherst, where he chaired the college newspaper—an activity that seems typical for a future writer—but he also spent two summers riding the rails in Depression-era America. Graduating in 1942 as America entered World War II, Wilbur married his college sweetheart, Charlotte Ward, and joined the U.S. Army. He initially trained as a cryptographer, but his leftist associations led the army to transfer him to infantry. For the next three years he experienced some of the war's most brutal combat, from the Allied landing on the beaches of Italy to the final push into Germany. He often read in the lulls between battles and once even wrote a poem in a foxhole.

After the war Wilbur started graduate school at Harvard, where he became friends with Robert Frost. Wilbur had written poems since childhood, but the aspiring scholar now began working on them seriously. His literary success was almost immediate. He was from the first a natural poet with a distinctive and powerful personal style. With the publication of his first two books, *The Beautiful Changes* (1947) and *Ceremony* (1950), Wilbur was recognized as one of the finest poets of his generation, a judgment that has never been seriously challenged. Even his detractors recognize his abundant talent; their complaint is only that he was not sufficiently ambitious in exploring it. His champions have no hesitation in acclaiming him one of the major American poets of his age.

Awards came early in his career and continued almost until his death. Wilbur won the Pulitzer Prize twice—in 1957 for *Things of This World* and in 1989 for *New and Collected Poems*. He was also awarded the National Book Award in 1957 for *Things of this World*, and his translation of *Tartuffe* won the Bollingen Poetry Translation Prize in 1963. In 1971, he won a second Bollingen Prize, this time for his poetry collection *Walking to Sleep*. In 1983, he won the Drama Desk Award for his translation of *The Misanthrope*, and the same year he took home the PEN Translation Prize for *Molière: Four Comedies*. In 1987, he was named U.S. Poet Laureate. In 1994, President Clinton awarded him the National Medal of Arts. And in 2012, Yale University conferred on him an honorary Doctor of Letters.

Wilbur's work is elegantly formal and deeply intelligent—two literary qualities that in a lesser talent might undercut the poetry's emotional immediacy or lyric force. But Wilbur's language is so fresh and sensuously alive that his poems never seem stiff or preordained. He possessed the lyric poet's irreplaceable gift of bringing the reader directly into an experience in all its heady complexity. While Wilbur is alert to the dark side of human existence, he is more receptive to the brighter emotions of compassion, love, and joy. Few American poets since Walt Whitman have offered such compelling optimism.

Wilbur's involvement with the theater began in 1952 when he won a Guggenheim Fellowship to write an original verse drama. Working on his own plays, he despaired. "They didn't come off," he later admitted. "They were very bad, extremely wooden." To learn the craft of verse drama, Wilbur decided to translate an acknowledged masterpiece of the genre, *The Misanthrope* by Jean-Baptiste Poquelin Molière. Little did he guess that he had begun what would eventually grow into a major part of his life's work as well as one of the great translation projects in American literature.

Over the next forty years Wilbur produced lively, sophisticated and eminently stageworthy versions of Molière's verse comedies: *The Misanthrope* (1955), *Tartuffe* (1963), *The School for Wives* (1971), *The Learned Ladies* (1978), *The School for Husbands* (1992), *Sganarelle, or The Imaginary Cuckold* (1993), *Amphitryon* (1995), *Don Juan* (1998), *The Bungler* (2000) and *Lovers' Quarrels* (2009). The only Molière verse play that escaped his grasp is *Dom Garcie de Navarre*, which Wilbur conceded is "universally considered a lemon." From the moment his first Molière translation was staged, his versions have delighted and impressed audiences. Widely produced from Broadway to college campuses, Wilbur's versions helped create a Molière revival across North America that continues to this day. He also translated two neoclassical verse tragedies by Racine: *Andromache* (1982) and *Phaedra* (1986). He subsequently turned his attention to the works of Corneille: *The Theatre of Illusion* (2007), *Le Cid* (2009), and *The Liar* (2009).

It would be hard to overpraise Wilbur's special genius for verse translation. Whether re-creating the witty badinage of Molière or the high tragic music of Racine and Corneille, Wilbur has the uncanny ability to create English versions that never feel like translations. They read and play as if they were originally written in English. The same virtue is equally evident in his extensive translations of lyric poetry from French, Italian, Russian, and Romanian. (One famous poet told me that Wilbur's translations were as good as her originals—and this was a writer not given to flattery.) The distinction, variety, and extent of his efforts earned him a position as one of the greatest translators in the history of American poetry. His French translations alone fill half a bookshelf.

Happy to leave the drama on the stage, Wilbur led a generally quiet and settled life, making homes in Cummington,

Massachusetts, which he moved into with his wife and family in 1965, and Key West, Florida. He died at ninety-six on October 14, 2017, in Belmont, Massachusetts.

Dana Gioia: How did you first become interested in Molière?

Richard Wilbur: It wasn't in school, where my French studies were all about grammar, a subject to which I've always had a foolish resistance. During World War II, when my division landed in southern France and swept north, I became a halting interpreter for my company, and picked up a book or two to read in transit: something by Pierre Louÿs, some poems of Louis Aragon. After the war, when I went to Harvard on the G.I. Bill, my friends André du Bouchet and Pierre Schneider got me to reading such Frenchmen as Nerval and Villiers de l'Isle-Adam. But it wasn't until 1948, when my wife and I went to Paris on leave from Harvard's Society of Fellows, that I encountered Molière, in a stunning performance of *Le Misanthrope*, starring Pierre Dux, at the Comédie-Française.

What prompted your first translation of Molière?

By 1952, T. S. Eliot and Christopher Fry had brought verse drama to Broadway, and in Cambridge the Poets' Theatre was in high gear. I proposed to the Guggenheim Foundation that I write a verse play, but once I was funded, and established in an adobe study in New Mexico, I proved unripe for the task. It then occurred to me that by translating *The Misanthrope* I could keep my word and learn something.

Can you describe your process of translating Molière?

I read the play, mostly unassisted by scholarship or criticism, and get to know its characters and milieu. Then I render it couplet by couplet, aiming for a maximum fidelity to sense, form, and tone. My chief virtue as a translator is stubbornness: I will spend a whole spring day, a perfect day for tennis, getting one or two lines right. Now that I have seen some splendid productions of my Molière translations, I render them in what I hope is the manner of Brian Bedford or Sada Thompson.

What is the hardest part of translating Molière?

The hardest thing is to find, playing with and against the pentameter, just the right timing for a witty or comical line.

Do the rehearsals and production process change your work?

Because my translations are so slavish, I am not asked to do any rewriting at the rehearsal stage. But attending rehearsals and productions has gradually improved my ability to think and feel theatrically.

As a poet, do you think you approach translating Molière differently from the way a playwright might?

I'm sure that a playwright would more quickly visualize the scene, the action, the choreography, the authorized "business." But I would not defer to him about the text. Because Molière's comedies are so thoroughly *written*, I am not likely to be wrong about his drift and tone.

Poetry tends to be a very personal art, while theater is necessarily collaborative. How has the experience in the theater affected your work?

My lyrics for the musical show *Candide* were collaborative, and I enjoyed working with Lenny Bernstein, but I think that my poems were not altered by the process. In doing the Molière translations, however, I know that I have changed as a poet: I am readier to speak out of a single mood or mask, as in "Two Voices in a Meadow" or that long monologue "The Mind-Reader."

How does Molière speak to contemporary American audiences?

Molière's language is readily understood by any American audience. So are the plots of his major comedies, which study the effect of an unbalanced central figure on those about him. Molière's idea of what is normal, natural, or balanced is very much like our own, and so there is no need for "updating." I have no patience with the sort of director who, thinking to render Alceste accessible, has him dress and behave like a hippie who "tells it like it is." That did happen once, and I have not forgotten it.

You have also translated plays by Racine and Corneille. Is the old actor's adage true for translation, that playing comedy is harder than tragedy?

I've found it easier to translate Molière's comedies. The spare nobility of Racine is very challenging, and in rendering a heroic play like Corneille's *Le Cid* one has to be careful not to slip into the oratorical.

Have there been particular productions of Molière or your other theatrical works that remain particularly memorable?

There have been fine productions in big towns and small, and throughout our splendid galaxy of repertory theaters. Of course, no later performance could so amaze me as *The Misanthrope*'s premiere at the Poets' Theatre in 1955, in which the poet Peter Davison played the lead. To my great joy, the demand for tickets was such that the show had to be moved from its original garret-like venue to MIT's new auditorium. And then there was the next year's New York production, directed by Stephen Porter at Theatre East, and starring Ellis Rabb and Jackie Brookes.

Has working with any particular actor influenced your approach to translation?

Yes. Brian Bedford has been my friend for many years, and I have seen him in many roles. He was unforgettable as Richard II, to mention but one of his triumphs, and he has been the life of many Molière productions. If I think of him while translating, it enlivens the words and gives me a more palpable sense of the work.

Were there other translations or classical theater that inspired the direction of your own work?

When I was fifteen or so, I saw Walter Hampden do *Cyrano* at some New York playhouse. Whose translation was used I don't know, but I think the experience may have implanted in me the notion that old French plays could be viable in contemporary American theater.

What literary translators do you most admire?

The last century has been a great age of translation, and the list of heroes is too long to recite. Let me say just this: Yesterday I came upon a translation by Miller Williams of a poem by the great Trastevere poet Belli, and said to myself, That's it. It will never have to be translated again.

The translators whom I most esteem are those who do not translate *pro tem*, but work in the wild hope of doing the job once and for all.

You are a singularly remarkable translator of poetry. Why do you devote so much creative energy to translation?

Translation must be faithful, and so it can't be creative *ab ovo*. But at the very least it uses a poet's abilities between the visits of his Muse. I think it can limber his voice and range, and give him great satisfactions and, with luck, can bring him royalties.

Why are there so few literary translations published in the U.S.?

As chairman of the National Endowment for the Arts, you would know better than I whether publishers are reluctant to bring out literary translations. If that is true in all genres, they should be ashamed. As a translator of classic French drama, I have of course often heard the editorial adage, "Plays don't sell."

Do you have any advice for poets or playwrights who want to translate or produce classical theater?

I would urge such translators to do their work faithfully and straight, and to insist on the same qualities in any production. Death to adaptations and adulterations.

Poet Dana Gioia served as chairman of the National Endowment for the Arts from 2004 to 2009. This article was funded by the Sidney E. Frank Foundation. It first appeared, in a slightly different version, in American Theatre *magazine in April 2009.*

The text of the book is set in 10½ point Adobe Garamond, a digital typeface designed by Robert Slimbach in 1989 for Adobe Systems and inspired by a hand-cut type created in the mid-1500s by Claude Garamond, as well as the italics produced during the same period by Robert Granjon. The chapter headings and dramatis personae are set in Garamond Premier, a new interpretation of Claude Garamond's font issued fifteen years later by Slimbach and Adobe and touted by typography expert Thomas Phinney as "a more directly authentic revival."

The paper is acid-free and exceeds the requirements for permanence established by the American National Standards Institute. The binding cloth is Verona, a woven rayon fabric manufactured by LBS, Des Moines, Iowa. Text design and composition by Gopa & Ted2, Inc., Albuquerque, New Mexico. Printing and binding by Lakeside Book Company, Crawfordsville, Indiana.